Critical Comments on *Why You Can Disagree and Remain a Faithful Catholic...*

"Fr. Kaufman's book is a carefully reasoned and balanced presentation of a subtle and complex argument. His position on controversial issues in the church is one with which many laity already agree completely and which the clergy and the hierarchy cannot afford to ignore. The book demands careful and serious reading."

— ANDREW GREELEY

"Philip S. Kaufman's *Why You Can Disagree and Remain a Faithful Catholic* is an education in discrimination. With abundant historical examples he shows that not everything that is taught is infallibly taught. There are degrees of teaching, nuances. A Roman Catholic is definitively committed only to that to which the Church has definitively committed herself. The 'hierarchy of truths' of which the Second Vatican Council speaks has always to be kept in mind. Dom Philip focuses on three questions: the ban on birth-control, which he says is 'a non-received' teaching; the possibility of looking again at divorce and remarriage in the light of the practice of the Orthodox Churches; the need for bishops to be elected according to the practice of the first millennium. Although most Catholic bishops are today appointed by the Pope, this is a very modern development. The classic statement is that of Pope Leo the Great in the fifth century: 'He who governs all should be elected by all.'"

— PETER HEBBLETHWAITE, *London Times Literary Supplement*

"Richard A. McCormick, S.J., introduces this little book by a Benedictine who evidently shares the problem many Catholics have today: how to be true to the church when it creates crises in faith....Central doctrines are not at stake....There is no effort here to promote individualist dissidence, or arrogant, narcissistic 'going of one's own way.' This is for people of deep faith and alert conscience who find good reasons to disagree with the church; Kaufman also sees good reasons for them to stay in it."

— *The Christian Century*

"This is a plea for Catholics to use their conscience.... The book is not about 'doing your own thing,' but about 'the elusiveness of infallible teaching.' It is about the 'right to know moral options, not the "right" to reject moral teachings.' I'm convinced that he has made a most successful presentation."
— RICHARD WEBER, *Spirituality Today*

"Philip Kaufman makes a convincing case for conscientious dissent from official teaching — a happy combination of in-depth research and reasoning which insists on the right of the People of God to know."
— EDWARD S. SKILLIN, *Commonweal*

"Father Philip Kaufman is no disloyal rabble-rouser. He speaks as one would expect of a Benedictine monk — peacefully and serenely, meanwhile showing his deep pastoral concern for so many Catholics who have either left the Church or are finding it hard to remain. His concerns are for those 'bruised reeds and smouldering wicks' among Catholics, who are confused when some bishops and priests lump all Catholic teaching together as if everything they teach is infallible and unchangeable; Catholics disheartened when discussion of non-infallible and changing issues is closed off."
— WALTER PRINCIPE, Toronto School of Theology

"I can hardly think of a book more needed today. It is well-researched, to the point, clear, up-to-date, and helpful for the many Catholics today who are confused, on the edge, marginal, or suffering.... I just wish that there were some way of getting it to every Catholic. In our pastoral work today, your book is a great help."
— FATHER HENRY FEHREN, columnist for *U.S. Catholic*

"It is excellent: well-written, interesting, and sound. I hope it enjoys a wide distribution."
— JOHN M. HUELS, O.S.M., Associate Professor of Canon Law,
Catholic Theological Union, Chicago

Why You Can Disagree and Remain a Faithful Catholic

In faith, unity;
in doubtful matters, liberty;
in all things, love.

— Attributed to
St. Augustine of Hippo

Why You Can Disagree and Remain a Faithful Catholic

New Expanded
and Revised Edition

Philip S. Kaufman

CROSSROAD • NEW YORK

1996

The Crossroad Publishing Company
370 Lexington Avenue, New York, NY 10017

Copyright © 1995 by Philip S. Kaufman

Printed in the United States of America

Library of Congress Cataloging-in-Publication Data
Kaufman, Philip S., 1911-
    Why you can disagree and remain a faithful Catholic / Philip S. Kaufman ; foreword by Richard A. McCormick. — New expanded and rev. ed.
        p. cm.
    Includes bibliographical references and index.
    ISBN 0-8245-1472-6
    1. Catholic Church — Doctrines. 2. Catholic Church — Infallibility. I. Title.
BX1751.2.K335   1995
282–dc20   95-23365
                                                                    CIP

Contents

Foreword to the First Edition

One of the anomalies of Catholicism is the coexistence of two phenomena: a faith and trust in the enlightening and guiding presence of the Holy Spirit to the church, including individual believers, and yet an apparent distrust of the free flow of ideas in the church. Thus, for example, as recently as 1987 John Paul II stated that the church's teaching on contraception is not a matter of free theological discussion. That statement is not the result of broad consultation with theologians, priests, and laypeople. The Holy Father's phraseology, taken literally from Pius XII's *Humanae generis*, is theologically tricky and not without the need of interpretation. But its overall public impact is the provision of support to those who discredit any expression of dissenting opinion in the church as illegitimate or worse. That is when the Holy Spirit is sent packing.

Philip Kaufman, rightly I am convinced, will have none of this. Catholics, he argues, have a right to know not only official teaching, but also "other information in the church." He borrows this from the distinguished moral theologian Bernard Häring, who stated in the wake of *Humanae vitae:*

> Those who are doubtful whether they can accept it have to study it thoroughly, have to read it with good will, but they also have to accept other information in the church. They cannot dissociate the pope from the whole of the church. They have to study it, consider it, but not alone, not isolated.

Kaufman's book is, in a sense, an expansion of the "other information" on several burning issues. He first presented us with the central theme of this book in an article in *Commonweal* (September 12, 1980) entitled "An Immoral Morality?" in which he rejected as immoral an imposition of obligations that discounted theological opinion in the church. When the article appeared I reviewed it in "Notes on Moral Theology" (*Theological Studies*, March 1981). I wrote:

When dissent occurs against an official formulation and becomes "massive" throughout the church, it cannot be viewed as "isolated speculation" with no relationship to practical everyday living. That is exactly what Häring and Kaufman are underlining. To say anything different is to put truth in the service of authority and official formulations. It should be exactly vice versa.

Kaufman knows very well that there are powerful forces at work in the church attempting to reduce the reflections in his book to "isolated speculation." That is why his study is a courageous one, an odd adjective, one would think, to have to use in our day. Yet it remains apropos. For when the official attempt to achieve uniformity stumbles at the bar of experience and ideas, the next step is to disenfranchise the speculator.

The price of that step can be steep, as Kaufman makes clear in the last paragraph of his book. One can disagree with this or that sentence, this or that analysis in Kaufman's study. Indeed, his own attitude and principles toward "other information" warmly invite such responses on the part of the ongoing teaching-learning process of a pilgrim church. What one cannot do with historical or theological support is to dismiss the idea that there legitimately *can be* "other information" or that it is of continuing relevance, even urgency, in the church. And that is the idea that generates and organizes this thoughtful book. It is why it should be studied carefully.

RICHARD A. McCORMICK, S.J.
John A. O'Brien Professor of Christian Ethics
University of Notre Dame

Preface

On the one hand and on the other hand!
—*Fiddler on the Roof*

In matters of morality, the Roman Catholic Church tends to speak inconsistently to its members. At times, it emphasizes the role of conscience in decision-making. American bishops have stated that our spiritual tradition accepts "enlightened conscience, even when honestly mistaken, as the immediate arbiter of moral decisions."[1] Presumably, therefore, Catholics have the right to know legitimate options in order to make enlightened decisions on controverted moral issues.

Yet Rome issues authoritative statements on specific moral issues, statements that, as Karl Rahner has said, "can make no claim to be definitive" and yet "are nonetheless presented in such a way as though in fact they are definitive."[2]

To deprive Catholics of knowledge of legitimate choices in their moral decision-making, to insist that moral issues are closed when actually they are still open, is itself immoral. Bernard Häring, "one of the most influential Catholic moral theologians of our century,"[3] makes this point when he says that "to allow others to manipulate one's conscience" sins against liberty and sanity.[4]

Moreover, the problem extends beyond the Church's own members to the ecumenical dialogue. Again, speaking of Protestant difficulties with the Pope's role as teacher in the Church, Rahner wrote:

> On the one hand, the ordinary teaching office of the Pope, at least in its authentic doctrinal decisions, often contains errors, even up to our own day; and secondly, Rome normally presents and pushes doctrinal decisions that are per se reformable as though there were no doubt whatsoever about their definitive correctness and as though further discussion about the matter by Catholic theologians would be inappropriate.[5]

Whether one's concern lies with consciences of Roman Catholics or relations between the Roman Catholic Church and other Christian bodies, Rome's teaching authority is, therefore, of critical importance. Sometimes Rome teaches reformable doctrines as if they were definitively closed, seeking to apply "the cloak of infallibility" to teachings that have not been formally defined. Catholics as well as Protestants have been led to believe that many open issues have been infallibly decided.

So before addressing specific concrete issues we will, in chapter 1, look at conscience, "the immediate arbiter of moral decisions." Then in chapter 2 we examine infallibility. We will see that official Catholic teaching on the issues I have chosen to deal with — birth control, divorce and remarriage, and abortion — cannot justifiably be designated as defined, that is, infallibly taught.

In chapter 3 we will speak of "probabilism," an important resource in Catholic moral tradition. According to probabilism, when genuine uncertainty exists about a precept's obligatory nature, Catholics may justifiably use a minority, "probable" opinion of competent theologians to help inform their consciences.

Chapters 4–9 apply insights on infallibility and probabilism to concrete issues in Christian lives. Birth control is discussed in Chapters 4–6. Chapters 7–8 consider divorce and remarriage. Chapter 9 is primarily a call for dialogue on the difficult issue of abortion.

Underneath all discussion of conscience decisions lies the question: How is God's will made known in the Church? Since, according to Vatican II, God "distributes special graces among the faithful of every rank" (*Lumen gentium* §12), God's will may be made known through the whole Church. Chapters 10–11, "Democracy in the Church," explore this issue, particularly in relation to the election of bishops and the question of intercommunion.

To be authentically Roman Catholic it is not enough to be Roman, to listen only to the Vatican. It is also necessary to be catholic, to consider many ways, past and present, in which the Spirit has guided and continues to guide the Church to truth. History is a great liberator, and a recourse to history often helps us resolve problems in our own day. We need knowledge of the Church's wider history, both past and present, to make conscientious decisions.

Bernard Häring, a member of Pope Paul's "birth control" commission, spoke at Holy Cross Abbey, Canon City, Colorado, shortly after the promulgation in 1968 of the birth control encyclical *Humanae vitae*. In his talk Häring showed Catholics how to form their consciences in view of the encyclical's prohibition of all artificial contraception. He emphasized that no one need leave the Church because of inability to follow the Pope's teaching:

> Those who are doubtful whether they can accept it have to study it thoroughly, have to read it with good will, but they also have to accept *other information* in the Church. They cannot dissociate the Pope from the whole of the Church. They have to study it, consider it, but not alone, not isolated.

This book seeks to provide some of the "other information."

The title of the book, *Why You Can Disagree and Remain a Faithful Catholic*, has led some to think that the book was written to promote disagreement. This it not true. The polls reported on pages 5 and 6 show that even before the book was written the level of disagreement in the Church was very high.

The book has been written to help three groups of people who already disagree. (1) It has been written to help those who have left the Church because they were convinced that they could no longer remain as sincere Catholics if they could not accept the official teachings on such issues as birth control and divorce and remarriage. (2) It has been written for those still hanging on by their nails, not sure if they can sincerely remain. (3) But it has been written perhaps more for those who have made up their minds that this is their Church and they have no intention of leaving because of these controversial issues. The book is written to supply them with the information from Scripture and history that supports their honest decisions in conscience.

It has also been written to help in the ecumenical dialogue. There will be no reunion with the other Christian Churches until there is change in Rome on these issues.

This edition of *Why You Can Disagree and Remain a Faithful Catholic* is dedicated with gratitude to the many friends who have given of their time and insights. I have decided not to name names. I, not they, have to accept full responsibility for what I have written.

Chronology

30	Death of Jesus
54	Paul's first letter to the Corinthians
70	Gospel of Mark
80–85	Gospel of Luke
90	Gospel of Matthew
150–450	**THE PATRISTIC AGE: GREAT CHRISTIAN WRITERS**

West	*East*
Tertullian (d. 230)	Origen (d. 254)
St. Cyprian (d. 258)	St. Basil the Great (d. 379)
St. Ambrose (d. 397)	
St. Jerome (d. 420)	
St. Augustine of Hippo (d. 430)	

309	Council of Elvira, first Spanish church council
325	Council of Nicea I, first ecumenical council
450–1000	**EARLY MIDDLE AGE: COLLAPSE IN THE WEST**
440–61	Pope St. Leo the Great
d. 461	St. Patrick
476	Last Roman emperor in the West
d. 543	St. Benedict of Nursia, Rule of Benedict
590–604	Pope St. Gregory the Great
900–1350	**HIGH MIDDLE AGES:** **CHURCH REFORM AND SOCIAL REVIVAL**
1054	Great Schism, break between Greek and Latin churches
1049–54	Pope St. Leo IX, church reform begins
1059–61	Pope Nicholas II, reform of papal elections
1059–1122	Investiture Struggle over Lay Appointment of Bishops
1073–85	Pope St. Gregory VII, celibacy of clergy

Why You Can Disagree and Remain a Faithful Catholic

Introduction

Change

" ... to live is to change, and to be perfect is to have changed often."

—John Henry Newman,
Essay on the Development of Christian Doctrine

1943

There is no one who cannot easily perceive that the conditions of biblical studies and their subsidiary sciences have greatly changed within the last fifty years.... These our times have brought to light so many things, which call for a fresh investigation, and which stimulate not a little the practical zest of the present-day interpreter.

—Pope Pius XII, *Divino afflante Spiritu* §11, 32

1950

The Teaching Authority of the Church does not forbid that, in conformity with the present state of human sciences and sacred theology, research and discussions, on the part of men experienced in both fields, take place with regard to the doctrine of evolution, in as far as it inquires into the origin of the human body as coming from pre-existent and living matter....

—Pope Pius XII, *Humani generis* §36

1967

Since then an increasing number of theologians have come to respect the well-documented majority opinion among scientists concerning evolutionary origins. The trend is to leave astronomy to the followers of Galileo and biology to the followers of Darwin, and to allow as an acceptable working hypothesis the notion of cosmic evolution, including mankind's.

—*New Catholic Encyclopedia*[1]

1994

The question about the origins of the world and of man has been the object of many scientific studies which have splendidly enriched our knowledge of the age and dimensions of the cosmos, the development of life-forms and the appearance of man. These discoveries invite us to even greater admiration for the greatness of the Creator, prompting us to give him thanks for his works and for the understanding and wisdom he gives to scholars and researchers.

—*Catechism of the Catholic Church* §283[2]

These passages from the encyclicals of Pope Pius XII, the *New Catholic Encyclopedia* and the *Catechism of the Catholic Church* point to several changes in thought in modern times. First there is the change in our understanding of the origins of our universe.

The universe probably began between ten and fifteen billion years ago with the Big Bang. This was followed by the formation of the galaxies, of our solar system, and of its planets.

Next there is a change in our knowledge of the facts about the development of life-forms and the appearance of human beings. For centuries the separate creation of the species, including human beings, was accepted as literally true. It was Pius XII who very cautiously accepted the study of evolution in his encyclical letter in 1950, cited above.

Another change has occurred in biblical studies. At the beginning of this century we were taught in the biblical decrees of Pope Pius X that we had to accept a literal interpretation of the creation story in the opening chapters of Genesis. Pope Pius XII in an encyclical on Scripture studies told biblical scholars to use the best scientific methods to understand the true meaning of the Scriptures.[3] This has made it possible for us to accept the "many scientific studies which have splendidly enriched our knowledge of the age and dimensions of the cosmos, the development of life-forms and the appearance of man."[4]

This changed understanding of creation is an important background for still another significant change. This is the change from a static to a dynamic understanding of reality. This struggle between a static and a dynamic understanding of reality is a very ancient one. The Bible has a historical approach. It has a worldview that is dynamic and a vision of a God who changes and adapts to people and to events. The ancient Greeks tended to follow Parmenides. He taught that reality is "complete" and therefore unchanging. If it could change, that would show that it hadn't really been complete after all.

Although the development is not consistent, Christian thought, especially in more recent centuries, has leaned toward the Greek understanding of reality as static. This has been particularly important because it saw human nature as unchanging. This led to an emphasis on natural law as unchanging, absolute "laws" governing human conduct. The realization that human nature is not static but changing has led to the radically different approach in the treatment of moral issues. This influenced the Second Vatican Council.

For centuries the static view also influenced the understanding of the nature of the Church as a fixed hierarchical institution. In another important change, Vatican II described the Church as the "pilgrim people of God."

In the chapters that follow we will see how these changes have influenced the thinking of Catholics today.

New York Times/CBS NEWS Poll
(Excerpted from the *New York Times*, June 1, 1994, B8, col. 1)

AMERICAN CATHOLICS: A CHURCH DIVIDED

	18–29 years	30–44 years	45–64 years	65 and older
Someone can be a good Catholic if he or she:				
Does not believe Jesus was the son of God	17%	14%	16%	16%
Does not believe in the authority of the Pope	43	49	53	46
Engages in homosexual relations	69	60	54	42
Practices artificial birth control	98	91	85	72
Gets divorced and marries someone else	94	97	89	87

NCR/Gallup Poll 1993
PERCENTAGES OF TOTAL SAMPLE AND
OF MOST HIGHLY COMMITTED CATHOLICS
SAYING YOU CAN BE A GOOD CATHOLIC

	Total		Church most important		Mass weekly		Won't leave	
	1987	1993	1987	1993	1987	1993	1987	1993
1. Without going to Mass every Sunday	70	73	60	58	52	55	67	69
2. Without obeying church teaching on birth control	66	73	53	59	54	64	63	71
3. Without obeying church teaching on divorce/ remarriage	57	62	43	48	45	52	53	59
4. Without obeying church teaching on abortion	39	56	26	36	26	40	34	51*
5. Without believing in papal infallibility	45	50	34	40	35	40	39	45
6. Without church marriage	51	61	40	54	44	55	48	59*
7. Without donating time/money to poor	44	52	42	47	41	50	45	53
8. Without contributing to Peter's Pence	68	79	62	72	63	76	66	76*

*From 1987 to 1993 there was increase in disagreement among highly committed Catholics on all items. However, the increase was especially great on abortion, the need for church marriage, and financial support for the Pope.

Chapter 1

CONSCIENCE

Conscience is the most intimate center and sanctuary of a person, in which he or she is alone with God whose voice echoes within them. In a marvelous manner conscience makes known that law which is fulfilled by love of God and of neighbor.

— *Pastoral Constitution on the Church in the Modern World* §16[1]

The judgment of conscience also has an imperative character: man must act in accordance with it.

— John Paul II, *The Splendor of Truth* §60

The thesis of this chapter is very simple. Everyone is obliged to follow a sincerely informed conscience. This definitely does not mean that we can do whatever we please. It does mean that once we have made an honest effort to determine what we should do or avoid doing, we have an obligation to act according to that conviction.

The reaction of the American Church to Pope Paul's condemnation of artificial contraception is a good place for Catholics to begin a discussion of conscience in human behavior. The condemnation was not new. Artificial contraception had been strongly condemned by Pope Pius XI in the 1930 encyclical *On Chaste Marriage*. That condemnation had been repeated by Pope Pius XII. However, devout Catholics found that the Popes' teaching did not fit their experience in their personal lives. Their difficulties came to the attention of Catholic theologians, and then to Pope John XXIII, who appointed a commission to study the issue. However, John died in 1963 before the commission met. Before he died Pope John had called Vatican Council II.

The Council Tries to Discuss Birth Control

At the third session of Vatican Council II, the bishops began to discuss family life. On October 29, 1964, three cardinals and an Eastern-rite patriarch called for a change in the Church's condemnation of artificial contraception. They received enthusiastic applause from the rest of the council members. That same day Archbishop John F. Dearden of Detroit announced that there was to be no further discussion of birth control by the council. Pope Paul VI had reserved the question of the birth control pill to himself.[2] In the meantime, the birth control commission, originally established by John XXIII, had been meeting. On June 24, 1966, after two and a half years of study, the sixty-five commission members took a vote on whether to change the official prohibition against artificial contraception. Of the fifteen cardinals and bishops who had been added for the last session, nine voted to permit artificial contraception, three opposed and three abstained. Of nineteen theologians, fifteen voted for change with four opposed. All thirty-one lay members voted for change. Their final report entitled "On Responsible Parenthood" was presented to Pope Paul on June 28, 1966. The four theologians from the commission who had voted against change, with others from outside the commission, submitted documents to the Pope opposing the official report. After less than a year the official report and the opposing documents were leaked to the press.[3]

Another year passed before the publication (July 29, 1968) of the birth control encyclical *Humanae vitae*. In it Pope Paul VI rejected the recommendations of his own commission. He wrote:

> It is never lawful, even for the gravest reasons, to do evil that good may come from it — in other words, to intend directly something which of its very nature contradicts the moral order, and which must therefore be judged unworthy of man, even though the intention is to protect or promote the welfare of an individual, of a family or of society in general. Consequently, it is a serious error to think that a whole married life of otherwise normal relations can justify sexual intercourse which is deliberately contraceptive and so *intrinsically wrong*.[4] (emphasis added)

Response to the encyclical was immediate and dramatic. In this country a group of theologians at Catholic University in Washington, D.C., under the leadership of Father Charles E. Curran, obtained a copy of the encyclical on the afternoon of its publication. After careful study they drafted a statement opposing the encyclical's prohibition of artificial contraception. This they discussed by phone with colleagues all over the country. By 3:00 a.m. of July 30, they had obtained eighty-seven signatures — later to reach over six hundred. At a press conference that morning they said that theologians had the duty to dissent from authoritative but not infallible teachings of the magisterium when there are sufficient reasons. They recognized that the encyclical had very good things to say about marriage. However, after the advances of Vatican II, they disagreed with how this decision had been reached on a subject like marriage. It had ignored the witness of married Catholic couples, of the separated Christian Churches, and of many people of good will. In addition, the theologians didn't accept the encyclical's specific rejection of artificial contraception. They claimed that it was based on an inadequate, static view of natural law.[5]

The following day Archbishop Dearden, president of the National Conference of Catholic Bishops, issued a preliminary statement that recognized the Pope's unique role in the Church. He asked "our priests and people to receive with sincerity what he has taught, to study it carefully, and to form their consciences in its light." Father Curran immediately pointed out that the "admonition to Catholics to form their consciences *in the light of the encyclical* implied the possibility of dissent and was therefore in substantial agreement with the statement of the theologians." Many interpreted this to mean that they were still free to follow their consciences.[6]

The editor of *America* wrote:

Theologians and married couples who are convinced, after careful study, that other conclusions than those drawn by the Pope are possible for them are not only free to follow their consciences, they must do so. No one can account to God for his talents simply by pleading that he acted as an agent of Peter. The abdication of personal moral responsibility has never been a doctrine of the Church.[7]

In an essay in *Commonweal* Daniel Callahan wrote:

People should of course be free to follow their conscience. But there is much sense in the traditional corollary that they should have an informed conscience; a lot of mischief is done in the name of conscience. In this instance those opposed to the encyclical would seem to have the positive duty of trying to inform the consciences of those who might feel an obligation to follow it: to inform them that they should know all the good theological arguments in favor of contraception; to inform them that they cannot cast off the obligation of making up their own minds on the shoulders of popes and bishops; to inform them that it is possible that good morality might require that they use contraceptives.[8]

What Is Conscience?

What is this conscience that must be obeyed even against the clear but not infallible teaching of the Pope? When the American bishops met in November 1968 they turned for enlightenment to Thomas Aquinas, who "describes conscience as the practical judgment or dictate of reason by which we judge what here and now is to be done as being good or to be avoided as evil."[9]

It is true, as the bishops write, that Aquinas teaches that conscience is the decision to act here and now to do good and avoid evil. However, Aquinas went further. He wrote that (1) conscience makes us recognize what we should have done or not done in the past. (2) With conscience we judge whether we did something well or badly. And (3) it also shows us what we ought to do or not do in the future.[10]

For us it is important to recognize that conscience is not a separate organ like the heart, lungs, or liver. Conscience is one's self deciding the rightness or wrongness of all these activities. The whole person including intellect, emotions, and will is involved in making all of these decisions in conscience.

In addition, Aquinas would use the word "conscience" to designate the *inborn* predisposition within the individual that makes possible the decisions and performance of moral acts. So in a broader sense, we can call "conscience" this inborn capacity that makes us moral beings. It is this inborn capacity that James Q. Wilson calls "the moral sense."[11]

The Origin of Conscience

We will be concerned with two histories: first, the history of the origin of conscience as found in all human beings and, second, the development of conscience in each of us individually.

Evolutionary psychologists recognize the fundamental unity of the human family. We are truly one species. A single human nature is responsible for all the capacities for good actions and evil that are universal in the human family. They exist in cultures that are as far apart and as different as two cultures can be. People in every culture on this planet worry about social status. They not only gossip, but gossip about the same kinds of things. They not only feel guilt, but feel it in broadly predictable situations. Members of every culture have a deep sense of justice.

Moreover, evolution explains basic differences between men and women in all cultures.[12] Notable among these differences is the difference in patterns of aggression.

> Men are more aggressive than women. Though child-rearing practices may intensify or moderate this difference, the difference will persist and almost surely rests on biological factors. In every known society, men are more likely than women to play roughly, drive recklessly, fight physically, and assault ruthlessly, and these differences appear early in life.... As they grow up, men are much more likely than women to cause trouble in school, to be alcoholics or drug addicts, and to commit crimes.[13]

As we look at what is the same throughout the human family we discover that there are many shared characteristics, "universals of expression." Darwin questioned missionaries and found that "scorn, disdain, contempt, and disgust are expressed in many different ways, by movements of the features, and by various gestures; and that these are the same throughout the world."[14] Everywhere, people stand straighter after a social triumph and children lower their heads after losing a fight.

> People in all cultures feel pride upon social success, embarrassment, even shame, upon failure, and, at times, anxiety pending these outcomes.[15]

Behind these remarkable similarities is a scientifically established fact. Every race and ethnic group in the world shares significantly more than 99 percent of its DNA. The genetic material responsible for physical characteristics, personality, or thinking is almost the same throughout the entire human family.[16]

Moreover, the predisposition of humans to care for their young or for aggression among males is shared with other mammals. Even the "universals of expression" are found among our closest relatives on the evolutionary scale.

> Nonhuman primates send some of the same status signals as people. Dominant male chimps — and dominant primates generally — strut proudly and expansively. And after two chimpanzees fight over status, the loser crouches abjectly. This sort of bowing is thereafter repeated to peacefully express submission.[17]

All of these shared characteristics go far back in the evolutionary process that has reached its present level in the human family. These similarities with our nearest relatives on the evolutionary scale are a preparation for the inborn human reason and emotions that are involved in conscience and found everywhere in the human family.[18]

Indeed, Aquinas suggested that in our human "practical intelligence" we have inherited the habit or predisposition that is the source of moral activity. We are born with a predisposition to think and act morally.[19] It is part of "being human" to be born with a moral sense.

Conscience — witnessing, binding, inciting, and also accusing, tormenting, or rebuking — is found by anthropologists everywhere among human beings. Not only conscience but also capacities for altruism, compassion, empathy, love, the sense of justice — all important elements in moral decision-making — can "confidently be said to have a firm genetic basis."[20]

Genes, of course, do not witness, incite, accuse, rebuke. They do not perform the universally characteristic acts of friendship, dislike, compassion, aggression, sympathy, lying, trustworthiness, and love. Genes do not have feelings of guilt over wrongdoing, or create a desire to do what is right. The work of genes is to program the developing fetus to produce the needed structures in the brain. It is these structures that supply the *capacities* to act — do good or avoid evil. Those capacities are shared by all members of our human family. The capacities in the brain are compared by Wright to "knobs" that still need to be tuned.[21]

Conscience is the product of a marvelous evolutionary process.

The Individual Conscience

So a long evolutionary process has produced the genes. The genes are responsible for development in the brain of the equipment used to perform the acts of intellect, will, and emotion involved in moral actions. How will these capacities, which Wright describes as knobs, be tuned? Environment will make the critical difference in the way the inborn capacities develop.

Environment here is to be understood in a very wide sense. Tuning the knobs begins in the womb. Evidence now exists that the mother's use of alcohol, drugs, and tobacco can seriously influence development of the areas of the brain involved in acts of conscience. These are primarily the limbic area, which is the seat of emotions, and the cortex, seat of reason.[22]

Still, as Callahan points out:

> More is required for moral development than a foundation of satisfactory biological equipment. Children must also have adequate parenting in average, expectable child-rearing environments.[23]

How this genetically programmed human nature develops depends upon a certain level of nutrition, emotional bonding, and positive experiences from those who care for the developing children. They must be protected from neglect and abuse, which can do irreversible harm in critical periods of psychological development. It is well known that abusers are likely to have been abused themselves or brought up in a home where they witnessed abuse of others. Neglect can seriously prevent the development of healthy self-confidence. The family background must give enough emotional care and intellectual stimulation to produce a minimum level of self-esteem. Where there are single mothers mired in poverty or "no-parent children" abandoned by drug-addicted mothers there is likely to be an impaired development of self and a warped conscience.

Environmental influence on the development and use of the inherited capacities is wide. Indeed, as Callahan writes:

> Babies are intimately connected to mothers, who are connected to fathers and their extended families, who in turn, through economics, employment, and the media, are connected to everyone and everything else in the country at large. Obviously, structural and political factors in the society affect the family and

other intermediary institutions that stand between the state and the individual. There are always implicit moral agendas given in the socioeconomic arrangements of class, race, age, and neighborhood.[24]

Here is how the *Catechism* expresses it:

> Thus sin makes men accomplices of one another and causes concupiscence, violence, and injustice to reign among them. Sins give rise to social situations and institutions that are contrary to the divine goodness. "Structures of sin" are the expression and effect of personal sins. They lead their victims to do evil in their turn. In an analogous sense, they constitute a "social sin."[25]

All kinds of hidden influences are important in the formation of consciences. What of the explicit social pressures in certain populations? I think here of the gangs in deprived urban areas with high unemployment. Their consciences are formed in their actual environment. They have group loyalties and obey group codes. Does it matter if their environment is changed by new and different influences? James Galipeau, a former gang member turned law officer, had over 50 percent success in rescuing gang members in Los Angeles. His high rate of success was due to the use of "a dying art — one-on-one probation."[26] This important work of changing the way young consciences had been formed was seriously undermined when tax cap Proposition 12 brought a 50 percent reduction in the Los Angeles Probation Department.

What happens to the consciences of children raised in homes where the emphasis is on how many things you can get? In strong contrast, there is the noticeable effect on young people of homes with high moral standards and an emphasis on self-giving. Their daughters and sons often serve in activities such as volunteering in deprived areas here and in the third world.

All of these environmental influences act on those inherited capacities of emotion, will, and intellect present in the brain. They affect the formation of the consciences involved in making moral decisions. The communities in which we grew up, or now live, influence and continue to influence the formation of our consciences.

However, neither the genes nor the environment finally control our conduct. They only predispose. At the core of each human being there is a radical freedom to choose "to do good and avoid evil." Or in the gray areas where the only choice is between two evils they dispose us to try to choose the lesser of the two evils.

In practice, however, both inherited characteristics and the influences of environment can seriously limit the extent of that freedom. Psychopaths are an extreme example of people who are born without consciences. These are individuals found in small numbers in every society. Due to a failure in the development in the brain they lack the emotional capacity required for the development of conscience.[27]

The *Catechism* lists several impediments that limit the freedom to achieve fully human acts:

> *Imputability* and responsibility for an action can be diminished or even nullified by ignorance, inadvertence, duress, fear, habit, inordinate attachments, and other psychological factors.[28]

The *Catechism of the Catholic Church*

How does the *Catechism* deal with the origin of these capacities for good and evil? In a paragraph entitled "The Fall," the *Catechism* gives its explanation for the presence of sin in a world created by a good God.[29] Like the evolutionary psychologists, the *Catechism* recognizes the universal human tendency to do evil. It gives this tendency the traditional name "original sin." However, it goes beyond the insights of the scientists. It shows us the meaning of the Church's teaching on original sin.

> The doctrine of original sin is, so to speak, the "reverse side" of the Good News that Jesus is the Savior of all men, that all need salvation, and that salvation is offered to all through Christ.[30]

However, compare the *Catechism*'s explanation of the *origin* of the universal, human tendency to do evil with the scientific explanation. The scientific evidence is that those dispositions developed through the evolutionary process. The *Catechism* accounts for "original sin" by a fundamentalist reading of the creation account in Genesis 2–3. The *Catechism* speaks of Adam and Eve as if they were historical persons. It tells us that they "were constituted in an original 'state of holiness.' "[31] Of original sin the *Catechism* writes:

> The account of the fall in *Genesis* 3 uses figurative language, but affirms a primeval event, a deed that took place *at the beginning of*

the history of man. . . . Revelation gives us the certainty of faith that the whole of human history is marked by the original fault freely committed by our first parents.[32]

This literal reading of the Bible fits the biblical decrees of Pius X early in this century. But it is not justified by a contemporary reading of Genesis.

Since Pius XII's 1943 encyclical promoting biblical studies, Roman Catholic Scripture scholars have been able to use the "historical/critical" method in their study of the Bible. This method emphasizes that the Bible contains material from many different sources. It uses many different kinds of writing — poems, myths, fables, history, etc. — to convey its message. A careful reading of any biblical passage must consider the intention of the author, the kind of writing, and the historical situation in which it was written. (Perhaps it is no coincidence that Pius XII's encyclical on biblical studies is never mentioned in the *Catechism*.)

When he wrote about original sin, Bruce Vawter, a leading Catholic authority on Genesis, agreed with the *Catechism:*

> The doctrine affirms that man is born into a sinful world and into a sinful race, and that from both of these he stands in need of redemption. This is quite plainly the sense of biblical religion, the teaching of both the Old and New Testament, and with it there can be no quarrel.

However, Vawter then continued,

> It is rather another matter, however, to imagine that we can construct a history of how this state of affairs came to be or to suppose that Genesis does, indeed, record that history. Genesis did not, in fact, attempt such a history. . . . [The author of Genesis] presupposed that mankind was capable of transgression from the beginning, even without outside help. There was, therefore, no "fall" in the sense that men and women became something other than what they had been created. The story does try to account for man's alienation from God, why his life is bounded with frustrations, and why he is under the sentence of death. According to the story, however, immortality was not a gift that he forfeited but rather one that he failed to attain. . . . The man and the woman of Genesis 2–3 are intended to represent everyone, but an everyone no different from that of the Yahwist's time or our own.[33]

The *Catechism*'s fundamentalist approach is particularly unfortunate. This is a book that is designed to provide important information for all levels of religious instruction. The *Catechism* does not even mention Pius XII's approval of the study of evolution that was quoted in the introduction.

In fact, the *Catechism* in its treatment of original sin ignores its own earlier section on "Catechesis on Creation." There, even though in small print, it acknowledges the

> many scientific studies which have splendidly enriched our knowledge of the age and dimensions of the cosmos, the development of life-forms and the appearance of man.[34]

Catholic students in competently taught science classes will learn about all of these wonderful scientific discoveries. They will learn of the great age and size of the universe, the development of life forms, and the appearance of the human family. They will learn the scientifically established *facts* of evolution and its explanation for so much in human nature. Their catechism classes should not deliberately ignore these insights or seem to contradict them. To do so would almost certainly undermine the credibility of other elements in the religious instruction.

The *Catechism* has missed an opportunity to show that in this important area of human knowledge there is no opposition between science and religion.

The Decision in Conscience

As our consciences are formed in community, so moral rules that we apply are developed and communicated in community. History understood in an extremely broad way supplies the elements from which the rules are developed. This includes insights from the past and present — religious, social, political, and economic sources.

For Roman Catholics that history will include Scripture and tradition. Since Pius XII's encyclical on biblical studies, the historical-critical method is required for understanding and using Scripture.

When we resort to history for insights we must look outside of Church history as well as inside. The early Church fathers used Plato and Neoplatonism from Greek and Roman sources. Thomas Aquinas used the Greek philosopher Aristotle. In our day we use Gandhi, Martin Luther King, Jr., Dorothy Day, and many others as sources that can influence development of rules of conduct and the formation of conscience. It will also include new insights from psychology and science generally.

For the Roman Catholic, the Church is a very important source for moral rules. Moreover, the teachers in the Church who develop the moral rules must use this same broad range of sources. As we learned from the impact of the Protestant observers at Vatican II, this must include the insights of the other Churches. The Spirit speaks through the whole Church and in many ways through what is happening in God's world.

We should also use a reverent historical-critical approach to understand the Church's official teaching. We must realize that some teachings in the past, such as official approval of slavery, have been wrong. In the chapters that follow we will use the historical-critical approach as we apply Scripture, tradition, and experience to such important issues as birth control and divorce and remarriage.

Let us return to the American bishops' use of tradition as they wrote about conscience in their letter about the birth control encyclical. They turned to Thomas Aquinas for their description of conscience as "the practical judgment or dictate of reason by which we judge what here and now is to be done as being good or to be avoided as evil."[35] But in the concrete situation how do we judge what is good and what is evil?

To understand Aquinas it is important to note the word "practical" in "the practical judgment or dictate of reason." In Aquinas this refers to the important distinction between "speculative" and "practical" reason. For Aquinas, *speculative* reason deals with the theoretical truths that we can learn by studying the world around us. Aquinas takes his example of speculative reason from plane geometry: the three angles of a triangle are equal to two right angles, 180°. In Euclid's geometry this would be a universal truth. We may never be able to make a perfect triangle, but in theory, if we could, the three angles would always equal 180°. According to Aquinas, the theoretical conclusions we reach in the speculative order are always true, absolute, and without exceptions.

Practical reason, on the other hand, deals with human affairs that don't necessarily have to happen. There is always the possibility of an exception in human affairs. For an example of practical reason Aquinas gives a moral rule. There is a moral obligation to return property on deposit to its rightful owner. However, it would not be reasonable to return it in a specific case if we knew that the owner planned to use it to do some grave harm. Unlike the case of speculative reason, in every practical situation one must take the circumstances into account. Aquinas writes:

> The more you descend into the detail the more it appears how the general rule admits of exceptions, so that you have to hedge it with cautions and qualifications. The greater the number of conditions accumulated the greater the number of ways in which the principle is seen to fall short, so that all by itself it cannot tell you whether it is right to return a deposit or not.[36]

Aquinas mentions first principles of natural law that apparently cannot change.[37] However, he immediately shows that the secondary conclusions deduced from those principles can change under certain circumstances. He applies this to very specific actions. Thus, he could agree that murder and theft are wrong as a matter of natural law.[38] Yet circumstances could so change the individual actions that they did not fit the definitions of what the natural law prohibited.[39] Killing in self-defense and stealing food when starving would be permitted. Unlike the area of speculative reason, in every practical situation we have to take the circumstances into account. There are no absolutes.

Contrast Aquinas's use of the words "absolute" and "absolutely"[40] with our contemporary use. We often mean "finally" and "with no possible exceptions." Aquinas, on the other hand, can describe an action as wrong *absolutely or evil in itself*.[41] He is not declaring, however, that it is wrong necessarily and universally, invariably and without exception. Quite the reverse:

> A thing taken in its primary consideration, *absolutê,* may be good or bad; yet when additional considerations are taken into account may be changed into the contrary.[42]

When it came to conclusions and applications in the practical realm, Aquinas allowed flexibility that later moral theology did not wholeheartedly accept. John Mahoney describes what has happened in later moral theology to Aquinas's natural law teaching. Moral theology has stressed his logical approach and the way he makes things hold together. It has neglected or ignored Aquinas's awareness that when you start applying the general principles of the natural law, the closer you get to the particular situation the more you have to consider the exceptions and different circumstances.[43]

Paul VI showed that lack of flexibility in the way he condemned all use of artificial contraception in his birth control encyclical. He would not allow it "even though the intention is to protect or promote the welfare of an individual, of a family or of society in general."[44] Moreover, he says it is "intrinsically wrong."[45] It is sometimes said that Paul doesn't follow Pius XI and speak of "intrinsic *evil*." But if he doesn't allow it for the good of the individual, of the family, or of society, then we have an absolute to which there can be no exceptions. The language is milder, but the meaning is the same.

In *Human Life in Our Day* the bishops deliberately rejected the word "intrinsically." In its place they substituted "objective."[46] The bishops left room for the possibility that artificial contraception might not be wrong in all circumstances. The bishops don't say this, but we may realize that in given circumstances it might be the only moral solution. By rejecting the word "intrinsic" when speaking of a moral evil, the bishops have followed Aquinas in allowing room for exceptions and flexibility. On the other hand, Pope John Paul II speaks of *intrinsic* evil sixteen times in his recent encyclical *The Splendor of Truth.*[47]

In *Human Life in Our Day*, the American bishops discussed the possibility that we might be compelled in conscience to oppose the supreme, though *not infallible*, authority of the Pope. They quote Newman's teaching that if in a particular case conscience

> is to be taken as a sacred and sovereign monitor, its dictate in order to prevail against the voice of the Pope, must follow upon serious thought, prayer, and all available means of arriving at a right judgment on the matter in question.... That is, the burden of proof of establishing a case against him lies, as in all cases of exception, on the side of conscience.[48]

This corresponds quite well with the American Canon Law Society's commentary on canon 752 in the 1983 Code of Canon Law. This canon describes the proper response to teachings of the Pope and college of bishops that are *not infallible*. To teachings that are not infallible canon 752 calls for prayerful respect but not "the assent of faith." To this teaching that is not infallible, the Canon Law Society's commentary first calls for a "basic attitude of religious assent based on a presumption of truth and good judgment" on the part of the Pope and the college of bishops. But then the commentary continues:

> However, since teachings are included that are not infallible and can be erroneous, the principles of the pursuit of truth and the primacy of conscience still come into play. In other words, dissent is possible because the teachings mentioned in the canon can be and de facto have been mistaken. To search for the truth is everyone's *duty* and right (c. 748).[49] (emphasis added)

Even before being recognized as a *right* there is the *duty* to search for the truth, especially in making the decisions of conscience that lead to actions that affect others.

The teachings that are not infallible can be and have been mistaken. It is therefore important to understand what is meant by infallibility and to know what has been infallibly taught.

Chapter 2

TEACHING INFALLIBLY
IN THE CHURCH

> No doctrine is understood to be infallibly defined unless it
> is clearly established as such.
>
> — *Code of Canon Law,* 1983

On August 18, 1986, Father Charles E. Curran, well-known ten-
ured professor of moral theology at Catholic University in Washington, D.C., received from Cardinal Joseph Ratzinger, prefect of
the Congregation for the Doctrine of the Faith, a letter that had
been approved by Pope John Paul II. The letter, dated July 25,
stated that Curran was "no longer considered suitable or eligible
to exercise the function of a Professor of Catholic Theology."[1]

Two days later a story in the *New York Times* read:

> An official familiar with Cardinal Ratzinger's thinking said: "This
> decision shows a deep rejection of Curran's distinction between
> fallible and infallible teaching. Ratzinger is stating that infallibility
> is not a category that can be collapsed simply to solemn declara-
> tions, and this raises powerful questions about how one identifies
> infallible teachings in the realm of moral doctrine...." Vatican of-
> ficials said that, to the extent that the priest's dissent had provoked
> severe punishment, Cardinal Ratzinger had implicitly applied the
> cloak of infallibility to such positions as the prohibition on homo-
> sexual acts and artificial birth control, even though that status had
> never been solemnly proclaimed.[2]

It will be helpful to make clear what is meant by "fallible and
infallible teaching." Infallibility has been described as a gift of
the Holy Spirit that protects the Church from error when it defines a matter of faith and morals.[3] By "defining" we mean that
the Church proclaims in a solemn fashion that a teaching must
be accepted on faith as revealed by God. The Pope and the "college of bishops," who have the power to define, are called the

22

"magisterium." In recent centuries the word "magisterium" has been "used almost exclusively of the teaching office of bishops."[4] This, of course, includes the Pope. All the bishops in the world are called "the college of bishops."

Both Vatican Councils I and II stated that doctrine can be taught infallibly in three ways. (1) It can be proclaimed by the Pope teaching ex cathedra, that is, in a most solemn and explicit manner on faith and morals. (2) It can be taught by the bishops when, in an ecumenical council and in union with the Pope, they solemnly define a teaching as a matter of faith. These two methods of teaching infallibly are called "extraordinary." (3) A third method is called the ordinary, universal magisterium. This is when, without coming together in an ecumenical council, all the bishops of the world in union with the Pope agree that a doctrine must be accepted as a matter of faith.

The Code of Canon Law clearly distinguishes between the response due to infallible teaching in canon 749 and to teaching that is not infallible in canon 752. Usually we contrast infallible with noninfallible. "Noninfallible" is a double negative for "fallible." If we use "fallible" as is done in the *New York Times* story, we must make its meaning clear. It definitely does not mean that the teaching is false. It means that such fallible teaching by the Pope and bishops can have been mistaken. To call "fallible" those teachings of the Pope and bishops that they have not designated as infallible in no way questions our presumption of the truth and good judgment on the part of the Pope and bishops. Nor does it lessen the respect we owe to them. It only recalls that matters not taught infallibly can be erroneous and in fact in the past have been.[5] With this clearly understood we can use the word "fallible" to designate teachings not taught infallibly.

It must be noted that Cardinal Ratzinger never claimed that the positions denied by Curran had been infallibly taught by the Church. In fact Ratzinger explicitly avoided making such a statement. What can be said of the statement attributed to Vatican officials in the *New York Times* report just quoted?

It is helpful here to discuss the birth control encyclical of Pope Paul VI. Msgr. Ferdinando Lambruschini, who introduced the encyclical to the press, was a personal friend of the Pope and a member of the birth control commission. We can be reasonably sure that he reviewed his statement with the Pope before he formally presented the birth control encyclical to the press. Lambruschini said that while most theologians think moral issues can be taught infallibly, no moral teaching has as yet been infallibly defined. He then explicitly stated that the birth control encyclical was not being taught infallibly.

Can the head of the Congregation for the Doctrine of the Faith *implicitly* apply "the cloak of infallibility" to issues that have not been solemnly defined by Pope or ecumenical council or the unanimous agreement of the college of bishops? In fact, according to the teaching of Vatican I, can the Pope alone do this without a formal ex cathedra definition?

Any implicit extension of infallible teaching must face the explicit statement of the Code of Canon Law: "No doctrine is understood to be infallibly defined unless it is clearly established as such" (canon 749 §3).

Curran's dismissal has widespread implications both within the Roman Catholic Church and in its dialogue with other Christian Churches. In ecumenical dialogue, Roman Catholic teaching on infallibility has long been a stumbling block for other Churches. Within the Catholic Church, Vatican reaction to Curran's dissent from what he considered noninfallible teaching raises a serious question. What does it mean to teach infallibly?

Teaching Infallibly in the Church

As to *what* is taught, the Theological Commission of Vatican II explained that this teaching

> extends to all those things, and only to those, which either pertain to the revealed deposit itself, or are required in order that the same deposit may be religiously safeguarded and faithfully expounded.[6]

By "the revealed deposit" is meant that which is contained in the truth that comes from God.

When we say that the Church teaches infallibly we mean that the Church proclaims in a solemn way that what is taught has been divinely revealed. If it is divinely revealed, as faithful members of the Church we must accept it with an act of faith that is binding forever.

It is important to note that the council first affirmed, in paragraph 12 in the *Dogmatic Constitution on the Church*, the infallibility of the People of God as a whole. Of them the council taught:

> The universal body of the faithful who have received the anointing of the Holy One (see 1 John 2:20, and 27), cannot be mistaken in belief. It displays this particular quality through a supernatural sense of the faith in the whole people when "from the bishops to the last of the faithful laity," it expresses the consent of all in matters of faith and morals.[7]

Only afterward in paragraph 25 did it take up the infallibility of the Pope and the bishops.[8]

As we have seen, the council described three different ways of teaching infallibly in the Church:

1. Pope solemnly defining (ex cathedra) on faith and morals.

2. Bishops solemnly defining in an ecumenical council.

3. Bishops exercising the ordinary, universal magisterium.

The "ordinary, universal magisterium," first taught officially by Pius IX in 1863 but not defined, is claimed for the bishops

> when they are dispersed around the world, providing that while they maintain the bond of unity among themselves and with Peter's successor, and while teaching authentically on a matter of faith and morals, they concur in a single viewpoint as the one which must be held conclusively.

The Pope solemnly defining and the bishops solemnly defining in an ecumenical council are called exercises of the *extraordinary* magisterium. The first time the bishops defined at an ecumenical council was the Council of Nicaea called by the Emperor Constantine in 325. The first time a Pope defined solemnly was Pius IX in 1854. Of the three methods of teaching infallibly only the first, the Pope teaching infallibly, has itself been solemnly defined by an ecumenical council. This was done in 1870 at Vatican Council I.

The Pope Teaching Infallibly

Although the doctrine on the Pope teaching infallibly was defined only in 1870, Brian Tierney has shown that it first developed toward the end of the thirteenth century. As late as the failed attempt at reconciliation with the Orthodox Church at the Council of Lyons in 1274, the question was not raised. Latin theologians at the council didn't believe in papal infallibility.

According to Tierney the doctrine of papal infallibility developed out of a dispute between two branches of the Franciscan order over the correct understanding of St. Francis of Assisi's teaching on poverty. The stricter Franciscans, called "Spirituals," claimed that Francis had taught an extreme form of apostolic poverty that was binding on all Christians. Pope Nicholas III adopted the Spirituals' rigoristic interpretation of apostolic poverty. He accepted their claim that Francis had been divinely inspired to teach it.

Pietro Olivi, leading theologian among the Spirituals, wanted to make sure that no future Pope would attempt to change Nicholas's teaching. He wrote that Nicholas had been "unerring in faith and morals." Indeed, he wrote that if a future Pope attempted to change that teaching, that Pope would be in heresy. He would thus be shown not to be the true Pope. So this first teaching on papal infallibility, according to Tierney, was developed to limit the ability of future Popes to change teachings of their predecessors.[9]

Definers of papal infallibility in 1870 had a radically different purpose. They wanted to strengthen the papacy in an embattled Church. The Church had been divided by the Protestant Reformation and undermined by nationalism in those countries that had remained Catholic. The Church had been criticized by the rationalists of the Age of Enlightenment and assaulted by the French Revolution. In Italy, the Pope's rule over the Papal States was threatened by the movement for unification of all Italy into a single national state.

Moreover, within the Church, liberal Catholics called for the Church to work with the spirit of the age. They sought recognition of religious and civil liberties and separation of Church and state.

Pope Pius IX and many bishops, who were often closely allied to contemporary autocratic governments, promoted the definition of papal infallibility to strengthen the papacy in the struggle against these "enemies." At Vatican I, the Pope and supporters of infallibility got a definition. However, opponents of a definition were able to narrowly restrict papal power to define infallibly. The Popes must make it clear that their intention is to define. Moreover, they can only define as doctrines to be held those things which, by God's help, they knew to be in keeping with sacred Scriptures and the apostolic traditions. For the Holy Spirit was promised to the successors of Peter not so that they might, by his revelation, make known some new doctrine, but that by his assistance, they might religiously guard and faithfully expound the revelation or deposit of faith transmitted by the apostles.[10]

With papal infallibility defined at Vatican I, it was widely presumed that councils would no longer be needed. Popes now had everything they needed to become the sole and supreme teachers in the Church.

Papal infallibility has been used only twice: the first time in 1854 when Pope Pius IX defined the Immaculate Conception; the second, when Pope Pius XII defined the Assumption in 1950. Both definitions were devotional acts by Popes who thought that the Papal States or the Vatican was threatened. They are the only two cases where the Popes have used explicit language to show their intention to teach infallibly. Moreover, they are the only two cases universally recognized.

Let us examine the meaning of the two defined dogmas in reverse chronological order. Pius XII defined the Assumption in 1950. It was an act of devotion to Mary against a possible communist takeover in Italy. This was thought to be a serious threat to the Vatican State. The faith content of that dogma would be the teaching on the resurrection from the dead. This is found in Scripture and in the creed. This teaching on resurrection from the dead is applied to Mary from the moment of her death, because she had such an important role in God's plan for our redemption.

For the Immaculate Conception, Pope Pius IX proclaimed in 1854:

The most Blessed Virgin Mary was, from the first moment of her conception, by a singular grace and privilege of almighty God and by virtue of the merits of Jesus Christ, Savior of the human race, preserved from all stain of original sin.[11]

As we have seen, the doctrine of original sin is not about a "fall" from a state of innocence. Rather it teaches that we are born into a sinful world and into a sinful people. From both of these we all stand in need of Christ's act of redemption. Mary's salvation and our salvation are the fruit of her Son's redemptive act.

Such ways of understanding both definitions — the Immaculate Conception and the Assumption — could make them more attractive to our ecumenical dialogue partners. Neither definition, however, affects moral decision-making in our everyday lives.

The Infallible Teaching of Councils

Recognizing the infallible teaching of councils is not as easy and certain as we once thought. Consider the use of the phrase "let him be anathema" used by the Council of Trent. Trent used this to condemn as heretics and declare accursed those who refused to accept certain teachings. As recently as the middle of this century it was taught that you could identify as infallible the teachings that were rejected by the heretic. Now, careful studies of the Council of Trent have revealed that there are cases where Trent attached an anathema to decrees that dealt with mere customs. Here is one example from a canon of Trent: "If anyone says that it is not necessary to put water in the wine at the offertory of the Mass..., let him be anathema."[12] This could not possibly be a matter that Trent taught we had to believe in order to be saved.

A celebrated controversy involved a decree of Pope Eugene IV at the Council of Florence (1439).[13] This council was called to restore unity between the Western and Eastern Churches. At issue was: what in the rite of ordination is essential for a valid ordination? The decree confirmed the Western tradition that the handing over of the chalice and paten was necessary for a valid ordination to the priesthood. Some leading theologians thought that the teachings of the decree were infallible. After all, those teachings had to be accepted for reunion with Rome. Other theologians denied that this teaching on ordination was an infallible teaching. The Orthodox had always used only the imposition of hands in their ordinations and their ordinations had always been considered valid by the Roman church.[14] The controversy was not settled until over five hundred years later. Although the handing over of the paten and chalice was continued in the ceremony, in 1947 Pope Pius XII declared that this was no longer required for valid ordination. In the future the essential "matter" for ordination of deacons, priests, and bishops was to be "only the imposition of hands."[15]

Teaching Infallibly in the Church

That, however, is not the only problem with solemn conciliar definitions. The meaning of words or even of ways of thinking may differ in different generations or cultures. A clearly intended definition of a revealed truth may no longer communicate what was originally meant. The Council of Constantinople in 381, for example, clearly intended to define its teaching on the Trinity: one God in three Persons.

The Trinity is a mystery that can never be fully expressed in human language. When the Greek-speaking bishops of the council looked for a way to explain this mystery to their contemporaries, they used an example from Greek theater. An actor could play more than one role in a monologue. For example, he could play both the father and his son. When he played the role of the father he held before his face the mask of an old man — his *persona*. That let the audience know that he was speaking as the father. When he changed to the role of the son he changed to a mask that represented the *persona* of a young man. In a similar way God could be one in three Persons. Did this explanation completely and exhaustively explore the mystery of the Trinity? Of course not. But by using an example from their own experience it did give Greek Christians some limited insight into how the Bible could speak of the one God as Father, Son, and Holy Spirit.

For the typical Christian in our day, however, the meaning of the word "person" has completely changed. It is very likely that many of our good practicing Christians are accidentally believers in three gods. They think of "persons" as radically separate, independent beings. When they say that they believe in one God in three Persons, they are thinking of three separate, independent "Beings." That, of course, is the last thing intended by the bishops at Constantinople. So even when it is reasonably certain that a doctrine has been infallibly taught, it may be necessary to change the way it is stated so that its meaning can be conveyed to different generations or cultures. This could well be an unending process.[16]

The Birth Control Encyclical

An important issue in the Curran case is his dissent from the birth control encyclical. It is quite clear that the birth control encyclical was not issued by Pope Paul VI as an infallible definition. Here is Msgr. Lambruschini's, statement, almost certainly cleared with the Pope, when he presented the encyclical to the press.

> Most of the theologians, while admitting that the magisterium can define infallibly some of the aspects of natural law explicitly or implicitly contained in revelation, consider that this has not come to pass in the field of morals. Attentive reading of the encyclical *Humanae vitae* does not suggest the theological note of infallibility....It is not infallible.[17]

This clear statement by Msgr. Lambruschini is not accepted by the strong supporters of Pope Paul's condemnation of all artificial contraception. A letter to *The Tablet*, April 16, 1988, reports on a thousand-page book published by the Vatican Press in 1986. The book received "a warm, personally signed letter of commendation from the Pope." A favorable review in the Vatican newspaper claimed that the book

> sustains the "shocking" thesis that *Humanae vitae*, article 14, in condemning contraception, abortion and direct sterilization, fulfills the conditions laid down by Vatican I in 1870 for an infallible ...*definition*.

I suggest that a comparison of the birth control encyclical with previous definitions that are accepted as infallible is revealing. How do the only two accepted infallible papal definitions make clear both Pope Pius IX's and Pope Pius XII's intention to teach infallibly? The definition of the Immaculate Conception by Pope Pius IX reads in part:

> by the authority of Our Lord Jesus Christ...and our own, We declare, pronounce and define that the doctrine...has been revealed by God....Wherefore, if any should presume to think...otherwise ...they...have revolted from the unity of the Church.[18]

The definition of the Assumption by Pius XII is similar:

> by the authority of Our Lord Jesus Christ...and by Our Own authority We pronounce, declare and define that the dogma revealed by God....Therefore, if anyone...deny this...he has cut himself off entirely from the divine and Catholic faith.[19]

There isn't any language like this in the birth control encyclical.

What Lambruschini said of the birth control encyclical, that "it is not infallible," is just as true of the official teaching on other moral issues for which Curran was disciplined. None of them has been solemnly defined by Pope or council. Therefore a claim of infallibility for any of those teachings has to be based on the third method of teaching infallibly, the ordinary, universal magisterium.

The Ordinary, Universal Magisterium

According to John P. Boyle, former president of the Catholic Theological Society, the first official reference to the *ordinary* magisterium occurred in 1863.[20] This was in *Tuas libenter*, Pius IX's letter against independent tendencies among Catholic thinkers.

In mid-century, liberal Catholics had begun to call for change and adaptation in the Church to meet the challenges of the age. In August 1863, two important events occurred. First, a Catholic conference in Malines called for recognition of religious and civil liberties. Then another congress of theologians in Munich opposed Roman attempts to control contemporary thought through condemnations and the Index of Forbidden Books.

The theologians in Munich acknowledged that Catholic theologians are obliged to hold to the infallibly defined dogmas of the Church. Pius IX, however, didn't consider acceptance of defined dogmas enough. He insisted that their

> subjection...must be given in the act of divine faith to those matters which are handed down by the ordinary magisterium of the Church scattered throughout the world as divinely revealed and therefore held by the universal and constant consent of Catholic theologians to belong to the faith.[21]

Pius IX's teaching can be traced to the Jesuit Joseph Kleutgen. Kleutgen had written: "Can they deny without falling away from Catholicism that the Church scattered throughout the world is just as infallible as the Church gathered in Council?" By "Church" Kleutgen meant "the bishops in union with their head the Pope."[22] Kleutgen thought it was heretical to deny

> the sacrifice of Abraham, the swallowing of Jonas by the whale and similar things...always...treated and preached by the whole Church as historical facts and not as poetical allegories.[23]

In his encyclical, Pius IX wrote that while opinions opposed to decisions of the Roman congregations on doctrinal matters or to doctrines commonly held as true might not be heretical, they should nevertheless be condemned.[24]

Teaching on the ordinary magisterium entered the mainstream of Catholic thought at Vatican I in 1870, where Kleutgen was a consulter of the council's deputation for the faith. When the phrase "ordinary magisterium" was introduced, it was so unfamiliar that eleven bishops raised questions or called for changes. As a result of these actions, two changes were made. First, only those teachings were to be held binding that were presented "as having been divinely revealed." Second, the word "universal" was added to make the final text read: "ordinary, universal teaching office." The word "universal" made it clear that the ordinary magisterium referred to here was not to the Pope teaching on his own. Here the bishops approved a way that the Pope could teach infallibly in union with the bishops "of the whole Church dispersed throughout the world."[25]

Thus, in addition to solemn definition by Pope or council, Vatican I spoke of a third way of teaching infallibly. This is the ordinary, universal magisterium. Under it, without coming together in council, the Pope and the bishops around the world could agree that a teaching had been divinely revealed and "must be believed with divine and Catholic faith."[26] Vatican I didn't define this third way of teaching infallibly.

Creeping Infallibility

Eighty years later this radical expansion of the scope of infallible teaching was continued by Pius XII. In *Humani generis*, his encyclical letter dated 1950 ("Concerning Some False Opinions Which Threaten to Undermine the Foundations of Catholic Doctrine"), Pius XII demanded the same response to papal encyclicals that Vatican I had required only for solemn definitions by ecumenical councils and infallible definitions of Popes. Pius XII wrote of two kinds of papal teaching to which Catholics must give their assent. The first kind of teaching concerned solemnly defined dogmas. To that he now added encyclical letters where doctrine is "taught by the ordinary magisterium."[27]

I want to emphasize the word "assent" because of Vatican II's later careful distinction between "assent" due to infallible teach-

Teaching Infallibly in the Church

ing of Pope or council and "submission" due to other official Church teaching.[28] Assent is an act of faith that binds the believer to accept a statement as true. Submission involves only a response of obedience or respect but not an act of faith. In his encyclical, Pius XII demanded an unquestioning assent to the teaching in encyclical letters and he insisted that once Popes have expressed

> an opinion on a hitherto controversial matter, it is clear to all that this matter, according to the mind and will of the same Pontiffs, cannot any longer be considered a question of free discussion among theologians.[29]

This meant that theologians would have nothing to do but find proofs for what the Pope had already taught.

> Indeed, the divine Redeemer entrusted this deposit [of faith] not to individual Christians, nor to theologians to be interpreted authentically, but to the magisterium of the Church alone.[30]

As for the laity, they seemed to be referred to only as the "individual Christians," who, like the theologians, were not entrusted with the deposit of faith. In theory and in practice, only Popes were needed to exercise the gift of infallibility.

Resistance appeared at the episcopal level just before Vatican II. In a 1960 pastoral letter, the Dutch bishops wrote that the definition of papal infallibility at Vatican I had resulted in an "isolated dogma." Papal infallibility was, they wrote, "part of the infallibility of the world hierarchy, which in turn is supported by the infallible faith of the whole body of the faithful." Publication of the letter was forbidden in Italy.[31]

A Copernican Change

This highly centralized, autocratic view of papal teaching authority was challenged at Vatican II. The council introduced an understanding of the Church that was as different from the claims of Pius XII as the Copernican from the Ptolemaic theory of the motion of the heavenly bodies. Comparing the change with the two theories of celestial mechanics is apt. In the Ptolemaic system the earth was at the center of the universe with the sun, moon, planets, and stars revolving around it. Similarly, for centuries the

Church had been thought of as revolving around the papacy. Or, to vary the image, the Pope was at the top of a pyramid. He was the source. From him all knowledge and authority came down. He was "the teaching Church," the one who received special insights from the Holy Spirit. These he handed down through the bishops and priests to "the learning Church," the laity.

As in astronomy, so in the Church a radical shift in understanding has occurred.[32] With Vatican II a different model of the Church became operative. During four years, before the eyes of the whole world, over two thousand bishops functioned as a learning and teaching assembly. They learned in dialogue with one another. They learned from theologians who had been silenced under Pius XII. They also learned from Protestant observers. Moreover, because their discussions were reported in the press, they learned from feedback into the council from the Church at large. Their documents were hammered out into acceptable compromises that could be approved by overwhelming majorities. Paul VI influenced but didn't dominate the council. On at least one notable occasion, he asked the council to explicitly repeat the statements of Pius XI and Pius XII on birth control. His request was respectfully turned aside.[33] The importance of this action by the bishops in the council will be seen when we come to the chapters on the birth control commission and the reaction of the national bishops' conferences to the birth control encyclical.

After Vatican II the Church could no longer be seen as a pyramid with the Pope at the top communicating to lower levels what he received by divine inspiration and guidance. Instead, the Church was seen as the "People of God." Among them certain members — Pope, bishops, and theologians — were called by God to special roles of ministry and leadership. The late Bishop Christopher Butler observed:

> The Church's life does not flow down from the Pope through the bishops and clergy to a passive laity; it springs up from the grassroots of the People of God, and the function of authority is coordination, authentication and in exceptional cases, control.[34]

Bishop Butler, himself a member of the council, claimed that Vatican II carefully distinguished between "assent" as the necessary response to infallible teaching and "respect or submission" as due to teachings not infallibly taught. Assent to infallible teaching involves an act of faith. It says, "I believe this is true." Only what comes from divine revelation, guaranteed by God who cannot deceive, can command an act of faith. To fallible teaching of Pope or bishops, which could be mistaken, the proper response is respect or submission. We have already seen that the American commentary on canon §752 in the Code of Canon Law makes the same distinction.

Recognizing Infallible Teaching

By what criteria can we judge that the ordinary, universal magisterium is in fact being used to teach infallibly? The norms for judging if the ordinary, universal magisterium has been used to teach infallibly must surely be as strict as the norms required at Vatican I for an infallible, solemn definition by the Pope. Three questions help us judge if the norms have been met. Who can solemnly define dogma? What can they define? How must the teaching be presented so that it is clearly recognizable?[35]

Who can solemnly define? All the bishops around the world united with the Pope can exercise the ordinary, universal magisterium.[36] It is generally agreed that this need not mean every single bishop, but must involve "moral," or virtual, unanimity.

There is, however, a warning with regard to the "who." Butler wrote of the possible existence of de facto unanimity, in which the bishops agreed but without adequate knowledge to reach a sound judgment. He gave as an example the probable de facto unanimity of eighteenth-century bishops on a doctrine of special creation of animal species as found in Genesis. Other examples of such de facto unanimity are the former teachings against freedom of conscience and religious freedom and on Church-state relations. As far as anyone can judge these teachings were firmly and universally held by the bishops right up to Vatican II.

Karl Rahner has pointed out:

It has often been assumed in the past...that a doctrine is irreformable in the Church simply because it has been generally taught without clearly notable contradiction over a considerable period of time. This view runs counter to the facts, because many doctrines which were once universally held have proved to be problematic or erroneous, and is fundamentally unsound.[37]

Four years before Paul VI's encyclical, Robert Blair Kaiser asked Bishop Willem Bekkers of 's-Hertogenbosch in the Netherlands if the bishops hadn't all opposed contraception. Bekkers replied that he was not sure there had ever been a real consensus among bishops. "What may seem like a consensus may be," he said, "a mere slavish and subservient parroting of the Pope's words."[38] Kaiser reports Cardinal Suenens speaking at a session of the birth control commission:

> We have heard arguments based on "what the bishops all taught for decades." Well, the bishops did defend the classical position. But it was one imposed on them by authority. The bishops received their directives, they bowed to them, and they tried to explain them to their congregations.[39]

In other words, simply because the bishops have spoken with one voice does not mean that they have reached a genuine agreement.

What can they define? Vatican I expressly taught the limits on the Pope's ability to teach infallibly:

> For the Holy Spirit was promised to the successors of Peter not so that they might, by his revelation, make known some new doctrine, but that, by his assistance, they might religiously guard and faithfully expound the revelation or deposit of faith transmitted by the apostles.[40]

According to Vatican II, the Popes and bishops when teaching infallibly exercise the gift that Christ bestowed on the Church. The council then placed careful limits:

> This infallibility, however, with which the divine redeemer willed his Church to be endowed in defining doctrine concerning faith and morals, extends just as far as the deposit of divine revelation that is to be guarded as sacred and faithfully expounded.[41]

Theologians break this down into two parts. The first part is limited to "the deposit of divine revelation." The second part is whatever is needed to religiously guard and faithfully explain what had been revealed.

Bishop Gasser, spokesman for the Deputatio de Fide of Vatican I, explained. It is a defined dogma of faith and must be believed that the Church and therefore the Pope can teach infallibly concerning "the deposit of divine revelation." On the other hand, it is not a defined dogma of faith, but is only theologically

Teaching Infallibly in the Church

certain, that the Church and the Pope can infallibly teach about what is not actually revealed but is needed to safeguard what has been revealed. Moreover, Gasser insisted that these secondary teachings must truly be "required for the defense and explanation of the deposit of revelation." It could not be just anything in some way remotely connected with revelation.[42]

Theologians before Vatican II included as infallible decisions the canonization of saints, solemn approval of religious orders, solemn condemnation of books.[43] Theologians today would limit the secondary object to what is strictly needed to defend and explain the Gospel.

Does the accepted use of the historical-critical method of interpreting Scripture have an impact on what can be considered "theologically certain"? Galileo's condemnation for teaching that the earth revolved around the sun and Pius XII's insistence that the entire human family is descended from Adam[44] are examples of actions that were once considered necessary to protect what had been divinely revealed in Scripture.

How must the teaching be presented so that it is clearly recognizable? If bishops dispersed around the world are to teach infallibly, not just any presentation of doctrine suffices. They must make clear their intention to guarantee that their teaching is divinely revealed by God. Karl Rahner wrote that

> we can speak of an absolutely binding article of faith coming from the "ordinary" magisterium only when the doctrine is clearly taught as divinely revealed.[45]

This is solid Catholic teaching as confirmed by the 1983 Code of Canon Law, canon 749, 3: "No doctrine is understood to be infallibly defined unless it is clearly established as such."

The Elusiveness of Infallible Teaching

Let us return to the issue raised at the beginning of this chapter. Curran claims the right and even duty, when the good of the laity and of the Church is involved, for theologians to dissent from teachings not infallibly taught. The Vatican insists that the line cannot be so clearly drawn between infallible teachings and teachings not infallibly taught. It claims that teachings from which Curran dissents have been infallibly taught by the ordinary magisterium. This can refer only to the ordinary, universal teaching of bishops dispersed around the world when "they agree about a judgment as one that has to be definitively held."[46]

Do the official teachings on issues in Curran's case meet the condition of unanimous agreement by the bishops for infallible teaching by the ordinary, universal magisterium? I will deal with three issues on which Curran ran into difficulty with Rome: artificial contraception, divorce and remarriage, and abortion. On divorce and remarriage, the bishops at the 1980 Synod on the Family appealed to the Pope to study the practice of the Orthodox Church allowing divorce and remarriage. This showed clearly that on this sensitive issue, not even what Butler called "a de facto unanimity" existed. I discuss this question in detail in chapters 7 and 8. For abortion, competent dissent from the strict official teaching that rejects all direct abortions is widespread. We will discuss the potential for dialogue on this difficult subject in chapter 9.

But what about the issue that affects the most lives — birth control? Pope Paul VI obviously did not solemnly define this in his birth control encyclical. So the official prohibition could be infallible only if it were taught by the ordinary, universal magisterium. We will see in later chapters that, before discussion was forbidden at the council, there was strong indication that a majority of bishops wanted change. Reactions of bishops' conferences around the world to the encyclical suggest anything but unanimity. A long and distinguished list of theologians think that the necessary conditions for an infallible teaching of the ordinary, universal magisterium on birth control have not been met.

Can an Infallible Ordinary, Universal Magisterium Work?

Historical evidence convinced Butler that the concept of the ordinary, universal magisterium is too vague to be of practical use. He points to bishops at Vatican I. When they came to the council they didn't have the necessary distinctions already developed to define papal infallibility. They had to work out the final decree

Teaching Infallibly in the Church

in their debate. They significantly scaled down the papal claims originally presented for their approval.

Vatican II's experience points in the same direction. Bishops learned in the conciliar process, and significant changes of mind resulted from dialogue and debate. All of the documents presented to the council by the preparatory commission, except a very brief one on communications, were returned for radical revision. Results would have been very different if the Vatican officials had simply polled the bishops around the world on the documents that they unsuccessfully tried to force through the council. Greater assurance of the Holy Spirit's guidance exists if bishops teach together in council rather than in isolation.

Infallibility of the ordinary, universal magisterium has been taught only since 1862. It has never been defined. Is it ever likely to be?

Bishop Butler suggested that Catholics could be assured that the bishops of the whole Church teaching in agreement would not lead them fundamentally astray. But what does it mean not to be led fundamentally astray? Were people not led astray for centuries by false teaching on slavery? How valuable is a teaching authority that assures us of the reliability of the doctrine "that Relations in God are really identical with the Divine Nature,"[47] but for over fourteen hundred years, not only failed to instruct Catholics on the gross immorality of slavery, but by official teaching actively supported it? (The official teaching on slavery will be treated in greater detail in chapter 3.)

Pope Pius XII could correct the teaching of Pope Eugene IV and the Council of Florence on the "matter" of the sacrament of orders. He changed the thousand-year-old way of ordaining in the Western Church. Yet the Western Church cannot find a means to solve the serious pastoral problem of broken marriages. This is especially pertinent since no defined dogmas support the present eight-hundred-year-old discipline on marriage in the Western Church.

To summarize: there exist no solemn conciliar decrees or solemn definitions by Popes on moral issues. Pope John Paul II's claim that the ordinary, universal magisterium "is truly considered as the usual expression of the Church's infallibility"[48] is without basis in any Church tradition before the middle of the last century. No exercise of the ordinary, universal magisterium can be cited that meets the necessary conditions for infallible teaching. This, like Ratzinger's rejection of Curran's distinction between infallible teachings and teachings not infallibly taught, are prime examples of creeping infallibility.

Pope John XXIII shocked a group of seminarians by saying: "I am not infallible." When that statement had had the desired effect, Pope John explained: "The Pope is infallible only when he speaks ex cathedra. I will never speak ex cathedra; therefore I am not infallible."

Rahner has written that it is not possible in the foreseeable future for the magisterium to produce new infallible definitions as was done in the past.[49] However, creeping infallibility has not stopped. In his May 1994 apostolic letter, "On Reserving Priestly Ordination to Men Alone," John Paul II used the strongest language yet used for the teaching of the "ordinary papal magisterium." As Francis Sullivan points out:

> The papal letter says: "This judgment is to be definitively held by all of the Church's faithful." The Note of Presentation says: "It will always require the full and unconditional assent of the faithful." It even says: "No one, not even the supreme authority in the Church, can fail to accept this teaching without contradicting the will and example of Christ himself." This last statement would rule out the possibility that even a future Pope or ecumenical council could reverse the judgment being taught in this papal letter. One does not find, even in the documents of the Second Vatican Council, any comparable claim to the definitive character of its teaching.

However, as Sullivan concludes:

> It would be a very small step, from saying that this papal teaching is definitive and irreformable, to claiming that it is infallible. I am surprised that until now I have not seen any statement made to that effect.[50]

Up to now this claim has not been made.

Yet all the faithful are to accept and *act upon it as if* it had been taught infallibly.[51]

There is a well-known story from the birth control commission. Father Ford said that the prohibition against contraception had not been taught infallibly, but was almost infallible and therefore

Teaching Infallibly in the Church

could not be changed. A doctor on the commission said this reminded him of the situation in his own family. His wife wasn't pregnant, but she was almost pregnant.

The issues on which Curran was disciplined have not been, and are not likely to be, defined infallibly. This has important implications not only in the Curran case, but even more for Catholics' right to know of the existence of options as they make conscientious decisions on moral issues.

Chapter 3

PROBABILISM
The Right to Know
of Moral Options

The ordinary teaching office of the Pope, at least in its authentic doctrinal decisions, often contains errors, even up to our own day.

—Karl Rahner

The Pope, bishops, clergy and faithful must all be true to conscience. But we are bound to do everything in our power to make sure that our conscience is truly informed.

—Bishops of England and Wales

An ancient adage, attributed to St. Augustine of Hippo, holds: "In faith, unity; *in doubtful matters*, liberty; in all things, love."[1] What resources do Catholics have to form their consciences about doubtful matters? I am going to write about a system called "probabilism" that was developed to help priests advise in doubtful matters in the confessional. I will suggest that Catholics can use that system as they form their consciences in such doubtful matters.

Probable and More Probable

For two centuries there was a battle between two opposing groups of theologians in the Church. Both advised priests how to handle doubtful matters in the confessional. The Jesuits taught a system called "probabilism." They were called "probabilists" because they said that in doubtful matters people could follow the *probable* opinion of a competent *minority* of theologians. The Dominicans said no. In doubt you had to follow the *more probable* opinion of the *majority* of theologians. Their system was called "probabiliorism" from the Latin word for "more probable." They were called "probabiliorists." The Dominican probabiliorists stood on the side of law, traditions, Church authorities, and rigoristic confessors. The Jesuit probabilists were concerned more for the needs of the individual conscience.

The end of conflict between probabiliorists and probabilists and the adoption of probabilism throughout the Catholic Church was due largely to St. Alphonsus Liguori, the great eighteenth-century moral theologian. He had been trained by a rigoristic probabiliorist of the Dominican order. However, his pastoral experience turned him toward the Jesuit probabilists. He promoted a moderate probabilism. St. Alphonsus's influence increased greatly when he was declared a doctor of the Church in 1871 and later made patron of confessors and moralists by Pope Pius XII.

St. Alphonsus taught that probabilism must not be followed if it led to serious harm for others. If an action would seriously endanger the life or well-being of someone, the safer course of action must be followed. Thus, for example, war could not be justified on the ground of a probable right. Infanticide could not be justified in the case of a retarded newborn child. In such cases the serious rights of others are involved.

Bernard Häring expressed the present discipline of the Church when he wrote that the confessor may not refuse absolution to a penitent who sincerely follows an opinion held by prudent and learned moralists.[2] My own careful, competent professor of moral theology in the early 1940s taught: "Gentlemen, no matter what your personal convictions, in the confessional you should be a probabilist."

I propose that Catholics can use the system of probabilism as they form their consciences about doubtful matters. When we make important decisions of conscience we should apply "serious thought, prayer, and all available means of arriving at a right judgment on the matter in question."[3] According to probabilism a confessor should allow us to follow the *probable opinions* of prudent and learned moralists. We can peaceably use that same information in following our conscience when making decisions. And we have the right to know that those scholarly opinions exist.

Probabilism safeguards the individual's free exercise of conscience from rigoristic confessors. It protects the liberty of Catholics in "doubtful matters." Richard McCormick wrote that probabilism supports the claims of human freedom against systems and ideologies that would unduly restrict that freedom. Moreover, it has helped moral theology by preventing the closing of difficult moral questions prematurely.[4]

As we shall see, reputable theologians defend positions on moral issues contrary to the official teaching of the Roman magisterium. If Catholics have the right to follow such options, they must have the right to know that the options exist. It is wrong to attempt to conceal such knowledge from Catholics. It is wrong to present the official teachings, in Rahner's words,

> as though there were no doubt whatever about their definitive correctness and as though further discussion about the matter by Catholic theologians would be inappropriate.[5]

The Birth Control Encyclical

The birth control issue illustrates the problem in an area of great practical concern to the laity. Vatican Council II acknowledged that many Catholic couples

> find themselves in circumstances in which the number of their children cannot be increased, at least for a time, and the constant expression of love and the full sharing of life is maintained only with difficulty.[6]

Against their needs, Paul VI spoke with great firmness and clarity: "Each and every marriage act must remain open to the transmission of life."

In response to those who would allow the use of artificial contraception as the lesser of two evils in a conflict situation he added that

> it is never lawful, even for the gravest reasons, to do evil that good may come from it — in other words, to intend directly something which of its very nature contradicts the moral order, and which must therefore be judged unworthy of man, even though the intention is to protect or promote the welfare of an individual, of a family or of society in general.[7]

We have seen that when Msgr. Lambruschini presented the birth control encyclical to the press, he was clear:

> Attentive reading of the encyclical *Humanae vitae* [the birth control encyclical] does not suggest the theological note of infallibility.... It is not infallible.

Lambruschini did insist, however, that a probable opinion could not be used against the teaching of the encyclical. But it is legitimate to ask: How great is the competent opinion opposed to the teaching of the birth control encyclical? Does a simple denial that probabilism can be used close the issue?

The condemnation of all use of artificial contraception by Pope Paul VI was not new. Pius XI had prohibited contraception in his 1930 encyclical, *On Chaste Marriage.* His prohibition had been confirmed by Pius XII. As we have noted, Paul VI had explicitly asked the bishops of Vatican II to repeat the teaching of Pius XI and Pius XII and his request was respectfully turned aside. Then at the last session of the council three cardinals and the Melkite patriarch called for change in the official teaching. They received spontaneous applause from a majority of the assembled bishops. All of this was clear evidence that there was strong desire for change. That same day Pope Paul removed the issue from the council and announced the existence of a birth control commission to study it.

The commission, as we shall see, was carefully selected to keep the old prohibition against artificial birth control. But, after two and a half years of thorough study, the overwhelming majority voted in favor of change. Of fifteen cardinals and bishops who took part in the final session of the commission, only three voted to keep the teaching of Pius XI.

Hundreds of theologians disagreed with the birth control encyclical when it came out. A majority of national bishops' conferences in their responses made changes in the encyclical's teaching, and many of the bishops at the 1980 Synod of Bishops on the Family asked that it be reconsidered.

At the very least we can say that a majority of competent theologians and a substantial number of bishops did not accept the birth control encyclical's rejection of artificial contraception. Can Catholics, then, conclude that there is indeed a *highly probable opinion* opposed to the Pope's teaching? Could they in conscience legitimately follow that opinion?

"No," say those who contend that there can be no probable

opinion opposed to a clear teaching of the Roman magisterium. Msgr. Lambruschini took this position when he gave the birth control encyclical to the press. He admitted that an act of faith was due only to solemn definitions. However, he asked Catholics to give "loyal and full assent, interior and not only exterior, to the encyclical." He insisted that the authoritative statement of the Pope prevented the formation of a probable opinion.[8]

In the same way the Congregation for the Doctrine of the Faith, in its 1975 ban on sterilization, denied that Catholics could follow the opinion of private theologians opposed to official teaching.[9]

But such a position can be maintained only if the Roman magisterium has never made an error in its authoritative moral teaching. If such errors have been made in the past, the possibility exists that they can be made again. In that case the doubt can arise that justifies the resort to probabilism.

We have already seen the commentary of the American Canon Law Society on canon 752 of the Code dealing with the fallible teaching of Pope and bishops. A high level of respect is due to that teaching. However, it can be erroneous. The obligation to seek and follow the truth is even greater.[10]

The list of moral questions on which the authoritative teaching has changed is long. Those who call for absolute obedience to all such teachings hold that they were correct for their own time and circumstances. They insist that changed conditions and further enlightenment led to the formulation of new positions. Here are three clear cases among many where that explanation won't hold: Pope St. Gregory the Great condemned pleasure in marital intercourse; Innocent IV approved the condemnation of witches and the use of torture in judicial interrogations. Pius IX condemned those who held "that freedom of conscience and of worship" were basic human rights.[11]

Slavery

One of the clearest cases of erroneous moral teaching is the Roman magisterium's authoritative approval of slavery.[12] It is true that the New Testament never explicitly condemns slavery, but neither does it attempt to justify the institution. Indeed, St. Paul's pastoral approach in Philemon and his statement in Galatians that in Christ there is neither slave nor free (Gal. 3:28) helped create the atmosphere in the West that led to the gradual elimination of slavery.

But St. Paul seemed to tolerate slavery. He wrote to the Corinthians, "Let each of you remain in the condition in which you were called. Were you a slave when called? Do not be concerned about it" (1 Cor. 7:20–21). As Raymond Brown points out, Paul does not have much social teaching. He is basically a missionary preacher and writer whose goal is to get people to believe in Christ. Paul dealt with social issues only if they blocked his preaching. Otherwise he left them alone, even when he disapproved. Paul was convinced that Christ would come in his own lifetime. He could advise slaves to remain slaves, because with Christ coming soon, the evil social institutions of the time were just not important.[13] But Christ did not come soon as Paul expected. And the magisterium would eventually use Paul's failure to condemn slavery as reason for supporting slavery, long considered an essential element in the structure of society.

Beginning with the local Council of Gangra in 362, affirmed by Pope Martin I in 650, the record is long and detailed. For example, in an attempt to enforce celibacy, the Ninth Council of Toledo in 655 decreed that the offspring of offending clerics should become permanent slaves of the Church. Pope Urban II in 1089 gave princes power to enslave the wives of clerics. During the Crusades, Pope Alexander III at the Third Lateran Council and Pope Innocent III at the Fourth Lateran Council authorized enslavement of captured Christians who had aided the Saracens. As the fifteenth- and sixteenth-century explorations began, Pope Nicholas V in 1454 granted to King Alfonso V of Portugal and his son, Prince Henry the Navigator,

> full and free permission...to capture, conquer and subjugate all Saracens and pagans whatsoever and other enemies of Christ... and to bring their persons into perpetual slavery. [This permission the Pope granted] with full knowledge by our Apostolic power.

Through these centuries there were Popes who worked against slavery, but even they didn't change the official teaching that slavery was moral.

When, in 1839, Gregory VI condemned the slave trade, the bishops in the southern United States claimed that it referred only to the transatlantic slave trade and not to domestic slavery. Many bishops' statements recommended freeing of slaves or, at least, better treatment of slaves, but none explicitly condemned slavery as immoral.

In fact, American bishops considered slavery a political, not a moral issue. They carefully avoided discussing it in their meetings. Even after the Civil War had begun, bishops at the Third Provincial Council of Cincinnati in 1861 wrote: "The spirit of the Catholic Church is eminently conservative. They do not think it their province to enter into the political arena."[14]

As late as 1866, after slavery had been abolished in the United States and several Latin American countries, the Holy Office (the Vatican predecessor of the present Congregation for the Doctrine of the Faith) issued an instruction reaffirming the moral justification of slavery. According to this instruction, slavery, considered in its essential nature, is not contrary to the

> natural and divine law, and there can be several just titles of slavery....It is not contrary to the divine law for a slave to be bought, sold, or given, provided that...due conditions are observed.

Finally in 1891, Pope Leo XIII spoke. He did not speak of slavery by name. However, he took a position that should have made it clear. Slavery is incompatible with universal and fundamental human rights. He wrote that human labor is

> personal, since the active force inherent in the person cannot be the property of anyone other than the person who exerts it, and it was given to him in the first place by nature for his own benefit.[15]

The erroneous doctrine so firmly held and promulgated by the Roman magisterium for so many centuries was implicitly corrected by the Roman magisterium in 1891. However, the correction by Pope Leo was so mute that some of the biggest men in moral theology—Lehmkuhl, Prümmer, Merkelbach, Génicot, and Zalba—didn't catch on. They still taught the morality of slavery down to the middle of the present century. Zalba wrote justifying slavery as late as 1958. He was one of the four theologians on the "birth control commission" who voted to keep the Church's prohibition of all use of artificial contraception.

The common Catholic teaching on slavery was not officially corrected until Vatican II in 1965.[16] Even then, however, there was no hint that the council was correcting centuries of false teaching and practice in the Church. Rather, the bishops condemned the practices of others, especially the forced labor and slavery of the totalitarian states. Finally, in stark contradiction to centuries of explicit Church teaching, Pope John Paul II, in his encyclical *The Splendor of Truth*, included slavery in a list of intrinsic evils.[17]

If the magisterium could be wrong in its approval of the morality of slavery, could it not also be wrong in its absolute prohibition of artificial contraception, sterilization, and marriage after divorce? If such a doubt exists, then probabilism could be used in these and other cases of conscience.

The history of moral theology provides ample reason for modesty on the part of all who teach on moral issues. In the decision in conscience, how do we judge between the "authoritative magisterium" and "the opinions of private theologians which dissent from it"? How do we determine whether the private theologians are indeed "prudent and learned," worthy of our respectful attention? I suggest that the criteria should be those used to judge the competence of scholars in other intellectual disciplines: economists, sociologists, biologists, physicists, etc. How do they rank with their peers? Are their articles and books taken seriously? How reputable are the schools in which they teach?

In our day there is serious dissent by competent theologians from the authoritative but not infallible teaching of the Roman magisterium on several important moral issues. Sincere Catholics must use "serious thought, prayer, and all available means of arriving at a right judgment" on their conduct in these issues. They would be justified in using these theologians' ideas to help them inform their consciences.

The right to this kind of information is not a favor granted to Catholics by a benevolent ruler but a hard-won victory of the forces of compassion over a rigoristic authority. Catholics have a right to that "other information" for the formation of their consciences. To deny that right is immoral. The next six chapters seek to supply information for conscientious decision-making in three issues of importance to the Catholics: birth control, the possibility of remarriage after a broken marriage, and need for dialogue on abortion.

Chapter 4

BIRTH CONTROL
The Call for Change

> The faithful are reduced to living outside the law of the Church, far from the sacraments, in constant anguish, unable to find a working solution between two contradictory imperatives, conscience and normal conjugal life.
> — Patriarch Maximos IV Saigh at Vatican II

Few events have had such a negative effect on the Church in the United States as Pope Paul VI's encyclical *On Human Life* (*Humanae vitae*), which forbade all use of artificial contraception. The authors of *Catholic Schools in a Declining Church* looked for the underlying causes of the dramatic decline in Catholic religious belief and practice in the American Church between 1963 and 1973. They decided that three changes could help explain the decline. These were the changes in the attitude toward birth control, toward divorce and remarriage, and toward the Pope's role as teacher and leader in the Church. The authors concluded that for the decline in Sunday Mass attendance: 48 percent could be attributed to the birth control issue, 26 percent to changing attitudes on divorce and remarriage, and 26 percent to papal leadership.[1]

The effect of the encyclical on individual Catholics is harder to measure. My own eyes had been opened in the 1977 contemporary moral issues class I had developed for permanent deacons. Like many priests, I had been convinced that most Catholics had worked out the problem of artificial contraception in their consciences. I assumed that they were no longer troubled. However, the future deacons and their wives convinced me that this wasn't so. They were in general agreement on the inadequacy of the Billings method of natural family planning (NFP).

A physician in the class taught NFP to engaged and young married couples. He told us that the percentage using it is small. Moreover, he was troubled by the number of young Catholic wives who resorted to sterilization by having their fallopian tubes tied. He thought that many who were sterilized had left the Church. They were under the impression that they could no longer be members in good standing.

Pope John Paul II and the Vatican treat artificial contraception, sterilization, and abortion as matters of equal gravity. John Paul II said to a group of American bishops in 1983: "Couples must be urged to avoid any action that threatens life already conceived, that denies or frustrates their procreative power or violates the integrity of the marriage act."[2] The Vatican, in the "Charter of Rights of the Family," Article 3, acknowledges the right of couples to determine spacing and number of offspring. It then specifically excludes "recourse to contraception, sterilization and abortion,"[3] as if these were issues of equal seriousness.

We had no way of measuring what was happening in lives of Catholics until our own period of sociological polls. Was the low level of reception of Holy Communion before Vatican II due, at least in part, to the official teaching that birth control was always a "mortal sin" that cut them off from communion? How many couples resorted to permanent sterilization, which some thought had put them out of the Church and others saw as one big sin for which they could seek absolution and thus solve their problem for life?

We do know that the birth rate dropped dramatically in modern times in northern Europe and America. For example, in Catholic Belgium it dropped from 31 per thousand in 1880 to 18.1 per thousand in 1929. Decline in the number of marriages can't explain the drop in birth rate. The number of births per marriage had dropped from 4.49 in 1880 to 2.29 by 1936. By 1936 birth rates in Belgium, France, Germany, Austria, the Netherlands, Sweden, Great Britain, Denmark, Canada, and the United States were all less than 20 per 1000.[4]

We gain further insights from current surveys. At the 1980 Synod on the Family in Rome, Archbishop John Quinn of San Francisco reported findings of a Gallup poll. Among U.S. Catholic women 76.5 percent practiced birth control; 96 percent of these used methods condemned by the encyclical. Only 29 percent of the clergy believed that use of artificial contraceptives was immoral.[5] The May 1993 *NCR*/Gallup poll (see page 6) shows that 73 percent of all American Catholics and 63 percent who attend Mass weekly say that "you can be a good Catholic without obeying Church teaching on birth control."[6]

Many cultural changes have contributed to the present situation in society and in the Church. A lower infant mortality rate and greater life expectancy have reduced the need for many children to perpetuate the family. The shift from a primarily rural to a primarily urban culture also radically changed the need for large families. On the farm, every extra hand helped distribute the burden of labor. In the city, each child increased the demand on limited resources of food, clothing, housing, and education. Expectation of higher levels of education prolonged the period of dependency. In the Third World, improvement in health and life expectancy has led to the population explosion that seriously threatens those regions and the world's limited resources.

In 1930, the Lambeth Conference of the Anglican Church became the first Christian body to approve of birth control. In reaction, Pius XI wrote an encyclical in which he condemned artificial contraception.[7] By the 1950s faithful married Catholics and then Catholic theologians had begun to raise questions about the official teaching. In 1963, John XXIII established a commission to study the birth control problem.

The Birth Control Commission

Robert Blair Kaiser, Rome correspondent for *Time* in the 1960s and author of *The Politics of Sex and Religion*[8] is my principal source on the birth control commission. John Marshall, a British physician on the commission, writes that Kaiser's book "is an authentic account of the events at the time."[9]

The complete title of the commission was the "Pontifical Commission for the Study of Population, Family, and Births." Kaiser suggests that the Pope was more concerned about the effect of the prohibition against contraception on the lives of Catholics than on overpopulation. In December of 1965, almost three years before the birth control encyclical, Cardinal Suenens told Kaiser that he had urged a commission on Pope John (and, later, on Pope Paul). Its aim would be to see if the Church could take an intelligent position on responsible parenthood. At least it should try to reform the old idea, "the more children the better." Suenens added: "The commission couldn't stop there. It went on to consider every aspect of the problem." Archbishop Gino Cardinale, who had been an undersecretary of state and a member of John XXIII's inner circle, assured Kaiser that John wasn't concerned only with population. "He wanted to see how solid the doctrine really was."[10]

The commission at first consisted of six members, but no theologians. Stanislaus de Lestapis was a French Jesuit specializing in sociology of the family. John Marshall, the British physician, had pioneered with the temperature rhythm method on the Isle of Mauritius. Clement Mertens was a Belgian Jesuit and population expert. Henri de Riedmatten was a Swiss Dominican and Vatican observer at the United Nations in Geneva. Pierre Van Rossum was a Brussels physician. Jacques Mertens de Wilmars was an economist from Louvain.

At its first meeting in October 1963, at Louvain, after the death of Pope John XXIII, the commission concerned itself only with questions of population.

Its second meeting in April 1964 was called to study the "pill." Pope Paul added two sociologists, Bernard Colombo of Venice, Italy, and Thomas K. Burch of Washington, D.C. In addition, he added five theologians. Joseph Fuchs, a German Jesuit, and Marcelino Zalba, a Spanish Jesuit, were moral theologians at the Gregorian University in Rome. Bernard Häring was a German Redemptorist, the secretary of the subcommittee of Vatican Council II that drafted the chapter on marriage and the family in the *Pastoral Constitution on the Church in the Modern World.*[11] Jan Visser was a Dutch Redemptorist, who had been a consultor at the Holy Office for about thirty years.[12] Häring and Visser were both moral theologians at the Pontifical Lateran University in Rome. Canon Pierre de Locht from Belgium was an adviser to Suenens. The enlarged group was "instructed to give priority to the study of certain matters of morals and doctrine."[13]

Häring and de Locht had been deliberately chosen by the Pope to bring diverse currents of opinion into the group. Both were well known for their belief in the need to change the official teaching.

However, de Riedmatten warned de Locht and Häring that the Pope wanted their participation to be highly confidential.

De Locht first raised questions about the Church's teaching on the meaning of marriage. The official teaching, reaffirmed by the Holy Office in 1944, was that the primary end of marriage was "the procreation and education of children" and the secondary end was "mutual love of husband and wife." De Locht asked if the Pope's commission wanted to challenge that. In his report at the end of the 1963 meeting, de Riedmatten wrote that the group unanimously affirmed that love is at the heart of marriage. A majority agreed that love of husband and wife should not be ranked among secondary ends of marriage. They agreed on very little else except that rhythm was the most desirable means of exercising responsible parenthood and that natural law wasn't adequate to solve the problem.

Active discussion on use of the pill in theological journals, and even in the secular press, was responsible for a hastily called meeting of the commission on June 14, 1964. Two new members were added: Tullo Goffi, a priest from the Pope's hometown of Brescia, and Ferdinando Lambruschini, a theologian from the Lateran University in Rome. He was close to the Pope. With Häring absent, the vote was nine of the fifteen against any use of the contraceptive pill and five in doubt. Two of those in doubt, Van Rossum and de Locht, leaned toward approval. None of them thought that papal approval of the pill was possible or desirable at the time. They again gave unconditional approval to rhythm.

On June 23 Paul VI told the college of cardinals that the norms of Pius XII must be considered valid, at least until he felt obliged in conscience to change them. He told them of the existence of the birth control commission.

Council Debates

The next significant development took place on the floor of the Vatican Council. On October 29, 1964, during the third session of Vatican II, debate began on the preliminary document that was to become the *Pastoral Constitution on the Church in the Modern World*. At the council, basic questions were raised about the nature of marriage, questions that so far the papal birth control commission had avoided.

The *Council Daybook* reported for October 29, 1964, that the ecumenical council began discussion of the long-awaited subject of marriage and responsible parenthood. However, the council avoided the question of birth control pills. Pope Paul had reserved the birth control issue to himself.[14]

Cardinal Ruffini led off the debate. He criticized a passage in the text on responsible parenthood. This stated that married couples, who for serious reasons limited the number of their children, must still manifest tender love for each other. Ruffini asked how such love can be expressed. Catholic teaching had always maintained that in such circumstances use of the act of marriage is unlawful. He cited St. Augustine, who claimed that parents who did not use marriage in a Christian way fell into debauchery and prostitution. Ruffini asked that the teaching of Pius XI and Pius XII be included in the document.

Paul Emile Léger, cardinal-archbishop of Montreal, spoke after Cardinal Ruffini. He said:

> We have had a pessimistic, negative attitude toward love. . . . Love is good in itself. It makes its own demands and has its own laws. . . . We must affirm that the intimate union of the couple finds its legitimate end in itself, even when it is not directed toward procreation.[15]

Léger praised the document for avoiding the old language of primary and secondary purposes of marriage. He approved its statement that marital fruitfulness must be governed by prudence and generosity.

Suenens suggested that the council's commission and the papal commission work together. He called for a broad inquiry to include renowned moralists, intellectuals, lay men and women, and married couples. He expressed the hope that the names of the commission members be well known so that they could receive the most ample information and truly be representatives of the People of God. "I implore you, brothers," he said. "Let us avoid another Galileo trial. One is enough for the Church."[16]

The eighty-seven-year-old Melkite-rite Patriarch Maximos IV Saigh of Antioch spoke after Suenens. He brought a new dimension to the discussion, since he came from a branch of the Church with the tradition of a married clergy. He immediately addressed a special aspect of morals: the regulation of birth.... Now, among the anguishing and sorrowful problems which agitate the human masses today, there emerges the problem of birth regulation, a problem most urgent since it is at the bottom of a grave crisis of the Catholic conscience. There is here a conflict between the official doctrine of the Church and the contrary practice of the vast majority of Catholic families. The authority of the Church is once more questioned on a large scale. The faithful are reduced to living outside the law of the Church, far from the sacraments, in constant anguish, unable to find a working solution between two contradictory imperatives, conscience and normal conjugal life.

Patriarch Maximos called attention to the population problem which "condemns hundreds of millions of human beings to a shameless and hopeless misery." He asked if the Church's official position could not be

revised in the light of modern science, theological as well as medical, psychological and sociological?... The purpose of marriage therefore must not be dissected into primary and secondary purposes.... Do we not have the right to ask ourselves whether certain official positions are not subordinated to obsolete conceptions and possibly to the psychosis of bachelors who are strangers to this sector of life?

Maximos asked for inclusion of Christian married people in the proposed council commission. Representatives of other Christian Churches and even thinkers from other religions should be included in the search for a solution.[17]

Cardinal Bernard Alfrink spoke of difficulties that can lead to alienation from the Church. They could be harmful to fidelity, "the highest value of marriage." He continued:

Difficulties of married life are often of such a nature that in fact a difficult conflict of conscience arises between two matrimonial values, that is, between the values of procreation and that of the human and Christian education of offspring, which is possible only when conjugal love is present between the parents, a love which is normally supported and increased by carnal relations.

Alfrink said that the Church could never approve means of preventing conception "which are certainly *intrinsically* evil." He said, however, that married couples, scientists and theologians had an *honest doubt* about complete or periodic abstinence as the only moral solutions to the problem. The Church could bind consciences of Catholics only when there is real certitude about the divine law.

Auxiliary Bishop Joseph Reuss of Mainz, West Germany, in the name of 145 bishops of many countries, supported Alfrink's emphasis on the difference between merely biological sex and human sex. He asked that the text include this emphasis.[18]

Cardinal Alfredo Ottaviani responded that the council could not approve the freedom granted by the document to let married couples decide how many children they should have.

The *Council Daybook* reported that applause for some of the speeches was the most enthusiastic in three years of the council. In case there is any question about which speakers received this applause, Häring, speaking at Holy Cross Abbey, reported on speeches of Léger, Suenens, Maximos IV, and Alfrink:

> There was a great upset and the moderators were told not to allow any more talks in this direction, especially since these men had received the applause of the majority of the council. It was on one of these days I was asked by the press panel whether Ottaviani did not also receive a strong applause and I said, yes he did, only with the difference, that he received a strong applause from very few hands. But [for the others] there was applause and a manifestation from many hands.

Häring referred to the reaction "of the great part of the hierarchy, the very moment when they thought they had a free expression."[19] Four leading members of the hierarchy had addressed the crisis for married Catholics on the birth control issue and clearly called for change in the official teaching. By their applause, the majority of bishops signaled their approval. This was the last chance the bishops had to show where they stood on this critical issue until four years later. Then the statements of their episcopal conferences on the birth control encyclical would show their real convictions.

Broader Consultation

The call on the council floor for a broader consultation was met by an enlargement of the commission from fifteen to fifty-five for the meeting scheduled for Rome in March 1965. Thirty-four lay men and women, nine members of the secular clergy, and twelve members of religious orders were included. There were professors from great universities, the Gregorian and the Lateran in Rome, Louvain in Belgium, Georgetown, Johns Hopkins, and Notre Dame in the U.S., Catholic University in Chile, some from Paris, one from Oxford, and two practicing psychiatrists. John T. Noonan, Jr., from Notre Dame University, well-known for his writings on change in Church teaching on usury, was made a consultant to the commission. His classic book on contraception would be published that same year.

Loyalty, however, seems to have been more important than professional credentials. Dr. John Rock from Boston, leading authority on the pill, and Mill Hill Missionary Father Arthur McCormick, important authority on demographic questions, had both taken public positions that seemed to differ from traditional Catholic teaching. They were not included.

Two bishops were also added to the commission at this time, Leo Binz, archbishop of Minneapolis–St. Paul and Joseph Maria Reuss, auxiliary bishop and rector of the seminary in Mainz, West Germany. Binz had caused the cancellation of a television series that would update American Catholics on the contraception situation. Reuss had publicly supported an article by Canon Louis Janssens of Louvain in favor of the pill. Appointment of Reuss indicated the desire to keep some balance on the commission. Häring considered Reuss, de Locht, and himself the only theologians on the commission open to change.[20]

Of the three married couples, the Potvins of Ottawa and the Rendus of Paris, ran rhythm clinics. The third couple, Patrick and Patricia Crowley of Chicago, were leaders in an international organization called the Christian Family Movement (CFM). They had used the calendar rhythm method. However, Patricia had been sterile since 1947, when she lost their fifth child and nearly died.

In his letter to the new members de Riedmatten asked for a brief note stating "what goes on in your own field of work or of study and what would be *answers* you can see ahead." He warned them that "the Group and its shape should remain *confidential.*"

The Crowleys wondered why they were asked to keep their appointment secret. They thought they should at least be able to talk to their own CFM members. They contacted Dr. André Hellegers, the gynecologist from the medical school at Johns Hopkins, who had also been appointed to the commission. With his help they put together a questionnaire to be sent to members of CFM. They thought that a study would prove, not that rhythm did not work, but that it had not actually been tried. What was needed were expert rhythm advisers.[21] In their report to de Riedmatten, the Crowleys said that they had "made some discreet and confidential inquiries of various members of the Christian Family Movement." One paragraph of their report read:

> The couples of whom we have inquired have demonstrated allegiance to the Church and her teachings through long services in the work of the Christian Family movement. Many of these couples have large families (six to thirteen children). Most of them have been able to educate and suitably support these children. Some have had intermittent physical, and in a few cases, psychological problems and many indicated that they are deeply troubled by this problem. Many expressed the hope that the Church will change. A very few have given up and practice some form of birth control. Most expressed dissatisfaction over the rhythm method for a variety of reasons, running from the fact that it was ineffective, hard to follow, and others had psychological and physiological objections to rhythm. None admitted lack of knowledge about rhythm but most felt it was a distraction from the proper development of married love.

The enlarged commission began its meetings in late March 1965. Their mandate was to provide the Pope with means of responding with "immediate action" to unresolved problems on the birth control issue. At the first meeting, John Noonan showed how the Church's teaching developed and changed in response to changing historical and cultural situations, always retaining basic respect for dignity of human life.

De Riedmatten divided the members into three major sections: one of sociologists, demographers, and economists; another of medical professionals; a third of theologians. The question was raised for the theologians: Could the solemn teaching of Pius XI, reaffirmed by Pius XII, be changed? Zalba insisted that because of "a practically uninterrupted tradition," those statements were infallible and could not be reformed. When he was challenged with Noonan's evidence of change, he contended that for 150 years, all bishops, in agreement with Rome, had taught many things infallibly against artificial contraception and direct sterilization. Perico and Visser agreed but wanted to remain open to new developments.

John C. Ford, a Jesuit theologian from the Catholic University of America, did not agree that there was a possibility of new developments. He quoted Pius XII quoting Pius XI:

> No indication or necessity can change an intrinsically immoral act into one that is moral and allowable.... This proscription is in full force now as it was before, and so will be tomorrow and forever, because it is not a mere human enactment but the expression of a natural and divine law.[22]

Delhaye, however, claimed that Pius XII had already changed the teaching when he approved the rhythm method.

De Riedmatten called for a vote of theologians: Could the teaching of Pius XI and Pius XII be reformed? The vote: twelve yes, seven no. Visser, one of the seven, said irreformable teaching could be open to explanations that did not contradict the original teaching. Seven of the twelve who voted for change claimed that moral matters

> do not lend themselves to irreformable statements "because the human data develop and change." Tradition is not static, it is life and history. In matters of morals, the magisterium can give directions, but not determine behavior once and for all.[23]

Natural law, unless it is clearly contained in revelation, is only as binding as the reasons on which it is based. Häring noted Vatican II's teaching: "infallibility extends as far as...the deposit of divine revelation."

How significant was this vote? Recall Häring's opinion that among twenty-one theologians in the enlarged commission, only three seemed to be open to change. Now among theologians present and voting, the vote was twelve to seven for the possibility of change.

Theologians on the commission had come a long way. Fuchs had been influenced by Marshall, the British physician on the commission, whose research showed that the temperature method could be used among illiterate people. Marshall explained to Fuchs that he doubted that the Church should promote it as the only method. "Because," as he told Fuchs, "it just doesn't work for everyone."

On specific issues, theologians could agree on only four points: parenthood should be responsible; marriage is for love; sex has a positive value; the Church should educate young people.

They had not yet heard results of the Crowleys' survey of devout CFM couples in the United States and Canada. Some of those couples were shocked at the idea of consulting the laity about a teaching that they had learned could never be changed. Most couples, however, hoped for a new approach. Statements like those of a couple married thirteen years with six children were seriously thought-provoking for some celibate members of the commission. The husband, a scholar, wrote:

> Rhythm destroys the meaning of the sex act: it turns it from a spontaneous expression of spiritual and physical love into a mere bodily sexual relief; it makes me obsessed with sex throughout the month; it seriously endangers my chastity; it has noticeable effect upon my disposition toward my wife and children; it makes necessary my complete avoidance of all affection toward my wife for three weeks at a time. I have watched a magnificent spiritual and physical union dissipate and, due to rhythm, turn into a tense and mutually damaging relationship. Rhythm seems to be immoral and deeply unnatural. It seems to me diabolical.

His wife, writing independently, reported:

> My doctor advised me, recommended the basal temperature combined with the calendar method, and was constantly consulted. The psychological problems worsened, however, as we had baby after baby. We eventually had to resort to a three-week abstinence and since then we have had no pregnancy. I find myself sullen and resentful of my husband when the time for sexual relations finally arrives. I resent his necessarily guarded affection during the month and I find that I can't respond suddenly. I find, also, that my subconscious dreams and unguarded thoughts are inevitably sexual and time consuming. All this in spite of a great intellectual and emotional companionship and a generally beautiful marriage and home life.[24]

In his formal report to the commission Patrick Crowley spoke of how shocked he and his wife were to realize that even the most dedicated, committed couples were deeply troubled over the problem. Hundreds of statements from the United States and Canada showed a strong consensus in favor of some change.[25]

In advance of an audience with the Pope at the end of this session, de Riedmatten asked commission members for suggestions for further work. The list was long. At the audience the Pope assured them that he understood why they needed more time. This was March 1965.

The Church in the Modern World

In the fall of 1965, the bishops at Vatican II changed the teaching about marriage that had been approved for centuries at the highest level in the Church. Marriage was no longer spoken of as a contract, but as a covenant of conjugal love. Coitus, so long treated as indecent and needing reasons to justify it even within marriage, was recognized within marriage to be a noble action. Speaking of conjugal love, the bishops wrote:

> This devoted love finds its unique expression and development in the behaviour which is proper to marriage. The acts by which the married couple are intimately and chastely united are honourable and respectable, and when they are carried out in a truly human way they express and encourage a mutual giving in which a couple gladly and gratefully enrich each other.[26]

Consciously and carefully the bishops avoided any reference in their document to primary and secondary ends of marriage. They said only that in this covenant, spouses would find their vocation to transmit life and educate those to whom life had been transmitted.

A serious effort at the very end of the council to introduce the teaching of Pius XI and Pius XII on procreation as the primary purpose of marriage was clearly rejected. The council fathers accepted the importance of transmission of life "without making the other purposes of marriage of less account."[27]

Moreover, parents were not to fulfill this task fatalistically. They should decide how many children to have and how often.

> They will accordingly discharge their task with human and Christian responsibility, and will reach a right decision for themselves in humble reverence for God and by shared counsel and endeavour, with an eye to their own good and that of their children, whether those already born or those foreseen, discerning the material and spiritual conditions of the times and their condition of life, and bearing in mind the good of the family community, of human society and of the Church. Ultimately married couples ought to make this decision themselves before God.[28]

"Responsible parenthood" was now officially accepted in a document overwhelmingly approved by an ecumenical council and signed by the Pope. How this goal was to be achieved wasn't spelled out in the council, since the Pope had appointed a commission to work on that issue. The council insisted on objective standards for morally harmonizing conjugal love and responsible transmission of life. These standards were "derived from the nature of the human person and its acts." These take into account "the whole meaning of mutual giving and human procreation in the context of true love."[29]

Fourteen years later, in 1979, the Congregation for the Doctrine of the Faith claimed that the council had retained the traditional ordering of primary end of marriage as the procreation and education of children and the secondary end as mutual love of husband and wife.[30] However, the 1983 Code of Canon Law confirmed the teaching of the council. It speaks of the marriage covenant "which by its very nature is ordered to the well-being of the spouses and the procreation and upbringing of children."[31] Contrary to the old custom, "the well-being of the spouses," is mentioned first.

Dialogue and Change

For the fifth and last session of the commission, the Pope added fourteen cardinals and bishops. Ottaviani, head of the Holy Office, was appointed commission president. Cardinal Julius Doepfner, archbishop of Munich, known to be a liberal, and Cardinal John Heenan, archbishop of Westminster, a conservative, were named vice presidents. Four other cardinals were Suenens, Valerian Gracias of Bombay, Joseph Lefebvre of Bourges, and Lawrence Shehan of Baltimore. Bishops were Carlo Colombo, the Pope's theologian, John Dearden of Detroit, chairman of the subcommittee of Vatican II that drafted the council's chapter on marriage and family, Claude Dupuy of Albi, France, Thomas Morris of Cashel, Ireland, José Rafael Pulido-Méndez of Merida, Venezuela, Jean Baptiste Zoa of Yaounda, Cameroon, and Karol Wojtyła of Krakow, Poland (future John Paul II). Wojtyła didn't attend any meetings.[32] Could his participation in the meetings have made a difference? It is interesting to note the case of Cardinal

Heenan. He seemed to have been even more conservative in outlook than Wojtyła. "Yet he, through his attendance at the debates, changed his own views on birth control."[33]

There is no explanation why Wojtyła chose not to attend the meetings of the commission. The accepted explanation has been that he chose to stay home out of solidarity with Primate Wyszyński, who had been denied a passport to go to Rome. However, the passport incident didn't occur until three months after the end of the session.[34]

On May 6, after four weeks of discussions, de Riedmatten had put two questions to theologians for a trial vote. First, can the teaching of Pius XI be changed? Second, "is contraception intrinsically evil, according to natural law, so that it can never be permitted in any case?"[35] A vote on the possibility of change the year before had been 12–7 that the teaching of Pius XI could be changed. Now the vote was 15–4 against the teaching of Pius XI on both questions. Three theologians had changed sides.

In his report de Riedmatten noted that the two sides were not evenly divided. Only 21 percent thought that change was impossible. He pointed out that the Pope himself had picked the members. Their conclusions had been the result of a long and careful study. He also pointed out that the minority who thought contraception intrinsically evil admitted that they could not prove their position. The commission would not recommend any particular method. They were influenced by the negative attitude toward rhythm that showed up in a number of surveys.[36]

At this point, the Crowleys presented results of another more thorough survey of three thousand dedicated Catholic couples from eighteen countries.[37] The survey sought to determine success in practicing rhythm: how it helped regulate the size of families and helped or hurt married relationships. Soon the Crowleys were swamped with mail, mostly from women unloading their burdens as they faithfully tried to follow the rhythm method. One wrote:

> I am on the verge of a nervous breakdown with worry, and my doctor also tells me that it would be unwise to have more children. My husband suffers from colitis, which is a nervous disorder aggravated by continued worry of this immense problem.

Another wrote: "This terrible situation can't but adversely affect the attitude between husband and wife toward each other and reflect on the children." And another: "My husband is away on long business trips and unfortunately his company doesn't take our calendar into consideration." Shaken by what they read, the Crowleys sent letters to the commission secretary with hope that they would be passed on to the Pope.[38]

A second questionnaire to CFM members asked: "What should the Church do?" Seventy-eight percent said, "Change." Only 42 percent said that rhythm helped regulate the size of their families. But 63 percent said that it

> harmed their marriages in varying degrees because of tension, frustration, sexual strain, loss of spontaneity, arguments, irritability, discouragement, insecurity, fear of pregnancy.

Of these couples 290 had also responded to questions in an article in *St. Anthony's Messenger*, "The Church Calls for the Facts." Less than 10 percent said, "Rhythm works and we have a positive reaction to it." About 25 percent said, "Rhythm works and we have a negative reaction to it." About 65 percent said, "Rhythm does not work and we have a negative reaction to it."[39]

Dr. Hellegers reported that women had the greatest difficulty using rhythm during menopause. This made it least applicable when it was most needed to prevent dangerous late-life pregnancy. Dr. John R. Cavanagh, psychiatrist and professor at Catholic University in Washington, had surveyed twenty-three hundred women who used rhythm. Seventy-one percent experienced their greatest sexual desire during ovulation, their most fertile period. Cavanagh concluded: "Rhythm is more psychologically harmful than other methods because it deprives a woman of the conjugal act during the time of her greatest desire." In a note to Heenan he wrote:

> Abstinence as the only means of controlling conception has left Catholics immature emotionally and impoverished financially. It has left them insecure, rebellious and frustrated. Serious psychiatric disorders have arisen as a result.[40]

Delhaye then presented an official Vatican report of a worldwide survey of bishops, requested by the Pope. Bishops' conferences in the "developed countries" reported that birth control was the principal pastoral problem. In "undeveloped countries" a majority of Catholics practiced withdrawal, and abortions were common.

Dr. Albert Görres, physician and professor of psychology at the University of Mainz, West Germany, shared insights he had received at professional gatherings and in talks with priests and lay people. First, apparent unanimity among theologians on the birth control issue was deceptive. Scholars who disagreed with the official teaching had been condemned or silenced. For generations, the scholars kept away from the study of moral theology. They knew what could happen to them if they wrote honestly on the subject. Those who did write saw their role as only to defend the status quo.

Church teaching on birth control, Görres continued, had been based on natural law. When natural law was seen as no longer adequate, it was justified because that is what the Church teaches. Teaching on sexual morality for centuries after Augustine had been subject to serious errors. These distortions were due in part to underlying, but still present and active, Manichaeism, Platonism, Stoicism, and fantastic medieval biological ideas. It was also due to a

> celibate psychosis...a state of mind arising out of the psychic situation of the cleric, one which keeps him from viewing marriage and sexuality with an unprejudiced and comprehensive mind.

Görres asked whether some moral theologians might be "emotionally handicapped...even by unconscious stirrings of resentment, envy and aggression." He questioned appeal to "the consensus of the bishops" and asked if there had not been such a consensus at the time of Galileo.[41]

Two women members of the commission tried to educate the celibate theologians. Mrs. Crowley said: "We have heard some men, married and celibate, argue that rhythm is a way to develop love. But we have heard few women who agree." Mrs. Potvin, married seventeen years and the mother of five, explained frankly and plainly what lovemaking meant to her and her husband.

Dupuy, who arrived before other cardinals and bishops, put some questions to the commission members. "What do you think has been agreed upon?" All but five asserted the need for change and that rhythm was "suitable only for the relatively few, an elite, who have a very strong Christian formation and a low sex drive."

Patrick Crowley was explicit:

I think we agreed that the sense of the faithful is for change. No arguments were presented on the other side of the status quo other than the one that Rome had spoken once and to change would undermine the magisterium. I must say I heard no other argument and I don't think this is a good argument to support an otherwise objectionable position in what we like to call the pilgrim Church.

Crowley asked that the commission create a pastoral statement. He then added:

The preponderance of testimony from the lay members showed that change is anticipated and great problems will arise if no change is made. If the Church fails in this, much of the progress made by the council will be lost. If the Church, that is, the members, learn that change was refused when reason seemed to dictate change, I think the authority will be undermined more than by any change.[42]

On May 23, de Riedmatten brought in Ernest Vogt and Stanislaus Lyonnet, two of Rome's leading Scripture scholars. They assured commission members that the Bible had no teaching on birth control. The Genesis story about Onan wasn't about withdrawal, the oldest form of birth control. It was about Onan's refusal to carry out the obligation under Judaic law to maintain his brother's line.[43] Lyonnet showed that no references to sexual sin in the New Testament had anything to do with contraception.

Another vote on June 3. Was it opportune for the Church to speak without delay? All said yes. Was the Church in a state of doubt about the agreed teaching on the intrinsic evil of contraception? Thirty said yes, five said no. The population experts all favored change in view of the catastrophic problems posed by population growth in many parts of the world. They thought that if the Church took a reasoned position in favor of birth control, it could help prevent massive government sterilization and abortion programs.

Why had cardinals and bishops been added to the commission for its final session? Was this a political maneuver to reinforce the small minority who were certain that contraception was intrinsically evil and that therefore the Church's teaching could never be changed?

John Noonan, who has since been appointed to a federal judgeship in San Francisco, tried to figure out where the new cardinals and bishops stood before they had been involved in any discussion:

For change:	Doubtful:	Against change:
Dearden	Gracias	Binz
Doepfner	Pulido-Méndez	Colombo
Dupuy	Shehan	Heenan
Reuss	Zoa	Lefebvre
Suenens		Morris
		Ottaviani[44]

During extended discussion with input from both sides, cardinals and bishops put serious questions to the theologians. Here is the final vote of the cardinals and bishops on the question: "Whether all contraception was intrinsically evil?"

No	Abstained	Yes
Dearden	Binz	Colombo
Doepfner	Gracias	Morris
Dupuy	Heenan	Ottaviani
Lefebvre		
Pulido-Méndez		
Reuss		
Shehan		
Suenens		
Zoa		

Nine for change, three opposed, three abstained. After thorough discussion with the theologians, several episcopal minds had changed.[45]

How this remarkable shift came about during study and dialogue can be illustrated from accounts of two theologians, Häring and Fuchs.

At Holy Cross Abbey, Häring told how for fifteen years he tried to convince others, and tried even harder to convince himself, without success, of the validity of the Vatican's teaching on the primary and secondary ends of marriage and the rejection of birth control. The reason he could not accept Rome's position was because he had never published anything on marriage without consulting married people. He tried to keep to traditional teaching, explaining it pastorally and pointing to doubts when they were evident.

His conversion came when he was called to the Holy Office several times from 1959 to 1962. He was told that he could not deny that married love was secondary in marriage. Häring, the eleventh of twelve children, said to Ottaviani:

> I repeat and I will repeat to the honor of my parents...that for them married love wasn't a secondary thing. That they could educate us in harmony was greatly due to the fact that for them married love was a great reality.

Gracias, aware that Fuchs had not originally held views he now expressed, asked what had happened. Fuchs explained that theologians on the commission had "made this change, some sooner, some later." His doubts began in 1963. In the academic year 1965–66, he stopped teaching at the Gregorian University because he could not teach a doctrine he himself did not accept. In 1965 he forbade reprinting his textbook that contained the old teaching. His understanding of natural law had changed. He saw that Pius XI's teaching on marriage had been changed in the teaching of Pius XII and Vatican II. There was a development away from the idea that each contraceptive act is intrinsically evil. Everyone on the commission, he said, "both from the right and the left, agreed that the pill presented no special moral case."

On June 28, 1966, Doepfner and de Riedmatten took the commission's final report to the Pope. The commission agreed not to submit majority and minority reports. However, Ottaviani and Ford took it upon themselves to present their opposing position to the Pope. This mistakenly became known as the "minority report" of the commission.[46]

The Long Delay

It would be two years, one month, and a day before the Pope spoke. The story of maneuvering in that period is well told in Kaiser's book. A powerful clique in the Vatican, under the leadership of Ottaviani, had fought bitterly at the council against change in Church teaching on marriage. At the last minute they had tried to force through without debate four amendments to the *Pastoral*

Constitution on the Church in the Modern World that would have explicitly reaffirmed the teaching of Pius XI and Pius XII on marriage and contraception. They failed. So ended the last attempt at "railroading" the council.[47]

Opponents of change had lost the battle in the council. The section on marriage was approved by a vote of 2,047 to 155 and signed by the Pope. Now they had again lost the battle in the birth control commission. Could they persuade the Pope, not only to reject findings of his birth control commission, but to act against clear direction of a great council?

Häring reported at Holy Cross Abbey that, as far as he knew, the commission wasn't further consulted. Only that small minority that supported the teaching of Pius XI was consulted. "I have evidence," he claimed, "evidence for the formation of my own conscience, [that] it was a test case for the curia to affirm that encyclicals stand higher than the council decrees."

Häring received four warnings from the curia. The first was in January 1967. In an interview he had said that the Pope's decision would be in accord with the teaching of the council and not simply a return to Pius XI. He was told by Archbishop Parente that he could not say this. The Pope was totally free to return to the teaching of Pius XI. He wasn't bound by the council.

On another occasion Häring was told that doctrine wasn't to be taken from the council since the council's document was only a pastoral text while the encyclical of Pius XI was pure doctrine. Häring explained that he could not reconcile that with the opening address of John XXIII, who insisted that the genuine teaching office of the Church is thoroughly pastoral. To assert that the encyclical of Pius XI is not pastoral, only pure doctrine, asserts that it is wrong doctrine. Häring continued:

> We had no possibility to approach the Pope. In my eyes he was walled in and thus came to this document which, in my eyes, is a test case of non-collegial exercise of papal authority.

The encyclical letter on birth control was finally published on Monday morning, July 29, 1968. The long wait was over.

Chapter 5

BIRTH CONTROL
Old Wine in New Wineskins

The mutual molding of a husband and wife, this determined
effort to perfect each other can, in a very real sense, be said
to be the chief [*primaria*] reason and purpose of matrimony,
provided matrimony be looked at not in the restricted sense
as instituted for the proper conception and education of the
child, but more widely as the blending of life as a whole and
the mutual interchange of sharing thereof.
> —Pius XI, *On Chaste Marriage*, §24,
> paragraph omitted from the 1930 translation
> of the National Catholic Welfare Conference

The long-awaited encyclical had arrived. With its statement that
"each and every marriage act must remain open to the transmission of life" (§14) it was immediately clear that Paul VI had
ignored significant developments in the teaching on marriage at
Vatican II and had rejected his own birth control commission's
recommendations.

The birth control encyclical is written in the language of Vatican II. However, it actually reaffirms the teachings of Pius XI and
Pius XII, which the council (despite great pressure) had refused
to accept. Thus, while the language of the birth control encyclical
is derived from contemporary personalist philosophy accepted by
the council, the doctrinal teaching at the heart of the encyclical
comes from the teaching of Pius XI and Pius XII. That teaching
comes from a particular understanding of natural law that is derived ultimately from Stoicism, especially from the Roman jurist
Ulpian (d. 228). It is the old wine in new wineskins.

Why did Paul VI ignore the more humane and personalistic
teaching on responsible parenthood that his own birth control

commission, following Vatican II, had recommended? Why did he return to a rigoristic teaching based on a Stoic understanding of natural law? As Rahner wrote:

> It becomes clear in the encyclical itself that the real and primary reason for adhering to this position is the need that is felt to hold firm to the traditional teaching of Pius XI and Pius XII.[1]

This was the teaching that Paul VI, as Cardinal Montini, had publicly upheld when he was undersecretary of state under Pius XII.

The Pope gave as his own reasons: lack of unanimity within the birth control commission and, he continued,

> especially because certain approaches and criteria for a solution to this question had emerged which were at variance with the moral doctrine on marriage constantly taught by the magisterium of the Church.[2]

In paragraph 4 of the birth control encyclical, Paul referred to the Church's "consistent teaching on the nature of marriage, on the correct use of conjugal rights and on all the duties of husband and wife."

What is to be said about these two reasons: lack of unanimity within the birth control commission and departure from the constant, consistent teaching of the Church on marriage? Although not quite unanimous, the vote for change by the birth control commission, whose members he himself had chosen, had been overwhelming. As for the Pope's need to sustain the magisterium's constant, consistent teaching, ample evidence exists of dramatic shifts in that teaching over the centuries.

First, we will review the history of the Church's teaching on "the correct use of conjugal rights" and the encyclical's misuse of the teaching of Vatican II. This will help us evaluate the encyclical and its meaning in the lives of married Catholics. Reaction to the encyclical and the significance of that reaction will be treated in the next chapter.

The Stoic Tradition and Clerical Power

From Justin Martyr early in the second century to the *Roman Catechism* in the sixteenth century, all Christian writers taught that the use of the marriage act could be justified only for procreation.[3]

Justin Martyr wrote in his *Apology for Christians:* "We Christians either marry only to produce children, or, if we refuse to marry, are completely continent."[4] Athenagoras, in his address to the emperor in 177, explained that like a farmer who does not sow seed into his already planted field until after harvest, so Christians avoid intercourse during pregnancy. They only marry to produce children.[5] This was the teaching of the Church fathers.

Since no basis for such a teaching is present in the Hebrew Scriptures or in Jesus' teaching, the question comes up: Where did it come from?

As James Brundage has pointed out, the immediate source of influence on Christian writers was the pagan Stoics, whose high ideals for morality challenged the Christians to copy them or even do better.[6] Natural law or the law of nature was the basis for these ideals. The famous Stoic jurist Ulpian supplied to Christian writers their understanding of natural law. For Ulpian, natural law consisted in the laws of nature that animals and humans had in common. Among the domestic animals with which Ulpian was familiar, the female accepted the male only when she was in heat. So it was the law of nature for humans and animals alike that sexual intercourse should only take place for breeding.

The Stoic Musonius Rufus taught that conjugal intercourse could be morally justified only for procreation. Even in marriage, intercourse for pleasure was reprehensible. For the Christian Clement of Alexandria, "To have coition other than to procreate children is to do injury to nature."[7] Indeed, with God's grace Christians can attain a higher ideal than pagan Stoics:

> The human ideal of continence, I mean that which is set forth by Greek philosophers, teaches that one should fight desire and not be subservient to it so as to bring it to practical effect. But our ideal is not to experience desire at all.[8]

Origen, in the next generation, taught that a man should have intercourse with his wife "only for the sake of posterity."[9] Clement, Origen, and the *Didascalia,* a collection of canons from Syria in the third century, forbade intercourse with a pregnant wife since this is not to produce children, but for pleasure.

In the fourth and fifth centuries, Stoic sexual ethics were combined with ideas about ritual purity from the Hebrew Scriptures. To these were added primitive ideas about the relationship between sex and the holy. From this came insistence on priestly abstinence from intercourse before celebrating the Eucharist. That led to a demand for priestly celibacy.[10]

There may, however, have been another reason to account for the strong anti-sexuality in the early Church. Samuel Laeuchli suggests that the clergy used control of sex to dominate the laity.[11] Laeuchli compares the treatment of sex in the Bible with the treatment of sexual offenses by the Council of Elvira (Spain, c. 309). In contrast with the Bible's minimal concern, more than 46 percent of Elvira's eighty-one canons deal with sexual transgressions, and the gravest punishments are applied to them.

The three capital sins, subject to canonical penance in the early Church, were murder, apostasy, and adultery. The seriousness of murder needs no explanation. In the century before Elvira, there were efforts to force Christians to take part in emperor worship. This was idolatry. To yield was apostasy, one of the gravest threats to the Church.

Now, however, persecutions came to an end. Under Constantine, Christianity would soon become the official religion of the empire. The issue of apostasy became less important. The clergy seem to have shifted their emphasis to controlling the laity in their sexual behavior. In the decrees of the Council of Elvira only 12.4 percent dealt with idolatry.

The bishops at Elvira imposed a rigid anti-sexual discipline on believers in general. But in canon 33 of Elvira these celibate bishops made an extraordinary attempt to control the lives of the married clergy. It decreed:

> Bishops, presbyters, and deacons and all other clerics having a position in the ministry are ordered to abstain completely from their wives and not to have children. Whoever, in fact, does this, shall be expelled from the dignity of the clerical state.[12]

Why did the celibate bishops command that married clergy not have intercourse with their wives? Laeuchli proposes that this was in an effort to distinguish the clergy as a purer, higher caste superior to the laity. Use of the phrase "dignity of the clerical state" betrays a mentality of belonging to a higher order. This is confirmed by fifteen decrees dealing with different ranks. The clergy, because they lived such ascetical lives, could claim a special right to leadership in the Church.

In the strongly anti-sexual atmosphere of the world in which Elvira was held, not to get married would have been the ideal. The apostle Paul had agreed, but, of course, not even he could eliminate the institution of marriage. Bishops and presbyters at Elvira, therefore, created a double standard: a superior, non-sexual way of life for the clergy, above that of the laity. The clergy determined what was permitted and what was forbidden in the laity's sexual behavior. They enforced their decisions with the threat of excommunication in this life and damnation in the next.

Later in the fourth century, Jerome enthusiastically accepted Stoicism's negative understanding of morality in marriage.[13] He saw the marriage act as lustful, unless for procreation. Jerome reworded a Stoic epigram to read: "An adulterer is he who is too ardent a lover of his wife." This saying, with others from the Stoic Seneca, became for centuries watchwords of those defending an exclusively procreative purpose for intercourse.

Augustine agreed. Only a spouse who had intercourse at the other's request could lawfully have intercourse without a procreative intention. Augustine went further. He integrated Stoic teaching with his theological understanding of original sin and concupiscence. Concupiscence and original sin were not identical, but rather concupiscence resulted from original sin. It was the "heat" that always accompanied copulation, the "confusion of lust," "the law of sin." Evidence for concupiscence's existence was reason's inability to control the generative organs. Original sin is passed on by concupiscence. So sexual intercourse, stained by concupiscence, could be justified only by a procreative intention. Augustine's teaching has dominated the Roman Catholic Church to our day.

Powerful reinforcement for this anti-sexual morality came from one of the most important early Popes, Gregory the Great (590–604). In his influential *Pastoral Rule* Gregory taught that not only was a procreative intention necessary, but that those who "mixed" any pleasure with the marriage act "transgressed the law of marriage." They had "befouled" their intercourse by their "pleasures."[14] Gregory wrote St. Augustine of Canterbury that "even lawful intercourse cannot take place without fleshly desire... [which] can by no means be without sin."[15] Stoic distrust of pleasure was pushed to the limit.

This tradition was maintained for centuries, first by the monks and bishops, writers and enforcers of the penitentials from the sixth through the eleventh centuries, then by the canonists and theologians. The twelfth-century theologian Peter Lombard stated that "coitus is reprehensible and evil, unless it be excused by the goods of marriage."[16] Only the good of offspring justified intercourse.[17] Those who went beyond the intention of procreating were guilty of venial sin.[18] Gratian considered intercourse with a contraceptive intent a very slight sin like excessive talking, eating after hunger is satisfied, being annoyed at a persistent beggar, or being late for divine services because of oversleeping.[19]

A few writers in the twelfth century began to suggest that marital sex had values apart from procreation. St. Bernard of Clairvaux considered it a legitimate outlet for sexual urges that otherwise lead to debauchery, incest, or homosexual activity. According to Anselm of Laon, love in marriage had its own value: even a childless marriage had merit if the couple loved one another. Nevertheless, these writers had reservations, and Hugh of St. Victor encouraged couples to subordinate sexual pleasure to the serious business of procreation.[20]

In spite of this tendency to be less harsh, the harsher teaching was carried to its ultimate extreme in the thirteenth century by the powerful Pope Innocent III. He agreed with some other theologians that seeking pleasure in intercourse could be mortally sinful. Indeed, it was always at least venially sinful. He saw no valid connection between love and intercourse. Here was a papacy that was gaining more and more control over the thought and life of the Western Church. It fully accepted procreation as the only justification for marriage along with Augustine's teaching on original sin and concupiscence.

In the same century, St. Thomas Aquinas developed a "natural law" understanding of marriage to which Pope Paul VI's thinking in the birth control encyclical is very congenial. Aquinas spoke of an order of nature, sacred and unchangeable because it comes from God. Therefore sins contrary to nature, by violating the order of nature, "are an affront to God, the ordainer of nature, even though no other person is injured."[21] In this view the biological structure and procreative purpose of coitus is part of the order of nature ordained by God, not to be altered by human intervention. Therefore, intercourse only for pleasure or without intention to procreate would be a sin against nature. This was common teaching through the fifteenth century.

Tradition Challenged, Prohibition Maintained

Gratian had written of "the second institution of marriage," after the fall, "so that the weakness which inclines to moral baseness may be rescued by the honorableness of marriage." Alexander of Hales, in the thirteenth century, used this passage from Gratian to justify marital intercourse to avoid fornication.[22] That now made three lawful uses: to procreate, at the other spouse's request, and to avoid fornication. This concession that intercourse could be used to avoid fornication received further approval in the sixteenth century in the *Roman Catechism* of Pope Pius V.

But, in spite of the *Roman Catechism*, controversy over this third lawful justification continued. It was finally ended in the late eighteenth century by St. Alphonsus Liguori. He pointed out that if Paul in 1 Corinthians 7 considered one of the purposes of marriage to be an outlet for the sexual impulse, then it must be lawful to seek intercourse in order to avoid fornication.

In the meantime, forbidding intercourse for pleasure was also under attack. It is true that the prohibition had been renewed by the Holy Office under Innocent XI in 1679. However, the language was weak. Theologians could get away with defending intercourse "for pleasure." This radical change in the motives for marital intercourse prepared for Pius XII's approval of rhythm. The stage was set for Vatican Council II's radical reevaluation of marriage.

In the sixteenth century, poverty and the educational well-being of children began to be recognized as reasons that justified a wife's refusal to have intercourse. By Liguori's time, theologians recognized the morality of economic and educational reasons for not wanting more children. Spouses could refuse the basic right to marital intercourse. So the ground was prepared for Vatican II's teaching on responsible parenthood.

Changes promoted by theologians during three hundred years, from 1450 to 1750, can be summarized. A procreative intention was no longer required. Intercourse for pleasure was tolerated. One spouse could refuse the marital debt because of the need to feed and educate existing offspring. These changes radically undermined the centuries-old teaching that only procreation justified intercourse.

With such significant changes in the reasons for lawful intercourse, why was the Church's condemnation of contraception not questioned?

Let us compare what happened to two prohibitions, both strongly maintained during the first fifteen hundred years of Church teaching: prohibition against contraception and prohibition against usury, that is, taking interest on loans. Both prohibitions had been taught by theologians and firmly upheld by the magisterium.

The prohibition against usury was dropped.[23] The prohibition against contraception was kept. The Church's condemnation of usury had a strong biblical basis. There is no basis for the condemnation of contraception in Scripture. Usury is very clearly forbidden in the Hebrew Scriptures and had been roundly condemned for centuries by Popes and councils. The only scriptural support for the condemnation of contraception had been based on a misunderstanding of the story of Onan in Genesis 38:8–10. Onan was not even mentioned by Liguori in his *Moral Theology*. Pope Paul VI didn't mention Onan in his birth control encyclical. None of his sixteen quotations from the New Testament were used to directly support his condemnation of contraception.

The reasons for the condemnation of both usury and contraception had by now been challenged. Why was the condemnation against usury dropped, while the prohibition of contraception continued in full vigor? I believe that the difference in treatment of the two moral problems was due to the difference in the two groups who were calling for change.

Unmarried churchmen up to the highest level were deeply involved in financial transactions requiring use of credit. Ecclesiastical organizations and individuals were involved in both borrowing and lending. The banking system was indispensable for an increasingly centralized Church. It became easy to justify financial methods so widely used by the Church itself. Moreover, the rationale for the condemnation of usury had been seriously undermined by the sixteenth century's commercial revolution and daring innovations of contemporary moral theologians. Change in teaching on usury was promoted by a relatively well-knit group of bankers involved with the Church. Notable among these were the Fuggers, who had become the Popes' bankers. Jacob Fugger of Augsburg claimed that he was involved in the appointment of every bishop in Germany.[24] The opposition to the laws against usury included celibate clergymen willing to work to get rid of such laws.

Quite different was the case of the "simple faithful." They were not represented at the levels in the Church where changes in the condemnation of contraception could have been made. Moreover, ordinary married people, unlike bankers, were not organized to work for change. So the condemnation of usury, even though it was biblically based and supported for centuries by Popes and councils, was reversed. The condemnation of contraception, with no basis in revelation, remained unchanged. A celibate clerical caste had begun to manipulate the laity through the control of their sex lives as early as the fourth-century Council of Elvira. It continued in full force. The condemnation of contraception was so strong that there was little opportunity for the development of a "probable opinion" contradicting official Church teaching.

Toward Vatican II

Meanwhile, the final stage in this history of change and development had begun with the discovery of the ovum by Karl Ernst von Baer in 1827. That discovery made it clear that not every act of intercourse could lead to conception. In 1853 the Roman congregation that dealt with moral issues was asked about some married couples who acted upon the medical opinion that the wife was sterile several days each month. If they had legitimate reasons for avoiding pregnancy, could they be left undisturbed if they had intercourse only on sterile days? The Roman congregation said yes.

In 1930, Pius XI removed any official doubt about the morality of intercourse during the sterile period in the encyclical letter *On Chaste Marriage*. In the encyclical the Pope seemed to accept Augustine's teaching completely, but actually he began to modify that centuries-old teaching at two critical points. First, the Pope no longer required a procreative intention to justify lawful intercourse. Then he weakened the teaching that procreation and education of children is the primary end of marriage while everything else is secondary.

As for need to have a procreative intention, Pius XI taught that sexual intercourse in the sterile period could be lawful. He wrote:

> Nor are those considered as acting against nature who in the married state use their right in the proper manner although on account of natural reasons either of time or of certain defects, new life cannot be brought forth. For in matrimony as well as in the use of the matrimonial rights there are also secondary ends, such as mutual aid, the cultivating of mutual love, and the quieting of concupiscence which husband and wife are not forbidden to consider so long as they are subordinated to the primary end and so long as the intrinsic nature of the act is preserved.[25]

Couples could have intercourse morally with the deliberate intention not to procreate because they knew that conception wasn't possible. The morality of the act now depended on whether intercourse was performed "in the proper manner" with "the intrinsic nature of the act...preserved."

Pius XI also prepared for an important development at Vatican II. The council deliberately refused to subordinate secondary ends of marriage to primary ends. For at least fifteen hundred years, from Augustine to the 1917 Code of Canon Law, this subordination had been central to Catholic teaching on marriage.[26] For Augustine, writing in 419, "the propagation of children is the first and natural and legitimate end of marriage."[27] Thirteen years before the encyclical *On Chaste Marriage*, the Code of Canon Law had stated: "The primary end of marriage is the procreation and education of children; its secondary end is mutual help and the allaying of concupiscence."[28]

This centuries-old teaching had been challenged in the late 1920s by European philosophers and theologians.[29] Now an important paragraph in *On Chaste Marriage* opened the way for a broader understanding of the meaning and purpose of marriage. Even though Pius XI spoke of primary and secondary ends, he wrote of conjugal love, which is so important for growth of conjugal faith:

> This conjugal faith, however, which is most aptly called by St. Augustine "faith of chastity," blooms more freely, more beautifully and more nobly, when it is rooted in that more excellent soil, the

love of husband and wife which pervades all the duties of married life and holds pride of place in Christian marriage.[30]

Then Pius concluded that "in a very real sense" marriage's primary purpose could be seen to be the blending of two lives and their mutual sharing. In a paragraph mysteriously omitted in the official American translation of the encyclical *On Chaste Marriage*, he wrote:

> The mutual molding of a husband and wife, this determined effort to perfect each other can, in a very real sense, be said to be the chief [*primaria*] reason and purpose of matrimony, provided matrimony be looked at not in the restricted sense as instituted for the proper conception and education of the child, but more widely as the blending of life as a whole and the mutual interchange of sharing thereof.[31]

This paragraph was still missing in the widely used 1939 Paulist edition of *The Five Great Encyclicals*, but is included in later editions. But when the passage was finally included, why was *primaria* translated "chief" rather than "primary"? Was it because the word "primary" had been used for many centuries in discussing one of the ends of marriage? To have translated *primaria* as "primary" would have called attention to an important change that was developing.

All that was needed to make the change was to recognize that perhaps marriage should be looked at from this wider viewpoint. The bishops at Vatican II would adopt the broader perspective in their treatment of marriage. They would deliberately reject the distinction between primary and secondary ends.

The final stage of the development before Vatican Council II came with Pius XII. In a 1951 speech to Italian midwives, Pius said that for serious reasons the sterile period could be used to avoid conception. Such reasons could be medical, eugenic, economic, or social. With these serious motives, he said, "it follows that the observance of the sterile period can be licit."[32] Economic motives were not limited to extreme poverty, and "social reasons" seemed wide enough to include population problems. A month later, Pius emphasized his intention to authorize regulation of births.

> We have affirmed the lawfulness and at the same time the limits — in truth quite broad — of a regulation of offspring.... Science, it

may be hoped, will develop for this method a sufficiently secure base.[33]

A practice whose intention was specifically contraceptive had been officially approved at the highest level in the Church.

The Preconciliar Teaching on Birth Control

With Pius XII, Church teaching had indeed come very far. For centuries intercourse without the intention to procreate had been condemned even during pregnancy. It was a nonprocreative use of a function destined by the Creator solely for generation of offspring. From Justin Martyr well into the nineteenth century a procreative intention or the use as a remedy for concupiscence had been required to justify marital intercourse. Moreover, Pius XI allowed intercourse in the sterile period.

Significantly, Pius XI shifted the emphasis for determining morality away from the intention to procreate to insisting that to be moral the act had to be performed properly. Pius XII even permitted intercourse with the deliberate intention not to procreate if serious reasons existed. However, the act to be moral had to be performed physically "in the proper manner." Pius XII's approval of a contraceptive intention prepared for further developments.

Vatican II emphasized "responsible parenthood."

> [The parents] will thoughtfully take into account both their own welfare and that of their children, those already born and those which may be foreseen. For this accounting they will reckon with both the material and spiritual conditions of the times as well as of their state in life. Finally, they will consult the interests of the family group, of temporal society, and of the Church herself.
>
> The parents themselves would ultimately make this judgment, in the sight of God.[34]

The council reaffirmed all the traditional values, but did so without demanding that each individual sexual act be done in the proper manner. "Harmonizing conjugal love with the responsible transmission of life" did not depend on how the act was performed. It depended on faithfulness to "the nature of the human person and his acts," carried out in a fully human way.[35] Morality in sexual matters as in all others depended on understanding what it meant to be human and how we treat one another as human beings.

There has been no "constant, consistent"[36] teaching from Justin to the present to which Paul VI could return. He returned to the static understanding of natural law taught by Pius XI and Pius XII. He leapfrogged back over the council's emphasis on persons to the previous emphasis on the structure of the act. He used the new language of the Vatican II *Pastoral Constitution on the Church in the Modern World* but repeated the teaching of his immediate predecessors Pius XI and Pius XII.

Canon Delhaye, one of the original drafters of the *Pastoral Constitution on the Church in the Modern World* and also a member of the birth control commission, has shown quite clearly how Pope Paul in the birth control encyclical used passages from the *Pastoral Constitution on the Church in the Modern World* to reinstate teaching from before the council.[37] He finds seven significant places in the encyclical where Paul used passages from the *Pastoral Constitution on the Church in the Modern World* in the birth control encyclical. In each case Paul used the council's language but undermined its changes in the teaching on marriage. The council bases objective norms for conjugal life and family planning "on the nature of the human person and his acts," that is, on the dignity of the human person. The encyclical changes the text so that "nature" refers not to human persons but to the institution of marriage.[38]

The birth control encyclical returned to a biological understanding of natural law based on Ulpian's statement:

> Natural law is what nature has taught all animals. For this law is not peculiar to the human race but common to all animals that are born on land or sea and to birds. From this comes the union of man and woman that we call matrimony, from this the procreation and upbringing of children.[39]

The council rejected this biological approach. It insisted that for Christians the standard for judging conjugal love in the marriage act is not biological, but psychological. The council emphasizes the difference between the human and the merely animal. "The sexual nature of man and woman and the human faculty of reproduction," wrote the council fathers, "are wonderfully superior to what is possessed in the lower stages of life."[40]

A word should be said about the council's use of the Bible. Vatican II presented its chapter on marriage as a meeting between

God's revelation in sacred Scripture and contemporary human ideals. It uses Genesis and the Gospels extensively. The birth control encyclical by contrast is entirely dependent on a "natural law" argumentation.

A "New and Distinct" Teaching?

Without Scripture to support his principal contentions and relying instead solely on a natural law theory derived ultimately from Stoicism, Pope Paul taught that it is "absolutely required that *any use whatever of marriage* must retain its natural potential to procreate human life"[41] (emphasis in original). He based his teaching on the *inseparability* established in the divine plan between the unitive and the procreative meanings of the sex act:

> This particular doctrine, often expounded by the Magisterium of the Church, is based on the inseparable connection, established by God, which man on his own initiative may not break, between the unitive significance and the procreative significance which are both inherent to the marriage act.[42]

Then in paragraph 14, which Lambruschini in his presentation of the birth control encyclical to the press called "the center, the nucleus, the apex, the heart and the key of the encyclical,"[43] Pope Paul spelled out specific, concrete norms that exclude all contraceptive activity. He taught that

> excluded is any action, which either before, at the moment of, or after sexual intercourse, is specifically intended to prevent procreation—whether as an end or as a means.

Nor did he permit choice of contraception as the lesser of two evils. For

> it is never lawful, even for the gravest of reasons, to do evil that good may come of it—in other words, to intend positively something which intrinsically contradicts the moral order, and which must therefore be judged unworthy of man, even though the intention is to protect or promote the welfare of an individual, of a family or of society in general. Consequently, it is a serious error to think that a whole married life of otherwise normal relations can justify sexual intercourse that is deliberately contraceptive and so intrinsically wrong.[44]

Every positive act which is deliberately contraceptive has been excluded. It doesn't matter if such acts are necessary to preserve the marriage itself or to protect the environment in which children could be wholesomely raised. There are no loopholes. Paul VI felt obliged to place these extreme limits on human freedom of choice in this important area of human life. He was reluctant to overturn the explicit teaching of his recent predecessors.

Noonan suggests that Paul VI advanced "a new and distinct" foundation for his doctrine. Where does Pope Paul get this new and distinct teaching on the "inseparable connection established by God" between "the unitive significance and the procreative significance" of the marriage act that cannot be broken by human choice?[45] In the first edition of *Why You Can Disagree* I had proposed *Love and Responsibility*, by Karol Wojtyła, as the source of Pope Paul's new teaching on the inseparability of the procreative and unitive meanings of the marital act. Wojtyła had written in 1960: "Love and parenthood must not therefore be separated one from the other. Willingness for parenthood is an indispensable condition of love."[46] We knew that Paul VI read *Love and Responsibility* while he waited for the report of the birth control commission.[47] Did it influence his appointment of Wojtyła to the commission?

Thanks to the critically acclaimed *Pope John Paul II: The Biography* by Tad Szulc we now know. Szulc writes: "Actually, Wojtyła was a drafter of the encyclical at the outset of his cardinalate, a fact that has never been publicly disclosed."[48]

Wojtyła hadn't attended the final session of the birth control commission when the bishops and cardinals were all present. However, he was in contact with the Pope. He had a private audience with the Pope on April 20, 1967, just before he was made cardinal, and then another on July 3, after being made cardinal. Szulc reports that a year later:

> Wojtyła had been working quietly in Kraców on the draft of the encyclical at least since returning as a cardinal a year earlier. He organized his own Kraców commission on birth control matters, which prepared material for *Humanae vitae* and forwarded it directly to the pope. He said later, "We had sent some materials to the Vatican." A Polish theologian who worked with Wojtyła on this matter says that "about sixty percent of our draft is contained in the encyclical."

Wojtyła was in Rome for a late-morning meeting with the Pope again on February 19, 1968, five months before the publication of *Humanae vitae.*[49]

Wojtyła was elected Pope in October 1978. Nine months later the Congregation for the Doctrine of the Faith began the process against Charles E. Curran. Curran had led the opposition against the birth control encyclical in the United States.

The statement about an inseparable connection between the unitive and the procreative significance, as Theodore Mackin, S.J., points out, is not a statement of a moral principle. It is presented as if it were a scientific fact that can be verified in anthropology. With no documentation or verification, the Pope presents it as if self-evident.[50] However, it cannot be verified biologically. Unlike mammals below the level of primates, human beings do not limit coitus to the fertile period. Nor can it be verified by a comparative study of marriage customs and sexual practices among various peoples.

This claim to an absolute linkage between unitive and procreative significance of human sexuality is based on the Stoic Ulpian's teaching that natural law is what the human race has in common with all animals "as it is manifested both in the sexual relationship and in the raising of children and whelps." Stoics like Seneca, and following him Christians like Clement, Ambrose, and Jerome, thought that what animals did was "natural." They were convinced that sexual activity in the animal world revealed a universal pattern. This was the ideal model of sex uncorrupted by sin. Their analysis was derived from the observation of sexual activity among domestic animals like cows, sheep, or horses where a female accepts the male only when in heat. Since such activity was reproductive, they concluded that coitus is inseparably connected with procreation.

This Stoic conclusion, however, was based on too narrow a field of observation. Like our own experience of primates until quite recently, the Stoics had contact with apes and monkeys only in captivity. Like us, they presumed that these primates' "abnormal" sexual play was due to the corrupting effect of captivity and human contact.

The Stoics were not aware, as we now are, of the sexual behavior of higher primates in their natural habitat. Among those mammals closest to us on the evolutionary scale, sexual activ-

Birth Control

ity is extremely complex and is not limited to the time of the female's heat. It performs significant functions in bonding and creating group relationships.[51] "Nature" actually teaches that the higher we go in the evolutionary scale, the more evident the *separability* of the unitive and the procreative becomes. This is true as consciousness and conscious decision-making supersede blind instinct. Indeed, as Rahner pointed out " 'nature' itself allows us to take these two aspects apart from one another and to take either one of them as our motive for the act."[52]

Mackin's point is that the Pope's major premise is an unproven hypothesis. But from hypothetical premises one can draw only hypothetical conclusions. Mackin asks how, in matters involving such heavy burdens and grave suffering, the Pope can bind consciences on the basis of reasoning only hypothetically true? Moreover, in this important case the evidence strongly suggests that the hypothesis is false.

In a similar vein, Father John Meyendorff, leading Russian Orthodox scholar and theologian, finds unacceptable the distinction between natural and artificial in contemporary Roman Catholic teaching. Speaking of periodic continence he asks:

> Is continence really "natural"? Is not any control of human functions "artificial"? Should it, therefore, be condemned as sinful? And finally, a serious theological question: is anything "natural" necessarily good? For even St. Paul saw that continence can lead to "burning."

Meyendorff concludes that

> it has never been the Church's practice to give moral guidance by issuing standard formulas claiming universal validity on questions which actually require a personal act of conscience.... The question of birth control and of its acceptable forms can only be solved by individual couples.[53]

I never see it mentioned but surely the teaching of the birth control encyclical is a serious obstacle to reunion with the Orthodox Churches.

Grave Sin or Venial Sin?

How binding is the teaching of the birth control encyclical? Joseph Selling says the encyclical makes no direct connection between contraception and sin. He compares Paul VI's encyclical to Pius XI's 1930 encyclical condemning contraception with its clear references to the "sinfulness" of contraceptive acts. Selling notes absence of the word "sin" in critical passages of Pope Paul's encyclical. Moreover, Pius XI made explicit the relation between use of contraception and grave sin. Paul VI, on the other hand, never speaks of "grave matter." Selling thinks this is a giant step forward.[54]

But we must ask if this benign interpretation of Paul VI's encyclical is justified. "Grave sin" is another way of saying "deserving of eternal damnation." In the birth control encyclical Paul VI justifies the Church's competence "in her Magisterium to interpret natural moral law," because "the natural law declares the will of God and its faithful observance is *necessary for men's eternal salvation*" (emphasis added).[55] The language is more benign than that of Pius XI, evidence of Pope Paul VI's compassion and anguish, but the moral evaluation of contraception seems to be unchanged.

No explicit statement in the encyclical suggests that contraceptive acts are only imperfections or slight faults. They seem rather to involve eternal salvation or damnation. This is confirmed by the gravity attached to all sexual sins in the 1975 *Vatican Declaration on Sexual Ethics* approved by Pope Paul VI. Only premarital sex, homosexuality, and masturbation are mentioned by name. But surely adultery, artificial contraception, and other unnamed sexual sins are included in the comprehensive statement:

> A person therefore sins mortally not only when his action comes from direct contempt for love of God and neighbor, but also when he consciously and freely, for whatever reason, chooses something which is seriously disordered. For in this choice... there is already included contempt for the divine commandment: the person turns himself away from God and loses charity. Now according to Christian tradition and the Church's teaching, and as right reason also recognizes, the moral order of sexuality involves such high values of human life that every violation of this order is objectively sinful.[56]

In this Declaration, as in all statements on sexual matters coming from the Vatican in recent years, tone and language are often those of the *Pastoral Constitution on the Church in the Modern World*, but the teaching is pre–Vatican II.

Why was this teaching so rigidly maintained? The members of the birth control commission who insisted on the intrinsic evil of contraception conceded that they could not prove their position. Ultimately the real reason was to safeguard the magisterium, the teaching of two Popes as recent as Pius XI and Pius XII. Häring was convinced that the birth control encyclical was a test case to show that papal encyclicals ranked higher than council decrees.

Pope Paul VI's implied intention is to maintain the teaching that contraception involves mortal sin. Häring spoke to this issue at Holy Cross Abbey:

> Behind all of this, of course, is the great problem...stated by Father Zalba. He cried out, and I understand it was the real anguish of a soul of a good man: "What then with the millions we have up to now sent to hell, if these things can be changed?" Mrs. Crowley, this nice and gentle American lady, responded: "Father Zalba, are you so sure that God executed all of your orders?"

Chapter 6

BIRTH CONTROL
A Teaching "Not Received"

> Certainly, if I am obliged to bring religion into afterdinner toasts (which indeed does not seem to be quite the thing) I shall drink, — to the Pope, if you please, — still to Conscience first, and to the Pope afterward.
>
> —John Henry Newman, "Letter to the Duke of Norfolk"

"Teaching is not a unilateral activity," said Bishop James Malone at the meeting of the American bishops in November 1986. "One is only teaching when someone is being taught. Teaching and learning are mutually conditional."[1] Moreover, teaching fails to be teaching when not accepted by those to be taught. It hasn't been received.

Response to the birth control encyclical's "teaching" was immediate and dramatic. Never in papal history had there been such negative response to a papal teaching. Karl Rahner wrote that opposition was "far greater, far swifter, far more decided and far more vocal" than had been reaction to any previous doctrinal pronouncements by Popes.[2]

In chapter 2, I very briefly indicated the extent of dissent from the birth control encyclical's teaching. Over six hundred theologians in the United States and twenty leading European theologians signed dissenting statements. Sixty percent of American priests did not think all artificial contraception wrong, only 29 percent were certain it is wrong, and only 13 percent were willing to refuse absolution to those practicing birth control. The Gallup poll showed that by 1992, 87 percent of all American Catholics favored use of artificial birth control.

The Bishops

More surprising than the response of theologians and the laity were statements from national episcopal conferences. Bishops rather than priests, or even theologians, are usually designated "official teachers" and spokespersons in the Church. Bishops are not like theologians who pick their own professions. They are all now appointed by Rome. One would therefore expect from bishops a high degree of loyalty to papal teaching. Unanimous agreement with the birth control encyclical from the world's bishops would have given strong endorsement to the encyclical. But, as Joseph Selling points out, "never before have so many bishops responded to a papal encyclical and never before have their responses been so varied, and sometimes critical."[3] To say only "sometimes critical" will be seen to be a decided understatement.

It will be recalled that the bishops at Vatican II had respectfully turned aside Pope Paul VI's request that the council explicitly repeat the statements of his predecessors, Pius XI and Pius XII, on birth control.[4] When three cardinals and the Melkite patriarch called for a change in the official teaching on birth control, Paul VI stopped discussion in the council and reserved the decision to himself. Now in their reactions to the encyclical, a great deal would be revealed.

In the statements issued by episcopal conferences, bishops almost unanimously repeated what the Pope wrote in the birth control encyclical. How they did this differed very much from conference to conference. Some merely repeated the teaching. Others presented the teaching and explained why it is valid, authoritative, and binding in conscience. Others first acknowledged the encyclical as an authoritative statement to which respect must be shown. Then they developed the teaching in their own way. Often they introduced new ideas that clearly qualified the papal position.

Selling has classified statements from national bishops' conferences in three groups. Group A includes bishops' conferences that clearly accepted the encyclical. Group B clearly changed the encyclical's teaching. Group C seemed to Selling to be uncertain.

I believe that Selling has been too conservative in his analysis. He has called some statements uncertain that were written am-

Table 1
BISHOPS' STATEMENTS ON
THE BIRTH CONTROL ENCYCLICAL

From Selling, *Reaction to Humanae vitae*, Appendix B3.
The numbers after some conferences refer to a particular statement
when a conference issued more than one statement.

Group A Clear Acceptance	Group B Clear Mitigation	Group C Uncertain
Interim Statements:		
Spain (1) Vietnam	Netherlands (1)	U.S.A. (1)

Statements issued during the first year after promulgation:

Group A	Group B	Group C
Australia (1)	Austria	Brazil
Ceylon	Belgium	Czechoslovakia
Colombia	Canada	East Germany
Dahomey	CELAM*	England/Wales
Ireland (1, 2)	France	India
Korea	Indonesia (1, 2)	Indonesia (3)
Malta (1)	Netherlands (2)	Italy
Mexico (1, 2)	Scandinavia	Japan
New Zealand	Switzerland	U.S.A. (2)
Philippines	West Germany	
Poland (1, 2)		
Portugal		
Puerto Rico		
Rhodesia		
Scotland		
Senegal		
Spain (2)		
Yugoslavia (1)		

Later Statements:

Group A	Group B	Group C
Yugoslavia (2)	Indonesia (4)	Austria (2)
Ireland (3)	Malta (2)	
	Mexico (3)	
	South Africa	

*Conferencia episcopal latinoamericana

biguously to obscure the fact that they did not fully agree with the Pope's teaching.

American statements illustrate the point. A preliminary statement issued by the National Conference of Catholic Bishops spoke of the Pope's unique role in the Church and asked "our priests and people to receive with sincerity what he has taught, to study it carefully, and to form their consciences in its light." Many interpreted this to mean that they were still free to decide in conscience how they could act. Then the conference's general secretary issued a "clarificatory" statement. He insisted that the bishops had not departed from the Pope's teaching. People had to form their consciences, but they had to form a *correct* conscience.[5]

Selling thinks that the American bishops' final statement, *Human Life in Our Day*, confirms the general secretary's "clarification." They in no way departed from the papal teaching. A careful reading, however, shows that change from papal teaching in the American document was quite definite.[6]

First, after serious discussion the bishops changed the Pope's language from "intrinsically wrong"[7] to "objective moral disorder," or "objective evil." So important is the word "intrinsic" in the natural law tradition used by the Pope, that change from "intrinsic" to "objective" is significant. For the Pope, contraception is "intrinsically wrong" because it frustrates "the design established by the Creator" and "contradicts the will of the Author of life."[8] It could not be justified "even for the gravest reasons."[9] The encyclical gives no hint that there could be a possible contrary decision in conscience.

Many American bishops, however, wanted to introduce the classic distinction between objective and subjective. Artificial birth control could be seen to be an "objective" or "premoral" evil. Subjectively, guilt could vary from zero to 100 percent. Objective evil would involve subjective guilt only for someone acting against conscience. Here conscience — not mentioned by the Pope — becomes the supreme guide. This distinction between objective and subjective was not used in the birth control encyclical.

The bishops included two statements about conscience in their November 1968 letter. They did emphasize importance of conforming conscience to the Church's interpretation of divine law. However, they recognized the possibility that Catholics might, in conscience, have to reject papal teaching that had not been taught infallibly. They quoted Newman's description of circumstances in which conscience could oppose the supreme, though not infallible, authority of the Pope. Newman wrote that for conscience to be "a sacred and sovereign monitor," it could prevail against the voice of the Pope only after serious thought, prayer, and use of all available means of arriving at a right judgment.

Moreover, when writing on conscientious objection, the bishops stated their own conviction about conscience quite clearly. They described themselves "as witnesses to a spiritual tradition which accepts enlightened conscience, even when honestly mistaken, as the arbiter of moral decision."[10] Not *correct conscience*" as in the earlier clarifying statement, but here changed to "enlightened conscience, even when *honestly mistaken*." The change is subtle, but unmistakable.

English and Welsh bishops, among those listed uncertain by Selling, also stressed conscience's role. In a context emphasizing the importance of listening to "the guidance of the Church," they stressed the primacy of conscience. Since the encyclical contained no sweeping condemnations and "no threat of damnation," these bishops seemed to think that it did not consider contraceptive acts gravely sinful.

The Swiss bishops reveal interesting contrasts in their episcopal statements. In an early individual statement, Bishop Adam of Sion said that anyone who did not accept the teaching was no longer a Catholic. He suggested that those who refused to obey the Pope "should have the loyalty and courage to leave the Church."[11] Later, Bishop Adam claimed no intention to exclude anyone from the Church. He only meant to remind Catholics of the consequences of rebelling against papal authority.

When the Swiss bishops finally issued their joint statement on December 11, 1968, they spoke to those who could not accept the encyclical's teaching in their lives. If they were not acting from selfish motives but were sincerely trying to obey God's will more perfectly, they should not consider themselves guilty. The bishops asked those whose difficulties were more intellectual to keep an open mind. They should be prepared to review their statements about the encyclical's doctrine.

Ways in which bishops' conferences expected papal teaching to be accepted differed significantly. Those in Group A fully accepted the encyclical and considered the issue closed. Its teachings were to be followed as set forth. However, the conferences classified under B (clear change) were concerned only that the Pope receive reverent and respectful attention. Many characterized the birth control encyclical as an opportunity for dialogue. Some suggested the possibility that the teaching on contraception might change. Almost all of these conferences leave room for individual conscience to dissent from the encyclical. Most consider that a serious possibility.[12]

All bishops in Group B (clear change), plus more than half in Group C (uncertain) considered the ban on contraception an open question when applied to individual cases. They introduced ways of getting around the Pope's clear teaching. These included the conflict of duties, the lesser of two evils, and the influence of motivation. Some suggested that, rather than a strict prohibition, a high ideal was proposed for married couples. Thus the Italian bishops wrote of "this norm, which is at once humble and sublime, an ideal goal to which they are pledged by their dignity and conjugal vocation." With some hesitation about doubtful cases, Selling concluded that the bishops' conferences that accepted the encyclical, to which he added Brazil, England/Wales, Italy, and the United States, made up slightly over half the conferences.

A More Democratic Scenario

I propose a different analysis of Selling's table. I have already questioned his conclusion that the American statement is uncertain. I consider its departure from the encyclical sufficiently clear to include it in Group B.

Then, is it statistically sound to give the same weight to New Zealand, with four dioceses, and CELAM, an umbrella organization that includes twenty-two national conferences with 442 dioceses in Latin America?

What would have happened if Paul VI, aware of the gravity of his decision, had sent a draft of his proposed encyclical to all the bishops *who head dioceses* around the world. With that limitation in mind I propose to reconstruct Selling's table, using the 1970 listing of dioceses from the Vatican Secretariat of State.[13]

This would give a rough approximation of how the presiding

Table 2
SELLING'S GROUPS ADJUSTED
WITH NUMBER OF RULING BISHOPS

Group A Clear Acceptance		Group B Clear Mitigation		Group C Uncertain	
Ceylon	5	Austria	9	Australia	26
Dahomey	6	Belgium	8	Czechoslovakia	12
Ireland	26	Canada	67	East Germany	7
Korea	13	CELAM	442	England/Wales	20
New Zealand	4	France	90	India	77
Philippines	47	Indonesia	31	Italy	270
Poland	26	Malta	2	Japan	16
Portugal	17	Netherlands	7		
Puerto Rico	4	Scandinavia	4		
Rhodesia	4	South Africa	20		
Scotland	7	Switzerland	6		
Senegal	5	U.S.A.	159		
Spain	63	West Germany	21		
Vietnam	12				
Yugoslavia	23				
Total	262		866		428
	17%		56%		27%

bishops of the dioceses from around the world might have voted if Pope Paul VI had given them a chance to respond to his proposed draft of the birth control encyclical.[14]

In our proposed survey only 17 percent would have strongly supported the birth control encyclical; 56 percent would have called for change; 27 percent would have been unreliable supporters. This is scarcely the moral unanimity required for infallible teaching of the ordinary and universal magisterium.

At the 1980 Synod on the Family, Cardinal Felici claimed that bishops of the West had been responsible for reservations expressed against the birth control encyclical.[15] The tables show, however, this was not the case. Indonesia and South Africa were clearly for change. Australia, India, and Japan were uncertain.

If the Pope had worked on the birth control issue with the bishops, beginning with getting help from the bishops at the council, the tragedy of the birth control encyclical would not have occurred. The birth control encyclical was an exercise of papal authority in a matter where the broadest involvement and extreme sensitivity to the "mind of the faithful" were essential for the building up of the Church.

The preamble to the definition of papal infallibility at Vatican I describes the process of consultation that the Pope should follow in order to teach infallibly:

> according to the exigencies of time and circumstances, sometimes assembling ecumenical councils, or *asking for the mind of the Church scattered throughout the world,* sometimes by particular synods, sometimes using other helps which divine providence supplied. (emphasis added)

It is critically important that a Pope find out "the mind of the Church" before he solemnly defines infallibly. Would not similar caution be advisable in his more ordinary teaching in a matter like birth control, that seriously affects millions of Catholics' lives? It is far from being absurd and uncatholic to ask how the world's bishops might have responded if they had been given an open opportunity to react to the proposed birth control encyclical.

In his book *Paul VI*, Peter Hebblethwaite discussed the insinuation made by Cardinal Karol Wojtyła (the future John Paul II) that the bishops had been improperly influenced by theologians. In Cardinal Wojtyła's response to a request for suggestions for a topic for the forthcoming 1974 Synod of Bishops, he wrote:

> The problem of the *Magisterium* has already emerged with the utmost clarity apropos of the birth control encyclical, which also illustrated the influence of theologians on the decisions of episcopal conferences.

Hebblethwaite wrote that this

> suggested that those episcopal conferences that introduced nuances of conscience into the interpretation of the birth control encyclical were pushed by aberrant theologians. This was as unjust as it was fanciful.[16]

Mind of the Faithful

What about the laity? The bishops at Vatican II devoted the entire second chapter of the *Dogmatic Constitution on the Church* to talking about the laity together with their pastors as "the People of God." Pastors here, of course, includes the Pope and bishops. Especially since Newman's groundbreaking *On Consulting the Faithful in Matters of Doctrine*,[17] Vatican I's phrase "the mind of the Church," surely includes the ancient idea of "the mind of the faithful." Indeed, some bishops' conferences wrote their statements on the birth control encyclical after direct consultation with the laity. There can be little doubt that all of the bishops' conferences that mitigated the teaching of the encyclical were indirectly influenced by their people's faith experience. In our day, cannot sociological surveys, carefully taken and carefully evaluated, be a tool for determining the "mind of the faithful"?

Rahner has called attention to a dilemma of the average Christian or theologian when asked to accept teachings whose basis in revelation is not clear, or which may even seem to be a new revelation. That is the situation Paul VI created when he called for obedience, not for the reasons he gave but because of special enlightenment associated with his office. He wrote:

> For, as you know, the Pastors of the Church enjoy a special light of the Holy Spirit in teaching the truth. And this, rather than the arguments they put forward, is why you are bound to such obedience.[18]

The Pope supported his appeal to the light of the Holy Spirit with a reference to the *Dogmatic Constitution on the Church*.[19] However, the passage from the *Dogmatic Constitution on the Church* asserts that the Holy Spirit's light is given to teach only what is in revelation. Both Vatican I and Vatican II make it clear that the infallibility of the Church, which the Pope exercises when defining solemnly, is limited in scope to the deposit of faith.

Pope Paul VI, however, based his encyclical not on revelation but on natural law. A case based on natural law can convince only by the power of its arguments. The birth control encyclical's failure to convince theologians and devout, thinking Catholics comes precisely from the weakness of its arguments. For Rahner the right approach calls for acceptance of papal teaching because of its truth, with minimal emphasis on the authority of the office.

A strange development since promulgation of the birth control encyclical has been the Popes' insistent appeal to theologians to explain the doctrine more clearly. They are asked to make it more acceptable not only to Catholics, but indeed, to all people of good will. In his 1981 encyclical *On the Family*, John Paul II issued a pressing invitation to theologians

> to collaborate with the hierarchical magisterium and to commit themselves to the task of illustrating ever more clearly the biblical foundations, the ethical grounds and the personalist reasons behind this doctrine...to render the teaching of the encyclical on this fundamental question truly accessible to all people of good will, fostering a daily more enlightened and profound understanding of it.[20]

But surely a major problem with the encyclical from the beginning has been its failure to convince a major part of the theological community. How are theologians to explain more clearly a doctrine about which they themselves are not convinced? One is reminded of Fuchs's testimony at the birth control commission. He had stopped teaching at the Gregorian University in the academic year 1965–66 and prevented the reprinting of his textbook. He could not responsibly teach a doctrine he himself could not accept.

Even more serious for priests and people is Pope Paul's call to those who are unable to live up to the demands of his teaching. Paul VI wrote:

> If, however, sin still exercises its hold over them, they are not to lose heart. Rather must they, humble and persevering, have recourse to the mercy of God, bestowed in the sacrament of penance.[21]

This advice raises a serious problem for a priest with experience of hearing confessions and counseling. In a typical situation a couple has decided in conscience that they must not have any more children. Periodic continence either does not work, or, like total abstinence, is destructive of their marital relationship. Often, with professional medical advice, they are using artificial contraception and expect to do so as long as the wife is fertile. They had been taught that they must have a firm "purpose of amendment" for their confession to be valid.

The confessor is urged to treat this penitent as a "habitual sinner" in need of time to convert, or as one with a sincere but incorrect conscience. In either case, penitents are told to continue to receive the sacraments "to overcome the hold that sin has on them." A penitent who has sincerely resolved to continue the use of contraception finds this a recommendation for hypocrisy.

In his 1968 talk at Holy Cross Abbey, Häring said those in doubt had to study the encyclical thoroughly and with good will, but be open to other information in the Church. If in sincere conscience Catholics decide that for them the use of artificial contraception is right and necessary, they must follow their consciences. Rahner, after describing a similar process of study and discernment, reached the same conclusion.

Here, however, the question must be frankly asked: how many of the laity can be expected to make this kind of thorough study of the encyclical? Has it not been the responsibility of the theologians to help them inform their consciences in this difficult matter? They should let the laity know all the good theological arguments in favor of contraception. They should inform them that they cannot cast the obligation of making up their own minds on the shoulders of popes and bishops. They should inform them that it is possible that good morality might require that they use contraceptives.[22]

At the 1980 Synod on the Family reaction to the encyclical was complex. Bishops from developing countries of the southern hemisphere worried about government attempts (their own and those of the north) to solve their very serious economic problems by reducing populations. The bishops were afraid that governments would concentrate on population control instead of seeking other ways to relieve human misery and poverty.

Many bishops from developed countries of the north expressed widespread concern over a gulf between the birth control encyclical's teaching and actual pastoral practice. We have already seen Archbishop Quinn's report on the United States. Consultation with sixty thousand Catholics convinced the French episcopal conference that "techniques of [ovulation] observation" are not practical for a large number of the laity. Bishop Jullien of Beauvais called upon the synod to make it possible for faithful couples to live without anxiety because of rigid Church teaching.[23] Bishops emphasized that opposition came from committed Catholics, including theologians and spiritual leaders — people undoubtedly dedicated to the Church.

Cardinal Basil Hume of England made a strong case for the synod to give serious attention to the experience of the married laity. He said that husbands' and wives' experience and understanding of the sacrament of matrimony was an authentic theological source.[24] Pastors, and the whole Church, should use it. Married couples had a twofold title to authority in matters concerning marriage. They are the sacrament's ministers and only they have experienced its effects. Cardinal Vicente Enrique y Tarancón, archbishop of Madrid, said that repeating old formulations was not enough. The Church must be open to new research in theology and the other human sciences. It must listen to married couples whose experience of faith bishops do not have. (In 1968 Spanish bishops had accepted the birth control encyclical.)

Was It Received?

Bishops, theologians, laity! Doctrine central to the birth control encyclical has not been received by a large part of the Church. How is this theologically significant? What does it mean that doctrine is received? What is reception? According to Yves Congar, a leading expert at Vatican II, reception is not concerned with whether the teaching is legal. Reception is concerned with the doctrine's content. Is the doctrine meaningful in the Church's life? Reception does not make teaching valid, but shows that this dogma, law, or ethical rule is for the Church's good. Non-reception does not mean that the decision is false, only that it "does not call forth any living power and therefore does not contribute to edification." Congar gives contemporary examples of non-reception and then asks of the birth control encyclical: "Is this 'non-reception,' or 'disobedience,' or what? The facts are there."[25]

Rahner proposes that the magisterium must wait to see if its teaching has been received. If teaching is received, the Church has recognized in it her already existing faith. In case of non-reception, it has not.[26]

Can Rome reverse this dissent among the bishops by carefully eliminating those who disagree from the ranks of the bishops it appoints? Thomas Reese, S.J., has published the confidential questionnaire used to screen out potential candidates for bishop who do not accept the official position on "the Ministerial Priesthood, on the priestly ordination of women, on the Sacrament of Matrimony, on sexual ethics."[27]

Under Paul VI, Archbishop Jadot, the apostolic delegate to the United States, was told to appoint pastoral bishops. John Paul II seems to be more concerned with uniformity and fidelity to Rome. During their visit to Rome in September 1983, he told the American bishops to seek "priests who have already proven themselves as teachers of the faith as it is proclaimed by the magisterium of the Church."

Does the Archbishop Hunthausen case show that waiting for bishops to retire in order to replace them with compliant appointees is not working fast enough for Rome? What of the dismissal in 1995 of Jacques Gailot, the popular French bishop of Evreux! Does such action by Rome further increase the laity's already well-documented loss of confidence in papal leadership? We recall that according to NORC 26 percent of the drop in Mass attendance from 1963 to 1973 could be attributed to loss of confidence in papal leadership.

There may be procedures to get theologians and bishops in line. With the laity this may be difficult. Paul VI upheld Pius XI's and Pius XII's teaching to protect the authority of the Roman magisterium. Does not evidence show that the birth control encyclical has had the opposite effect? Before the encyclical, how many Catholics would have thought that they could disagree with the Pope on birth control, divorce and remarriage, and abortion and still consider themselves good Catholics?

Vatican II taught that the Spirit "distributes special gifts among faithful of every rank." Newman showed how, during the fourth-century Arian heresy, it was the laity, not bishops, who upheld the orthodox faith. At the 1980 Synod on the Family, Cardinal G. Emmett Carter, archbishop of Toronto, asked if this movement to a new level of thinking and acting was an expression of the mind of the faithful.[28]

Under the Spirit's guidance, is history repeating itself: in the fourth century on dogma, today on moral issues?

Chapter 7

DIVORCE AND REMARRIAGE
The Problem and the
Teaching of Jesus

To the unmarried* and to widows I say: it is good for them
to stay as they are, like me. But if they cannot exercise self-
control, let them marry, since it is better to be married than
to be burnt up. (*Editor's note: Paul includes in this category
separated couples, see v. 11.)
— 1 Corinthians 7:8–9, New Jerusalem Bible

Many Roman Catholics have experienced the tragedy of divorce
in their own lives or among family or friends. Many have tried to
start over in a new marriage. They have been told that once two
baptized Christians enter into a valid marriage and have intercourse a bond is created between them. According to Rome no
power on earth can break that bond. If they try to marry again
and rebuild their lives, they are living in adultery and cut off from
the sacraments. Rome claims that this discipline is based on the
clear teaching of Jesus and has been followed consistently by the
Church ever since.

In this chapter we will show that the teaching of Jesus in the
Bible is not clear and certain. In the next chapter we will see that
the teaching and practice of the Church have changed through
the centuries. In fact, the present rigid discipline has been in
force only since the end of the twelfth century. It is my conviction that the present policy is harmful, unnecessary, and morally
unjustifiable.

How Many Are Affected?

How many Catholics around the world are divorced and remarried? No official figures are available. Divorce among Catholics in the United States, however, has increased from 16 percent to 26 percent in the last twenty-five years. The percentage of divorce for Catholics is now the same as for Protestants and Jews.[1]

The 1982–86 National Opinion Research Center (NORC) General Social Survey shows that about 26 percent of Catholics in this country have been divorced at least once.[2] Andrew Hacker reported in 1983 that 73 percent of all divorced Americans remarry.[3] It therefore seems valid to conclude that a high percentage of divorced Catholics have remarried. According to one estimate the number of divorced and remarried Catholics in the United States is between six and eight million.[4]

Whatever the exact figure, very many Catholics around the world are involved. At the international Synod of Bishops on the Family in Rome in 1980 the problem of divorced and remarried Catholics was "the cause of the most thought and concern for bishops from every part of the Church universal."[5]

The Official Teaching

The present teaching of the Roman Catholic Church goes back to Pope Alexander III at the end of the twelfth century: If two validly baptized Christians enter into a valid marriage and consummate that marriage, it cannot be dissolved by any power on earth.[6] Divorced Catholics from such marriages may not remarry. If they do remarry, they are living in adultery and excluded from the sacraments. They can receive the sacraments only if they live together without having intercourse. This official teaching prevents millions of Catholics around the world who have suffered the tragedy of broken marriages from rebuilding their lives as full-fledged Church members.

In chapter 3, I noted a survey that claimed 26 percent of the decline in Mass attendance between 1963 and 1973 could be explained by changing attitudes toward divorce. Evidence exists that 50 percent of the divorced and remarried continue to go to Mass at least once a month.[7] So divorced and remarried Catholics may not be responsible for the big drop in attendance at Mass. Perhaps other Catholics who are not divorced have been turned off in part by a Church that they see as insensitive to the genuine human needs and suffering of their divorced and remarried relatives and friends.

Moreover, decline in belief and practice among Catholics cannot be explained by general religious decline in the United States during this period. According to the surveys, the rate of loss of practicing members among Protestants was not nearly as great as that among Catholics. In fact, a previous divorce is one of the most powerful reasons why Catholics leave the Church.[8]

Official Church teaching on divorce and remarriage can be found in the 1983 Code of Canon Law. It states:

> The essential properties of marriage are unity and indissolubility, which in Christian marriage obtain a special firmness in virtue of the sacrament.[9]

Moreover, the Code affirms that a valid marriage between baptized persons is always a sacrament.

> The matrimonial covenant...between baptized persons has been raised by Christ the Lord to the dignity of a sacrament. For this reason a matrimonial contract cannot validly exist between baptized persons unless it is also a sacrament by that fact.[10]

Marriages Can Be Dissolved

Although the Code in canon 1056 says that a sacramental marriage cannot be dissolved, marriages can be broken. Here are the circumstances under which this can happen.

1. First, there is the marriage that has not been consummated, that is, the couple has not had intercourse after the marriage ceremony. Although a marriage between two baptized persons is a sacrament as soon as they exchange their vows, it does not become unbreakable, according to the official teaching, until they have *consummated* it by sexual intercourse. The Code describes consummation as "the conjugal act which is per se suitable for the generation of children...by which the spouses become one flesh."[11] Before they have had intercourse after getting married, the Pope can dissolve such sacramental marriages "by the power of the keys."

2. The marriages of non-Christians can also be dissolved under "Pauline privilege." This is when one of the partners enters the Church (1 Cor. 7:12–15). In addition, under what is known as "Petrine privilege," the Pope has dissolved consummated, non-sacramental marriages between baptized and unbaptized spouses "in favor of the faith."[12]

Therefore, according to official teaching only the valid, ratified, consummated marriages of baptized Christians can never be dissolved by any power on earth. This official teaching holds that this is God's will, revealed in Jesus' explicit teaching and developed and practiced in the Church's living tradition.

Annulments

The Church has courts called marriage tribunals that deal with broken marriages. While it denies the possibility of divorce for those in validly consummated Christian marriage, these courts grant what are called annulments. An annulment, usually called "a declaration of nullity," is based on the understanding that marriage is a contract. Just as civil courts throw out contracts where essential elements have not been fulfilled, so, if the essential requirements for a valid marriage weren't met at the time of marriage, marriage tribunals issue decrees of nullity. Only after receiving a decree of nullity can Catholics involved in broken marriages remarry in the Church.

James Provost, chairman of the canon law faculty at Catholic University, studied annulments in 1975 to find out how well the system works.[13] Provost's examination distinguished between two different types of marriage cases: (1) conflict situations and (2) hardship cases.

1. Conflict situations are those in which necessary requirements of a true marriage have not been fulfilled. Examples would be when there was no intention of entering into a permanent marriage or a clear intention not to have children. In such cases, if the facts can be proven, tribunals can grant an annulment. Provost concludes that in these conflict situations most Catholics throughout the world find no relief at all. According to the Church's General Statistics Office, 95 percent of all cases that received a hearing were reported from Europe, Canada, the United

States, Colombia, and Australia. That included the cases where the annulment was refused as well as those where it was granted.

With divorce statistics from the United Nations and figures from the Vatican on annulments granted, Provost estimated that only about 7.5 percent of potential cases around the world were even heard. The effectiveness of the system for the number of couples who needed relief ranged from 0.4 percent in France to 11.5 percent in Italy.[14]

American diocesan tribunals rendered decisions in 10 percent of the cases of people with a right to a hearing. Although there were an estimated 225,720 divorces affecting Catholics in the United States in 1975, diocesan marriage tribunals handed down only 23,034 decisions. With over 200,000 cases a year not considered, this could result in over 2 million cases not acted on in a ten-year period. So an estimate of 6 to 8 million Catholics in the United States involved in this tragic situation does not seem exaggerated.

Europeans are even less likely than Americans to seek annulments. In 1992, Europe — with a Catholic population of 288 million — had only 10,596 annulment cases introduced. In contrast, the United States with a Catholic population of 55 million had over 47,000 cases introduced. Germany — with a Catholic population of 28.4 million — had only 848 cases introduced (with 540 succeeding). About one-third of the Catholics in Germany are in second marriages but simply do not want to go through the annulment process. Italy, with 12,000 divorces, had only 1,500 applications for annulments.[15]

We have no reason to hope that divorces among Catholics will decrease in the foreseeable future. Nor does the drop in priestly vocations and shortage of funds and personnel make likely any increase in the number of annulments granted to those who are entitled to them.

Meanwhile, Pope John Paul wants the number of annulments reduced. A news item headed "Too Many Annulments" reads:

> Speaking to the 25 judges of the Rota [the highest marriage court in the Vatican] John Paul II deplored "the excessive proliferation and almost automatic annulments of marriages on pretexts of immaturity or diminished responsibility." Tribunals must not "become an easy way of finding a solution for failed marriages and irregular arrangements for marriage partners." The Pope deplored

the drift toward a sort of Catholic divorce and warned judges to watch out for those who presented their "slight mental troubles" or moral weakness as "proof of inability to carry out their conjugal obligations."[16]

2. Hardship cases are those in which the marriage was clearly valid, but where there is no possibility that the former marriage relationship can be restored. An example would be when both parties have entered into civil marriages and are now raising children in those marriages. Here, marriage tribunals can do nothing. According to the contemporary official Roman Catholic teaching, these marriages can be dissolved only by the death of a spouse.

Can anything be said about the official claim that indissolubility of valid, consummated, sacramental marriages is both the clear teaching of Jesus and the Church's firm and constant teaching and practice that cannot be changed?

As we shall see, neither Scripture nor the first thousand years of tradition supports official teaching that such marriages can be dissolved only by the death of one of the spouses. Evidence from Scripture is uncertain and has been interpreted in different ways from the Church's earliest years. As for tradition, a continuous, firm tradition in the Eastern Church, from long before the break between East and West, permits remarriage, especially of the innocent party, in a broken marriage. In the Western Church, the discipline against remarriage was not firmly established until the twelfth century.

At the 1980 Synod of Bishops on the Family there was a strong demand to study the practice of the Orthodox Church. That Church, in consideration of human weakness, continues to tolerate remarriage and reception of the Eucharist, although it does not consider the second marriage a sacrament. Pope John Paul II ignored the bishops' request.

What Did Jesus Teach?

The official position denying remarriage after divorce claims to be based on the clear teaching of Jesus and the constant, consistent practice of the Church. So it is important to know what Jesus taught.

We have four sources for the teaching of Jesus on divorce and remarriage: St. Paul's first letter to the Corinthians and the Gospels of Matthew, Mark, and Luke. There is agreement among Scripture scholars that neither Paul nor any of the authors of the three Gospels actually heard Jesus teach. Paul wasn't a witness during the life of Jesus and Luke tells us how he collected information. Scholars are agreed that the Gospels of Matthew and Mark weren't written by the Matthew and Mark mentioned in the Scriptures. The Gospel of John, the only Gospel that claims to be based on an eyewitness, doesn't treat the question of divorce and remarriage. So all of our sources are based on traditions that they received from others. And they don't agree.

In *Divorce and Remarriage*, Theodore Mackin, S.J., devotes forty-six pages to a discussion of verses in Scripture and the complex and often contradictory scholarly attempts to interpret them.[17] The late George W. MacRae, S.J., observed that no single interpretation of these biblical passages has won general consent of Scripture scholars, at least Catholic ones. Perhaps this is why the Church has never attempted to define their meaning.[18]

Paul and the Gospels

So we don't know exactly what Jesus taught. But we can study our sources. These are Paul in his first letter to the Corinthians (written around the spring of 54) and the Gospels of Mark (64–67), Luke (80–85), and Matthew (80–90).[19] They are likely to reveal to us what was happening in the Church at the time and in the place where they were written. This will help us in the next chapter as we study the teaching and practice on divorce and remarriage in the Church's history. But they may also give us insights into the original teaching of Jesus. Since the sources don't agree, we can't possibly hope to come up with final answers. But we may decide that some tentative insights make sense.

Our first problem is with language. Jesus almost certainly spoke in Aramaic. But our sources are in Greek and we are working with translations into English. There is always a problem in translation from one language to another and we are dealing with the English translation of a Greek translation of what Jesus said in Aramaic. This can affect our attempt to discover what Jesus taught.

Let me begin with our earliest source, Paul's first letter to the Corinthians. This was probably written in the spring of 54, just twenty years after the death of Jesus. We have two reputable translations that don't agree on what Paul wrote. The New Revised Standard Version (NRSV) reads:

> To the married I give this command — not I but the Lord — that the wife **not separate** from her husband (but if she does separate, let her remain unmarried or else be reconciled to her husband), and that the husband should not *divorce* his wife. (1 Cor. 7:10–11)

Here is the translation in the New Jerusalem Bible (NJB):

> To the married I give this ruling, and this is not mine but the Lord's: a wife **must not be separated** from her husband — or if she has already left him, she must remain unmarried or else be reconciled to her husband — and a husband must not *divorce* his wife.

The words in bold type show where there is a problem with the translation. The phrase in the NRSV, "That the wife *is not to separate* from her husband," suggests an action that is taken by the wife. However, the verb in the Greek, *choristhênai*, is passive. The NJB translates this passive: "a wife *must not be separated* from her husband." This suggests an action that is taken against her. However, Jesus was speaking to Jews among whom only the husband could get a divorce. So the translation in NJB is more likely to correspond to the teaching of Jesus.

The translation "divorce" also creates the wrong impression. This suggests a legal action, such as occurs in our day where either spouse can initiate the action and there is a hearing before a judge. No such action existed among the Jews at the time. Only a husband could end the marriage. As Matthew points out, all a husband had to do was to give his wife "a certificate of dismissal" and send her away. The translation "dismissed" or "put away" would be more accurate.[20] Since Jesus was speaking to Jews, this probably expresses his meaning. Mark allows either husband or wife to end the marriage. This is probably because he is writing in Rome. Among the Romans either husband or wife could end the marriage. Here are the passages from the Gospels:

> Mark 10:2–12: [2]Some Pharisees came, and to test him they asked, "Is it lawful for a man to divorce his wife?" [3]He answered them, "What did Moses command you?" [4]They said, "Moses

allowed a man to write a certificate of dismissal and to divorce her." [5]But Jesus said to them, "Because of your hardness of heart he wrote this commandment for you. [6]But from the beginning of creation, 'God made them male and female.' [7]For this reason a man shall leave his father and mother and be joined to his wife, [8]and the two shall become one flesh.' So they are no longer two, but one flesh. [9]Therefore what God has joined together, let no one separate." [10]Then in the house the disciples asked him again about this matter. [11]He said to them, *"Whoever divorces his wife and marries another commits adultery against her;*[12]*and if she divorces her husband and marries another, she commits adultery."*

Matt. 19:3–9: [3]Some Pharisees came to him, and to test him they asked, "Is it lawful for a man to divorce his wife for any cause?" [4]He answered, "Have you not read that the one who made them at the beginning 'made them male and female,' [5]and said, 'For this reason a man shall leave his father and mother and be joined to his wife, and the two shall become one flesh'? [6]So they are no longer two, but one flesh. Therefore what God has joined together, let no one separate." [7]They said to him, "Why then did Moses command us to give a certificate of dismissal and to divorce her?" [8]He said to them, "It was because you were so hard-hearted that Moses allowed you to divorce your wives, but from the beginning it was not so. [9]And I say to you, *whoever divorces his wife,* **except for unchastity,** *and marries another commits adultery."*

Luke 16:18: [18]*"Everyone who dismisses his wife and marries another commits adultery, and he who marries a woman dismissed from her husband commits adultery."*

Notice how the Gospels differ. Luke and Matthew speak only of the husband dismissing his wife. And Matthew introduces an exception. Mark speaks of husbands or wives dismissing their married partners.

Some scholars think Luke[21] is closest to the actual teaching of Jesus. Mark[22] would then have adapted the original teaching of Jesus to fit a Roman audience where either husbands or wives could obtain a divorce.

Most scholars think that the teaching in Luke is an absolute prohibition against divorce. However, as we shall see, there is a quite plausible way of understanding Jesus' saying in Luke that would not support an absolute prohibition against all divorce.

With Matthew,[23] attempts to recover Jesus' exact teaching become even more difficult. Matthew twice states an exception. "Whoever dismisses his wife, *except for unchastity,* and marries another commits adultery."[24] During many centuries the Greek, here translated "unchastity," has been understood to mean unfaithfulness or adultery. The teaching of the Orthodox Church that the husband who dismisses an adulterous wife can remarry is based on Matthew.

Joseph Fitzmyer, a Jesuit Scripture scholar at Catholic University, questions that the word usually translated "unchastity" in Matthew means "adultery."[25] He is convinced that it refers, not to adultery, but to marriages with close relatives. These marriages with close kin were common among pagans but forbidden to the Jews in Leviticus 18:6–18. This interpretation assumes that Jewish Christians in Matthew's Church would have been gravely offended if Gentile Christians in their Church were allowed to remain in marriages considered incestuous in the law of Moses.

George MacRae, a Jesuit Scripture scholar at Harvard Divinity School, disagreed with this recently developed interpretation.[26] He points out that the Greek word in Matthew refers to "every kind of unlawful sexual intercourse," as well as to "the sexual unfaithfulness of a married woman."[27] The evangelist may have chosen that word precisely to broaden the kind of unchastity that can break a marriage.

Another difficulty, however, arises because Jesus' teaching in Mark and Matthew is based on Genesis. It would therefore apply to all human marriages, not just Christian. Jesus had been challenged by Pharisees who quoted Moses' permission to write a certificate of divorce. In Mark and Matthew, Jesus referred them to God's plan in Genesis in order to reject Moses' permissive attitude toward divorce.

> But from the beginning of creation he made them male and female. This is why a man leaves his father and mother, and the two become one flesh. They are no longer two, therefore, but one flesh. So then, *what God has united, human beings must not divide* (Mark 10:6–9, NJB).

If Jesus intended to establish an absolute prohibition against all divorce based on God's plan "from the beginning of creation," it would apply to the entire human family. How can one justify Paul's exception or the current Church policy of dissolving non-Christian marriages?[28]

Divorce and Remarriage

Of Jesus' saying "human beings must not divide" Lawrence Wrenn, judge on the Hartford matrimonial tribunal, comments that Jesus could have said that what God has united no one *is able* to divide. This would have made clear the existence of an unbreakable bond. Rather, "let not" suggests that the marriage can be broken but should not be.[29] Wrenn thinks that Jesus taught that a bond existed, but that it is fragile and care should be taken not to break it.[30] In other words, the prohibition is not absolute.

Difficulty also arises from the position of the divorce clause in the Sermon on the Mount. In a series of six sayings on anger, lust, divorce, oath taking, resisting evil, and love of enemies, the Church has absolutized only the saying on divorce into a binding law. The other five sayings are considered ideals to be worked toward.

Another Interpretation of the Divorce Passages

Has the contemporary Catholic interpretation of these texts from Paul and the synoptic Gospels been influenced by seven centuries of teaching on divorce and remarriage in the Western Church? Do we read back into the Scriptures a meaning needed to support the present discipline of the Roman Catholic Church?

What happens if we try to understand the divorce passages in the Gospel in the situation where they occurred? We would begin with Mark, the earliest Gospel, to deal with the divorce problem. Matthew and Luke very likely had Mark before them when they wrote.

Mark's teaching on divorce occurs in an "entrapment story" (Mark 10:2–12). Already in the third chapter of Mark, Jesus' opponents made plans to destroy him. Part of their attempt can be found in the entrapment stories. His enemies tried to trap Jesus with questions about dangerous or controversial issues. They would put him in a position where no matter how he answered, he would antagonize and lose the support of those on one side or the other of the controversy. The best known of these stories involved payment of taxes to the Roman emperor. They asked him, "Is it lawful to pay taxes to the emperor, or not? Should we pay them, or should we not?" (Mark 12:14–15). If he answered yes, he would alienate the people who hated the Roman occupation of their country. If he answered no, he would be in serious trouble with the Roman authorities.

Was the question about divorce just such a trap to catch him on an issue on which there was serious disagreement between the followers of two respected Jewish teachers? Shammai allowed divorce only for a serious fault in the wife. Hillel permitted divorce for lesser reasons.[31] So a trap was set to catch Jesus between these two groups. "And the Pharisees came up and in order to test him asked, 'Is it lawful for a man to divorce his wife?'" (Mark 10:2).

In the Jewish society of the time there were only two places where a woman could live in decent respectability. She could live in her father's house until marriage and after marriage in her husband's house. "For emancipated women there was in the ancient world only one calling,"[32] prostitution.

Jesus answered the two disputing parties, "Because of your hardness of heart he wrote this commandment for you (Mark 10:5; see Matt. 19:8). Was he rejecting the whole controversy as involving a callous attitude toward women? Was his purpose to protect women in the social situation of his day from men's ability, for one reason or another, to throw their wives out and thus make them social outcasts?

Sayings in both Matthew and Luke seem to agree with such an interpretation of Jesus' intention. In Matthew and Luke, Jesus says nothing to condemn the wife. He only accuses the husband who casts out his wife and the man who takes advantage of her sad situation. Paul also speaks of what is not to be done against a wife, "a wife must not *be separated* [passive voice] from her husband.... And a husband must not divorce his wife" (1 Cor. 7:10–11, NJB). Jesus' teaching seems to be that men must not abuse their wives by sending them away.

This interpretation of Mark's entrapment story fits very well with Paul, Matthew, and Luke. It suggests that Jesus' concern was to protect women rather than to hand down an absolute law against divorce. Mark, then, would have adapted Jesus' original teaching to a Roman situation where there would be greater equality between men and women in obtaining divorces. Matthew followed Mark by using the entrapment story. He did not copy Mark's adaptation for a Roman audience.

But, some will say, perhaps Jesus intended to protect women and the family by prohibiting all divorces. This is doubtful. Both

Divorce and Remarriage

Paul and Matthew would then be guilty of permitting something that they knew the Lord had strictly forbidden. It is true that the exceptions could be ascribed to the Spirit of the Risen Lord who spoke through Christian prophets. But the exceptions to the Lord's teaching are more plausible if we do not insist that Jesus during his ministry laid down an absolute prohibition against all divorce based on a divine plan revealed in Genesis.

There is wide agreement that both Matthew and Luke wrote with Mark in front of them. Why did Luke leave out the entrapment story in Mark's Gospel and keep only a saying on divorce? Maybe his independent tradition led him to question the story's historical accuracy, with its emphasis on the use of Genesis. If he wanted to teach that marriages could never be broken, why did he leave out Mark's saying, "Therefore what God has joined together, let no one separate" (Mark 10:9; Matt. 19:6b)?

With Luke leaving it out, can we be sure that Jesus actually quoted the passage from Genesis? But, even if he did, we don't quote Jesus' saying, "For just as Jonah was three days and three nights in the belly of the sea monster" (Matt. 12:40) to prove that the story of Jonah and the whale is straight history. We no longer go to the opening chapters of Genesis for scientific information about the creation of the world or the origin of the species.

Some caution is justified in building a complete theology of marriage, binding for all times and all cultural situations, on a few verses from Genesis and a supposed saying of Jesus reported only by Mark and Matthew, one that Luke may have deliberately left out. Genesis may or may not have been quoted by Jesus, and "what God has joined together, let no one separate" (Mark 10:9) can have more than one interpretation. So also Jesus' divorce saying in Luke may also mean that wives must not be thrown out. It may not be meant as an absolute, eternally binding law on divorce and remarriage.[33]

In view of these differing interpretations of scriptural evidence, is it not reasonable to say that we simply do not know for sure what Jesus taught on divorce and remarriage? Paul certainly must have thought that the Spirit guided him when he changed a tradition that he attributed to the Lord. Some scholars think that it was the evangelist who added "except on the ground of unchastity" in Matthew's Gospel. If that is true, then he also seems to have made a conscious exception.

Biblical evidence for Jesus' teaching on divorce does not support the Western Church's present discipline on divorce and remarriage. Uncertainty about that teaching and what it means for consciences has continued in Church tradition down to our own time. That tradition must now be examined.

Chapter 8

DIVORCE AND REMARRIAGE
The Tradition and a Call for Change

He who cannot keep continence after the death of his wife, or who has separated from his wife for a valid motive, as fornication, adultery, or another misdeed, if he takes another wife, or if the wife takes another husband, the divine word does not condemn them or exclude them from the Church or the life; but she tolerates it rather on account of their weakness.

—St. Epiphanius of Cyprus

In chapter 7 we noted the official claim that the current Roman Catholic discipline on divorce and remarriage can never be changed because it is based on the clear teaching of Jesus and the constant, consistent practice of the Church ever since. But we saw that the teaching of Jesus is not certain. The biblical texts do not lend themselves to a single interpretation. The Bible shows a Church already adapting to human needs what Jesus is reported to have taught.

This adaptation began before the Gospels were written. It began with Paul. About twenty years after the death and resurrection of Jesus he wrote to the Corinthians,

To the rest I say, not the Lord...if the unbelieving partner desires to separate, let it be so; in such a case the brother or sister is not bound. For God has called us to peace." (1 Cor. 7:12–15)

Paul adapted to a missionary situation what he had received as the original teaching of Jesus. He was converting Gentiles, very many of whom were already married. Sometimes both became Christians, but not always. And sometimes the Gentile partner in the marriage abandoned the Christian. When that happened, Paul allowed abandoned converts to marry again. It had been a valid marriage and Paul allowed it to be ended. The Church has allowed Paul's exception to the teaching of Jesus and called it "Pauline privilege." Paul must not have thought that Jesus had taught an absolute commandment against divorce and remarriage. On his own authority he changed the teaching of Jesus to fit the needs of believers in his own Churches.

The uncertainty about the teaching in Scripture continued in the early Church tradition. It continues in the attempts of modern scholars to interpret that tradition. In his 1984 study, Theodore Mackin, S.J., concluded that the early Church allowed remarriage after divorce. The evidence reveals uncertainty among early Christian writers as they tried to apply the teaching of Paul and the Gospels in the Roman Empire with its easy divorce on consent.

We tend to think of the ancient pagan Romans as very immoral, especially in sexual matters. But the Roman Stoics had very high ideals. Influenced by Stoic idealism, the early Church fathers taught that marriage should be absolutely monogamous — one husband, one wife. Indeed, Athenagoras and Tertullian, after Tertullian joined the heretical Montanist sect, even considered remarriage in widowhood adulterous. But while they tried to promote a high ideal of monogamous marriage, the early Christian writers always had to contend with Paul's exception (1 Cor. 7:10–11) and the exception given twice in Matthew (5:32; 19:9).

The Early Church Fathers

The uncertainty appears in writings of the Latin Church father Tertullian (c. 155–220). Before joining the Montanists, Tertullian wrote two books on marriage for his wife. In the first he urged her not to remarry in case of his death, but to embrace the holiness of a life of continence. But in the second book, since second marriages could not be absolutely condemned, Tertullian asked that she at least not marry a pagan. He warned her with recent examples of women who, *after divorce* or their husband's death, not only rejected an excellent opportunity to lead lives of continence, but married pagans. For Tertullian, their fault seems to have been that they married pagans, not that they remarried after divorce.[1]

In a controversy with Marcion, Tertullian insisted that Christ's condemnation of divorce was conditional. He wrote:

> Thus if Christ has forbidden one to dismiss a spouse under a certain condition, he has not forbidden it entirely. And that which he has not forbidden entirely, he has otherwise permitted, when the reason for his forbidding it ceases.[2]

Yet in Book 5 of the same work, Tertullian seemed indecisive about what he had just written. Later, in fact, he condemned all remarriage.[3]

Around 240, Origen of Alexandria, a very highly respected early Church father, wrote:

> apart from or contrary to the Scriptures certain heads of the Church have permitted a certain woman to be [re-]married while her husband is still alive....However they have not acted altogether unreasonably. This accommodation is allowed in lieu of even worse ones.[4]

Whether Origen approved or disapproved of these concessions, he surely reported that the bishops in the Church of his time allowed them. Moreover, in the social conditions of the time it is inconceivable that such concessions were granted to women but not to men.

Almost all of the witnesses from about 180 to about 380 in both East and West make clear that a man dismissing an adulterous wife and remarrying could receive communion without having to do penance. Since this permission applied only to the husband, it seems to be based on a widespread acceptance of a literal interpretation of the exception in Matthew.

Around 380, Eastern and Western Churches diverged in their treatment of divorce and remarriage. The East used the canons of Basil the Great (d. 379) to support allowing remarriage after divorce. This practice is still in force in the Orthodox Church.

In the West a different tradition began to develop with the teaching of Ambrose (d. 397), Jerome (d. 420), and Augustine (d. 430). Eventually, in the twelfth century, this led to the teaching in the Western Church that Christian marriage could never be dissolved. Note that the present difference in discipline between Roman Catholics and Orthodox began to develop many centuries before the break between the two Churches in the eleventh century. Indeed St. Basil the Great, author of the Eastern canons, is listed as one of St. Ambrose's favorite authors and an influential source of his theological knowledge.[5] If Basil's letters had been better known in the West, would separate traditions on divorce and remarriage have developed?

There is disagreement between contemporary Orthodox and Roman Catholic scholars about the meaning of two of Basil's "Canonical Letters."[6]

Any doubt about the meaning is completely absent in St. Epiphanius of Cyprus (d. 403). He wrote about the same time:

> He who cannot keep continence after the death of his wife, or who has separated from his wife for a valid motive, as fornication, adultery, or another misdeed, if he takes another wife, or if the wife takes another husband, the divine word does not condemn them or exclude them from the Church or the life; but she tolerates it rather on account of their weakness.[7]

This has been the discipline of the Orthodox Church to the present day.

Evidence from other Fathers of East and West in the fourth century is mixed. When Gregory of Nazianzus and John Chrysostom in the East and Ambrose in the West dealt with marriage, especially in their sermons on Matthew or 1 Corinthians, they did not comment on the exceptions. They seemed to approach the issue and then back away. Ambrose had a brief statement in his commentary on Luke that suggested that a marriage was dissolved by adultery, but said nothing in that commentary about the possibility of remarriage.

How can we explain this reluctance of the Fathers to face a question that must have been just as practical for them as for us? Can the spouse who has dismissed an adulterous spouse remarry? It is possible that they were reacting to the Stoic ideal that rejected remarriage even in widowhood as a yielding to lust. We saw in chapter 5 that early Christian writers insisted that the Christian ideal was as high as the Stoic. Some said even higher. Did they think that the exception in Matthew pointed to a lesser ideal, which they decided to ignore?

The Western Tradition

The tradition of an absolutely unbreakable bond that finally prevailed in the West begins with Ambrose. In a baptismal instruction he clearly rejected remarriage after divorce:

> You are bound to a wife; do not seek for a dissolution, for you are forbidden to take another wife as long as your first wife lives. Attempting to cover an adulterous relationship with legal respectability through a divorce only added to the sin's gravity.[8]

Jerome, in his *Commentary on Matthew,* also seemed to deny that the exception in Matthew allowed the husband to remarry. But Augustine became the principal source for the teaching that was ultimately adopted in the Western Church. Christian marriages could not be dissolved.

Augustine spoke of the existence of an unbreakable "bond." In 401 he wrote that the marriage bond is so strong that for Christians, even after divorce, spouses remained joined to one another. He concluded, however, that this was true only for Christians. It was true "only in the City of God, in his Holy Mountain." This was Augustine's name for the Church.[9] Augustine's teaching supports the present teaching of the Roman Catholic Church that only the marriages of the baptized can never be dissolved.[10]

Not every bishop accepted Augustine's teaching that the marriages of baptized Christians could not be dissolved. Pollentius, another African bishop, claimed that in the case of adultery the innocent spouse could obtain a divorce unilaterally and remarry. Augustine's rejection of Pollentius's position was based on a complicated use of Scripture that would not be acceptable to modern Scripture scholars. Canon 8 of the Eleventh Council of Carthage included Augustine's teaching and sought, without success, to have it adopted in the law of the empire. In general the opposition to remarriage after divorce was part of a general effort by some Church authorities to restrict sexual activity.[11]

In fact, imperial law provides evidence of a different Christian attitude toward divorce and remarriage from this same period. Christianity had become the official religion of the empire and Christian Roman law continued for centuries to allow marriages to be dissolved by the mutual consent of the spouses. Christian emperors, from Constantine in 331 to Justinian in 566, all sincerely sought to make Christianity the law of the empire. Although they discouraged its widespread practice, they consistently allowed divorce by mutual agreement with the right of remarriage. These Christian emperors surely knew that some theologians taught that Christian marriages could not be dissolved. Yet for over two hundred years of imperial legislation there was no suggestion that remarriage after divorce is evil or invalid.[12] The Council of Carthage's request that marriage after divorce be forbidden was ignored. Christians in good faith could believe that marriages could be dissolved without fear of being considered heretics. Calm acceptance in Roman law from 331 to 566 that marriage could be dissolved is clear evidence that the indissolubility of marriage had not yet been definitively established.

The official teaching today is that valid, consummated Christian marriages cannot be dissolved because this is the will of God revealed in Scripture and tradition. But careful examination has shown that the evidence from Scripture is uncertain. Moreover, early patristic evidence continues that uncertainty.

Unsettled Questions

With the barbarian invasions and the collapse of the empire in the West, two different traditions developed in the East and West. The Church in the East, under the reasonably stable conditions of the empire, supported Basil's teaching that allowed divorce and remarriage. This has been maintained in the Orthodox Church to our day.

In the West, however, centuries passed before a single tradition was established. Among Western Fathers only Ambrosiaster clearly allowed remarriage after divorce. In his commentary on 1 Corinthians 7 he granted permission to remarry to husbands who dismissed adulterous wives, but not to wives of adulterous husbands.[13]

Decisions of two Popes provide an interesting contrast. In the fifth century, St. Leo the Great addressed the case of thousands of soldiers taken captive, whose wives had legally remarried. Asked what was to be done if their husbands returned, he replied that it was "necessary that the legitimate union be restored."[14]

Almost two centuries later in a letter to St. Boniface in 781, St. Gregory II wrote:

> You have asked what is a husband to do if his wife, having been afflicted with an infirmity, cannot have intercourse with the husband. It would be good if he could remain as he is and practice abstinence. But since this requires great virtue, if he cannot live chastely, it is better if he marry. Let him not stop supporting her.[15]

After the sack of Rome in 410, central authority broke down dramatically. For several centuries the decrees of local councils, anonymous writers of penitentials (handbooks used by priests to determine the penances to impose on repentant sinners), and writings of local canonists are our principal sources of information.

Two synods of St. Patrick and his fellow bishops, held in Ireland between 450 and 460, are of special interest. (This was before the Irish Churches had been forced to adopt the Roman way of doing things.) Both synods allowed remarriage after dismissal of an adulterous wife. Local councils of Frankish bishops in 755 and 756 listed several cases in which the innocent husband could remarry, including the case of a spouse's contracting leprosy.

But change was on the way. The Synod of Aachen, held in Charlemagne's palace in 789, simply quoted the Eleventh Council of Carthage, canon 8. This contained Augustine's teaching that forbade remarriage after the dismissal of a spouse. Then, in 796 at the Council of Friuli in northern Italy, a council for the first time taught explicitly that the innocent husband who dismissed his wife for adultery was forbidden to remarry. He was declared incapable of remarrying while his first wife lived. To justify their teaching, the bishops appealed to "that most expert and blessed man, Jerome," in his *Commentary of Matthew*. As late as 1031, however, the Synod of Bourges allowed remarriage after separation because of adultery.[16]

By the end of the eleventh century, the writings of Ivo, bishop of Chartres, show that Augustine had become an authoritative source. Ivo's *Decretum* was the most comprehensive compilation of sources up to his time. Ivo ignored the Eastern Fathers and like other writers left out all mention of Matthew.

The Western Position Solidified

To understand the next development it will help to review the present teaching on marriage in the Western Church. In this teaching the *sacrament* is present as soon as two eligible baptized Christians sincerely exchange their vows. However, the bond of the marriage can still be dissolved up until the time the marriage is consummated. Two twelfth-century scholars, the canonist Gratian and the theologian Peter Lombard, contributed to the final form of the Roman Catholic Church's law. In Gratian's time, unconsummated Christian marriages were being dissolved by religious vows or by papal dispensation. To account for these exceptions to the absolutely binding character of marriage vows, Gratian treated marriage as a contract. He then distinguished between two stages in the formation of the contract. The first stage was the exchange of final consent. This created a true but preliminary marriage. Consummation was the second stage. This was when the two have become one flesh. The marriage was now absolutely binding.

Lombard also contributed to the teaching that a consummated, *sacramental* marriage is absolutely binding. He used Augustine's teaching on the three ends of marriage: fidelity, offspring, and *sacrament.* He claimed that the *sacrament* made Christian marriage absolutely binding. The sacrament of marriage is an image of the union of Christ and the Church, a union that can never be broken. The elements of the Western Church's present discipline were in place, ready to be fixed:

> Only a marriage that is a sacrament is indissoluble, because it alone images the unbreakable union of Christ and the Church. And only a marriage that is consummated as well as a sacrament is indissoluble, because it alone images that union truly and completely.[17]

Since nearly everyone in Western Christendom was baptized, canon lawyers had reduced the possibility of dissolution to cases of nonconsummation, which they could carefully control.

Without a strong central authority to enforce the discipline, however, the scholars' work might have had no effect. Scholarly debate on the issues could have swung back toward a more benign interpretation. A strong reforming papacy intent on control in sexual matters kept that from happening.

Divorce and Remarriage

Why was a rigid discipline adopted in spite of (1) the exception in Matthew, (2) several centuries of diverse teaching and practice in the West, and (3) contrary development in the East? I believe it was due in part to important characteristic differences between the authorities that enforced discipline in East and West.

In the Church's early history in the Roman Empire, the Church in both East and West had accepted civil regulation of the legal aspects of marriage. Destruction of Western imperial power by barbarian invasions did not affect civil authority in the East. Civil courts continued to control the legal aspects of marriage and divorce in their own territory. So no special Church courts developed in the East to care for matrimonial cases. With the breakdown of civil government in the West, however, bishops took over functions of government in all aspects of civil life. This included marriage.

In the East, the emperor was the strong central authority who maintained Basil's benign teaching that allowed divorce and remarriage. Not only was the emperor himself married, but he was protector of a Church that cherished the right of its priests to be married. In the West, an increasingly centralized papacy began to impose celibacy on all clergy in major orders.

So a strong impulse to legalize and centralize the administration of the discipline of marriage came from a papacy also committed to celibacy for the clergy. This was just when Augustine's teaching on divorce and remarriage was becoming influential.[18] It began to be implemented at the highest level in the Church in the decrees of Alexander III (1159–81), the first canon lawyer to become Pope. The present teaching of the Western Church that consummated, sacramental marriage can never be dissolved was now firmly established. Subsequent events would show this to be one of those issues of which Rahner said: "Although they can make no claim to be definitive, [they] are nonetheless presented in such a way as though in fact they are definitive."[19]

Notwithstanding the absolute position in the West, neither the Council of Florence (1438–45?) nor the Council of Trent (1545–63) challenged the Eastern practice. The Council of Florence sought to promote reunion with the Greeks. From April 1438 to July 1439, every issue thought to be seriously divisive between the Eastern and Western Churches was studied in great detail. The Eastern practice of allowing remarriage after divorce was not even brought up in those discussions. Only eight days after solemn promulgation of the agreement between the two Churches did the Pope raise a question about divorce practice among the Orthodox. The only reply of the Orthodox was that the practice was allowed with good reason.[20] Clearly the Eastern practice on divorce was an issue on which the Latin Church could yield.

Over a century later the Council of Trent came close, without mentioning the Greeks by name, to condemning their practice on divorce and remarriage. At the last minute, at the urging of the Republic of Venice with its large Greek population, the council fathers drew back.

> Tradition on this point was not absolutely clear. Above all it was desired not to offend the non-united Greeks who allowed remarriage in such cases. The wording is thus carefully designed so that it only demands acceptance of the Latin standpoint without expressly condemning the other.[21]

Although Pius XI stated in the encyclical *On Chaste Marriage* that the Latin Church's teaching was binding on the universal Church, we will see from interventions at Vatican Council II and the 1980 Synod of Bishops that discussion is not closed.

Call for Change

In spite of the widespread severity of the divorce problem, there was practically no evidence of pastoral concern about the issue at Vatican II. The final documents contained only one reference "to the plague of divorce" and a statement that authentic conjugal love "is far removed from all adultery or divorce."[22]

One prophetic intervention, however, addressed the issue. Archbishop Elie Zoghbi, Melkite-rite patriarchal vicar in Egypt, asked if the Church couldn't dispense the innocent party in a broken marriage from the matrimonial bond as was done in some Eastern Churches?

> The counsel to live a life of solitude and continence is not for everyone because it calls for heroic virtue which cannot be imposed indiscriminately. Could not the Church, without prejudice to her doctrine on the indissolubility of marriage, use her author-

Divorce and Remarriage

ity on behalf of the innocent party in these cases as has been the case in the Christian Orient? This practice was also followed sometimes in the West.

Zoghbi noted how careful the Council of Trent had been not to offend the Orthodox on this issue.

Cardinal Charles Journet challenged Zoghbi. He insisted that divorce had only entered the Eastern Church through adoption of the law of Justinian. Thus it followed a human policy rather than the Gospel.

Zoghbi replied that

the Justinian Code, promulgated toward the middle of the sixth century and adopting Eastern discipline on marriage, could not in any way have influenced Origen, St. Basil, St. John Chrysostom and others who lived during a period ranging between 300 and 150 years before this code, which merely recorded the previous teaching and practice of the Churches of the East.

Furthermore, he noted, this teaching went back long before separation between East and West and had never been challenged in councils in which Eastern and Western bishops sat together.[23]

Journet's effort was a rather crude example of a tendency to make ancient evidence fit the Latin Church's present teaching and practice.

By the 1980 Synod of Bishops, the problem of divorced and remarried Catholics had become a principal concern of bishops from every part of the world.[24] Western and non-Western members of the synod alike expressed concern for the innocent party in divorces and for the problem of stable second marriages involved in bringing up children.

Archbishop Derek Worlock (Liverpool) presented the results of a presynodal consultation with priests and people of his diocese:

He said that the synod must listen to this voice of experienced priests and laity pleading for consideration of this problem of their less happy brethren,... spiritually destitute [though not physically starving]... Catholics whose first marriages have perished and who have now a second and more stable (if legally only civil) union in which they seek to bring up a new family. Often such persons, especially in their desire to help their children, long for restoration of full Eucharistic communion with the Church and its Lord. Is this spirit of repentance and desire for sacramental strength to be forever frustrated? Can they be told only that they must reject their new responsibilities as a necessary condition of forgiveness and restoration to sacramental life?[25]

Particularly significant was the appeal from every side for study of the centuries-old recognition of the validity of second, nonsacramental marriages by the Orthodox. Typical was the statement of Patriarch Maximos V Hakim of Antioch. Here is how he referred to the Eastern Church's very ancient practice as a solution in the present crisis:

> The Fathers of the Church at that time accepted that the divorced-remarried could again be admitted to the Eucharist. On the basis of the principle of "Oeconomia," often invoked and applied in the East, the Synod would be in a position to approach this question and find a practical solution.[26]

This ancient principle of "economy" is based on a conviction in the Eastern Church that God gives the Church the means to get around the harsh but unwanted side effects of a law.

Cardinal Basil Hume, speaking for the entire English-speaking group, called for objective norms for admission to the sacraments, based on study of the Eastern Church's practice. Bishop Etchegaray, for the French-speaking, asked for a special commission to study Eastern practice. Proposition 14, submitted to the Pope by all the bishops, even while excluding possibility of remarriage after divorce, called for study of the Eastern practice.

In his closing homily, John Paul accepted some of the recommendations in Proposition 14, stressing pastoral care of the divorced and remarried. He then reaffirmed traditional norms under which they could be allowed to return to sacramental penance and communion. They had to live together committed to complete abstinence from sexual intercourse under circumstances in which no scandal is given by their receiving the sacraments.

The Pope also effectively ruled out an "internal forum" solution widely recommended by many priests for those involved in hardship cases. This solution allowed those who in sincere conscience were convinced that their former marriage was truly dead and that their present marriage was right before God to receive the Eucharist.

The Pope departed from Proposition 14 in two ways. He forbade any pastor for whatever reason or pretext even of a pastoral nature to perform ceremonies of any kind for divorced people who remarry. Such ceremonies would give the impression of the celebration of a new, sacramentally valid marriage and would thus lead people into error concerning the indissolubility of a validly contracted marriage.[27]

Thus he ruled out a kind of ceremony recommended by theologians like Curran. While not Church weddings, such celebrations bring a sense of blessing and support to those attempting to rebuild their lives.

But most significantly, he completely left out any reference to Proposition 14f, where the bishops asked for a "new and extensive" study of practices of the Eastern Churches. The Pope closed the issue. He left no room for further study or pastoral adaptation.

In his encyclical letter the following year, *The Community of the Family,* Pope John Paul addressed the question of communion for the divorced who had remarried without obtaining an annulment. He wrote:

> However, the Church affirms the practice which is based on Sacred Scripture, of not admitting to Eucharistic communion divorced persons who have remarried. They are unable to be readmitted thereto from the fact that their state and condition of life objectively contradict that union of love between Christ and the Church which is signified and effected by the Eucharist. Besides this there is another special pastoral reason: If these people were admitted to the Eucharist the faithful would be led into error and confusion regarding the Church's teaching about the indissolubility of marriage.

The Pope would allow them to continue to live together only for grave reasons, such as the raising of children. However, they could receive communion only if they "take on themselves the duty to live in complete abstinence, that is, by abstaining from the acts proper to married couples."[28]

In September 1993 three German bishops, Oskar Saier of Freiburg, Karl Lehmann of Mainz, and Walter Kasper of Rottenburg-Stuttgart issued a pastoral letter. In it they advocated

> that the Church should offer pastoral help to divorced and remarried Catholics. They also recommended that these people should not be barred from the sacraments.... The bishops said that each case should be evaluated by a priest and that, "after considera-

tion," the priest might allow remarried divorcees to receive the Eucharist.[29]

None of the three bishops is considered progressive or a critic of the Vatican. Two of them, Lehmann and Kasper, are internationally respected theologians. They went to Rome three times to discuss the issue with Cardinal Ratzinger. Bishop Lehmann insisted that they went voluntarily. *The Tablet* claims that they may have been ordered to Rome for the last meeting on September 13–14, 1994.[30]

In October 1994 Rome responded with a seven-page letter. Actually there was no change from the Pope's teaching. This time that teaching was stated at much greater length and with greater emphasis.

In a paper issued simultaneously with the document from Rome, the German bishops spoke of the need in individual cases "to search for legitimate pastoral solutions for difficult situations." They repeated their earlier position

> that they still think that the possibility of admitting divorcees to Communion should "be available under certain clearly-defined conditions." They stress their conviction that care of divorced and remarried people is one of the "key questions" of present-day pastoral work.[31]

The Tablet for November 19 reported on other reactions to the Vatican letter. The Catholic bishops' conference in Belgium said that the "well-informed conscience of the individual" should determine whether communion should be received.

> The Belgian bishops recognize that the Vatican document points out the traditional teaching of the Church, they say, "but, as in other cases," the personal decision of the individual conscience is final. No priest or special minister "has the right to refuse giving the Eucharist publicly, except to avoid causing scandal or provocation."

The bishops' role was to help priest and people make decisions.

The Dutch bishops had not responded to the letter. However, one Dutch bishop, Johannes Moeller of Groningen, said in an interview that remarried divorcees ought not to be treated as "lepers." Priests in the Netherlands would not refuse to give communion. The decision on whether or not to receive rested "completely and exclusively with the individual." The Pope himself had said that the divorced and remarried were "full members of the Church."[32]

Cardinal König, the archbishop emeritus of Vienna, was joined by seven other Austrian bishops in supporting the German bishops. He stressed that the Church cannot control the individual conscience. Its duty is to interpret the Gospel and to explain and support moral values. However, in "certain tragic, difficult, individual cases" the upright conscience must be respected.[33]

Rights Denied

The strongest remaining argument against relaxing present discipline is that to do so would open the floodgates of divorce and promote further deterioration in family stability. But Catholic divorce rates in this country are now the same as those of Protestants and Jews, who are not under such a strict discipline.[34] Maintenance of rigid discipline has not prevented increase of divorce among Catholics.

Lay reaction suggests that among the People of God the official position is not accepted as the final, irrevocable answer. The Gallup poll of 1993 shows that 62 percent of all American Catholics say that they "can be a good Catholic without obeying Church teaching on divorce/remarriage." For those who attend Mass at least weekly the figure is 52 percent. Incidentally, a majority of those who do not accept the official teaching have not themselves been divorced.

It is often argued that scandal will be given by a relaxation of current practice. If available statistics give any indication, lack of compassion toward people in great suffering gives even greater scandal. It is a question of who is being scandalized. Should our concern be only for those who will not accept change in Church teaching? What of the scandal of those who ask: Is it moral, in the face of so much suffering by so many millions of the Church's own members, to maintain a discipline with such weak biblical, historical, and doctrinal foundations?

The right to marry is a fundamental, if sometimes limited, human right. Is it moral to deny the possibility of remarriage to those whose first marriages have been hopelessly ended? The right to the Eucharist is a fundamental right of the baptized.[35] It is not a privilege granted by the Church leaders, but a gift offered to his own by the Lord of the Church. Grave questions arise about an authority that claims that the consummated marriages of the baptized can never be dissolved[36] and yet dissolves true marriages where one or both parties are not baptized. There is adequate scriptural and historical basis for the opinion that the Church can dissolve the marriages of the baptized as well.

Chapter 9

ABORTION
Catholic Pluralism and
the Potential for Dialogue

An important goal of the Roman Catholic Church in the abortion debate should be to save unborn life. That goal can be achieved only if the Church is willing to enter into dialogue with other parties to the debate. Is the Roman Catholic position so completely settled that conversion of others to the Catholic position is their only possible goal? Or are there responsible differences among serious thinkers within the Roman Catholic Church that make it important for Catholics to begin meaningful dialogue on the abortion issue among themselves and with other people of good will?

It is not the purpose of this chapter to resolve those differences. I have the much more modest goal of bringing the differences out into the open and calling for honest dialogue during which we examine the differences and seek grounds for reconciliation.

The Official Teaching

The current official teaching is quite definite: (1) Human life begins at the moment of conception. From that moment all direct abortions are forbidden. According to the official teaching this is not the Church's law but the law of God. (2) Direct abortion may not be allowed even to save the life of the mother. Only indirect abortion can be permitted, and this is allowed only for grave reasons.

There have been and continue to be significant differences within the Church on both of these points.

1. The Beginning of Human Life. When we speak of the beginning of human life, it would be helpful to recognize that the scientific understanding of human life in general has grown greatly in recent times. Our concern is with the transmission of that life and the beginning of individual human lives. With the discovery of the ovum by Karl Ernst von Baer in 1827, we realized that this is accomplished through the union of the mother's egg and the father's sperm. The egg and sperm are both made up of living, human tissue. Nature produces both extravagantly to be discarded when not used.

When they combine, in a process lasting about twenty-four hours, they produce a fertilized egg, called a zygote. A normal, healthy zygote contains all of the genetic material needed to develop into a human being. Once fertilization is accomplished that first cell will begin to divide rapidly. However, only after the second week is it certain that the cell mass will develop as a single human being. Up to that point the cells can separate and have the potential to develop into twins or more.

Our concern is: at what point is there an individual human being with full human rights? The official teaching designates this as "the moment of conception." Presumably the end of the twenty-four hour period during which the sperm and ovum are combining to produce the zygote would be the moment when a newly created soul is infused into the new organism. In the official teaching this "moment of conception" is the presumed time of ensoulment when "*a human being* comes into existence as an individual person with his own rights."

This designation of the moment of conception as that point of ensoulment is quite recent. This is not a defined dogma and has not always been held. Augustine and Aquinas considered abortion unacceptable at all times, but did not consider it homicide in the early stages of pregnancy. Aquinas taught that ensoulment occurred only when the developing organism was suitably formed to receive a soul. This was after forty days for males and eighty days for females.

Karl Rahner asked if contemporary moral theologians can maintain this position on ensoulment at the moment of conception, when they know that

Fifty percent of all fertilized female cells never succeed in becoming attached to the womb? Will [they] be able to accept that 50 percent of all "human beings" — real human beings with "immortal" souls and an eternal destiny — will never get beyond this first stage of human existence?[1]

The embryologist Clifford Grobstein writes: "It is worth emphasizing that even in natural development only about one in four human zygotes [fertilized eggs] actually achieve development to birth."[2]

In an earlier work Grobstein suggested that there is a natural process in humans

> to cope with a surprisingly high percentage of "damaged" eggs …most of those eliminated disappearing prior to implantation, and most of the rest being aborted shortly after implantation. Abortuses show a considerably elevated frequency of chromosomal abnormalities compared with those found in infants at term, suggesting that embryo loss screens out abnormal embryos. The screening is not complete, since infants at term show a significant frequency of various defects, among which are chromosomal abnormalities, anatomical irregularities and more subtle biochemical deficiencies.[3]

Especially with the knowledge that twinning can occur during the first two weeks, the uncertainty over when an individual life begins continues today.

2. Direct versus Indirect Abortion. In the official teaching direct abortion may not be allowed even to save the life of the mother. Only indirect abortion can be permitted, and this is allowed only for grave reasons.

What is meant by "indirect abortion" is usually explained by the case of the cancerous womb. A woman in the early stages of pregnancy is diagnosed as having a life-threatening cancer of the womb. The competent medical opinion is that she cannot live long enough to bring the fetus to birth. It is permitted to remove the diseased organ, even though it has within it a human being that will die. The direct action was the removal of a diseased organ. The death of the fetus is a secondary outcome of a primary intervention that had a different purpose. Only indirectly is the death of the fetus a result of the necessary surgery.

Evidence of doubt among American cardinals about the official teaching on direct abortions occurred twenty years ago.

This happened at a hearing before the Senate Subcommittee on Constitutional Amendments on March 6, 1974. The hearing involved a human life amendment to the Constitution proposed by Senator James Buckley, a Catholic senator from New York. The amendment would have made all abortions illegal unless there is "reasonable medical certainty...that continuation of the pregnancy will cause the death of the mother."[4]

The spokesmen for the American Church at this important public hearing were four American cardinals: John Krol, archbishop of Philadelphia; Timothy Manning, archbishop of Los Angeles; Humberto Medeiros, archbishop of Boston; and John Cody, archbishop of Chicago. In his formal statement Cardinal Medeiros said that the Catholic conference could not endorse in principle or conscientiously support

> an amendment that would generally prohibit abortion but permit it in certain exceptional circumstances, such as when a woman's life is considered to be threatened.[5]

Senator Marlow Cook pressed the issue of the exception to save the life of the mother.

> Section 2 of Buckley's resolution says this article shall not apply in an emergency when a reasonable medical certainty exists that continuation of the pregnancy will cause death of the mother. Now as far as the organization for which you speak, the bishops throughout the nation, is that or is that not acceptable?

Medeiros replied: "I could not endorse any wording that would allow for direct abortion."

Cook then turned to Cody: "Cardinal Cody, how does that language strike you?" Cody answered:

> Well, since we're not going to make a decision here today, I think it needs further study. As Cardinal Medeiros has indicated, there is a very definite understanding about direct and indirect abortion; the Senator's proposal here, as it stands, I don't think it would be justified on moral grounds. However, this is something at least for myself I would not want to make a definitive judgment on here today. I would have to study and meditate on it and then come to some conclusion.[6]

Cardinals Manning and Krol agreed with Cardinal Medeiros. Cardinal Cody seemed to agree, but he still expressed some doubt or hesitation in making a judgment.

Here is an issue on which the teaching of the official Church is clear, absolute, unchangeable. Direct abortion, the direct taking of unborn life, is surely one of those acts that Pope John Paul II, in his *Apostolic Exhortation on Reconciliation and Penance,* describes as

> intrinsically grave and mortal by reason of their matter. That is, there are acts which, per se, and in themselves, independently of circumstances are always seriously wrong by reason of their object.[7]

As Pope Paul VI, in a different context wrote:

> it is never lawful, even for the gravest of reasons, to do evil that good may come of it — in other words, to intend positively something which intrinsically contradicts the moral order, and which must therefore be judged unworthy of man, even though the intention is to protect or promote the welfare of an individual, of a family or of society in general.[8]

Pope John Paul II considered a direct abortion so serious that he maintained an automatic excommunication in the new Code of Canon Law against all the active participants in such an abortion.

The Tubal Pregnancy

Could Cody's hesitation have been due to a closely related issue explored earlier in the hearing where Church teaching had quite recently been changed? This was the question of what could be done in the case of the tubal pregnancy. The tubal pregnancy is the case where the fertilized egg, which should go through one of the two fallopian tubes to the womb, becomes attached to the wall of a fallopian tube instead. Unlike the womb, the fallopian tube doesn't expand to accommodate the growing fetus. Therefore it will grow until it bursts the tube. This type of pregnancy now occurs in one out of every one hundred to two hundred pregnancies. If untreated it is almost always fatal. Until quite recently the tubal pregnancy was diagnosed only when the tube burst and hemorrhaging began. Now with ultrasound it can be recognized and treated at a very early stage.

Senator Birch Bayh had read from the *Ethical and Religious Directives for Health Facilities* of the Department of Health Affairs of the U.S. Catholic Conference dated September 1971. This instruction permitted the removal of the fallopian tube with a fetus attached in the tubal wall. This was a permitted *indirect* abortion. However, to open the tube and remove the fetus would be the forbidden *direct* abortion.

Under questioning from Bayh, Medeiros continued:

If the intention is to get at the human life which has a right to be in the mother, to destroy that life directly, that would be abortion and an immoral act. But if it is to save the life of the mother by removing an organ which is attached to the mother, and thus the child is destroyed, again, it is not direct abortion, because there is no direct intention to destroy the child.[9]

Cody may have recalled that when he was in seminary this procedure to remove the tube with a fetus inside had been forbidden. Here is a passage from a manual widely used in seminaries at that time:

The direct killing of the fetus is murder and therefore always gravely sinful. Even though it be to save the life of the mother, it is not permissible to destroy the living child, e.g., by a craniotomy, embryotomy, etc.... So too it is always mortally sinful to procure an abortion, even though both mother and child will otherwise die. This holds also for ectopic gestation [tubal pregnancy].[10]

Just two years before the Senate hearing Father John F. Dedek, professor of moral theology at Cardinal Cody's own seminary, had written the story of the change in the Church's teaching on tubal pregnancy. In a chapter entitled, "Abortion, the Christian Tradition" Dedek told how the issue of the tubal pregnancy had been raised. A question had been submitted to Rome on March 20, 1900: "Is it ever permitted to remove an immature ectopic fetus prior to six months of gestation?" On May 5, 1902, the Church office replied "no," since ordinarily a fetus at that stage could not survive. Dedek went on to show that Lehmkuhl and Bouscaren, two outstanding moralists of the day, argued that

the removal of a part of the fallopian tube along with a nonviable fetus is an indirect abortion...not a direct attack on the fetus but the removal of a pathological tube with the indirect consequence of fetal death.

Rome has never rejected their opinion.[11]

Could Cody have read this chapter from Father Dedek's book to prepare for the Senate hearing?

Bernard Häring, in his *Medical Ethics*, illustrates the confusion in the distinction between direct and indirect abortions with an actual case involving a Catholic gynecologist. His patient was recently married and in her fourth month of pregnancy. He had successfully removed a tumor from the exterior surface of the womb, but was unable to suture because of the condition of the veins. To save the woman from bleeding to death, he "opened the womb and removed the fetus. Thereupon the uterus contracted, the bleeding ceased, and the woman's life was saved."

Afterward he consulted a noted moral theologian. The theologian told him that he had not sinned because he had acted in good faith. However, what he had done was objectively wrong. It would have been perfectly proper to remove the diseased uterus. That would have been only a permitted *indirect* abortion. However, by deliberately and directly taking the healthy fetus out of the womb he had performed a forbidden *direct* abortion. He had directly removed a living fetus. For this moralist "preservation of the woman's fertility and in some cases, preservation of the marriage itself, played no decisive role."

Häring would say that "the malice of abortion is an attack on the right of the fetus to live." In this situation without the doctor's "direct" intervention both mother and fetus would have died. He saved the mother's life while he did not truly deprive the fetus of its right to live. It could not possibly have survived if the doctor had failed to save the life of the mother. Moreover, Häring adds, "the preservation of the mother's fertility is an additional service to life." By preserving the wife's fertility he may also have preserved the marriage.[12]

Dedek showed that for Aquinas it was not the physical nature of an act that determined whether it was direct or indirect. In the case of killing the unjust aggressor, Aquinas reached the conclusion that the killing was *indirect*. Whether the act was to be considered direct or indirect depended on the intention, not on the physical nature of the act. Even if the physical act was quite direct, since the intention was not to kill but only to stop the aggression, Aquinas would have described the act as an indirect act. This Thomistic understanding of "indirect" was applied by outstanding authors to the abortion issue right down to the end of the last century.[13] Häring would agree. The present official understanding of direct-indirect is quite recent. In the older tradition:

"The life-saving interruption of pregnancy, when it is impossible to save both lives, is to be called an "indirect abortion." In such extreme situations, Häring has said,

> the whole meaning and purpose of the action is nothing else than to save life. In ethical analysis according to our best tradition, you have to look at the whole meaning of the action, and not just on the directness or indirectness of the physical performance. . . . It does not at all have the "malice of abortion" as traditional authors, like St. Alphonsus, would say.[14]

Alphonsus Liguori would have asked why is it necessary to have a *direct* intention to expel the fetus when an *indirect* intention would suffice.[15]

So Dedek, following St. Thomas, and Häring, following St. Alphonsus Liguori and others, would restore the more traditional meaning of "indirect." It refers to the intention of the one acting and the end result of the action rather than to the physical structure of the act.

With John T. Noonan, Jr., we get a significantly different analysis. He would reject the use of the direct-indirect terminology altogether. He contends that

> the physician has to intend to achieve not only improvement of the mother but the performance of action by which the fertilized ovum becomes nonviable. He necessarily intends to perform an abortion, he necessarily intends to kill. To say that he acts indirectly is to conceal what is being done.

Noonan proposes that the cases of the cancerous uterus and the tubal pregnancy be acknowledged as

> true exceptions to the absolute inviolability of the fetus . . . special cases of the general exception to the rule against killing, which permits one to kill in self defense. . . . Characterization of this kind of killing as "indirect," does not aid analysis.[16]

But according to the present official teaching, the direct taking of innocent life is the one case where there can be no exceptions. Dedek has discussed the situation of conflict between innocent life and other values. He recognizes that, although traditional Catholic theology always allowed exceptions to most concrete rules, it saw the rule prohibiting the direct killing of the innocent as absolute. Acknowledging that innocent life generally deserves preference over other values, Dedek asked if we cannot conceive of values that could come into conflict with innocent life and still be preferred to innocent life? He writes:

> Physical life is fundamental. But it is neither an absolute value or the highest one. [We] should be willing and able to make responsible judgments of preference even in such basic areas.[17]

This "preference principle" can be simply stated: put in a position where we will unavoidably cause evil we must maximize the good and minimize the evil. If Lehmkuhl and Bouscaren had had the preference principle, would they not have preferred opening the fallopian tube and directly removing the fetus? This would have done minimal damage to the mother and preserved her fertility. To remove the tube would have been an unnecessary mutilation of the mother in order to uphold an abstract principle.

Robert Springer, S.J., puts it well: "The basic question, then, is not: Is it direct or indirect abortion? Rather it is: How great a value must be present to countervail the sacrifice of life?"[18]

The Other Churches

The Senate hearing also revealed that the Catholic Church's staunchest allies in the abortion debate do not accept the official Roman Catholic rejection of direct therapeutic abortions.

The Mormons, whose position was presented at the Senate hearing by David L. McKay, permit abortion

> in rare cases where in the opinion of competent medical counsel, the life or good health of the mother is seriously endangered or where the pregnancy was caused by rape and produces serious emotional trauma in the mother.[19]

Mrs. Jean Garten, official spokesperson for the Lutheran Church-Missouri Synod, presented a report that also included the exception to save the life of the mother.[20]

The strong pro-life position of Orthodox Judaism was expressed by Rabbi David Bleich, speaking for the Rabbinical Council of America. According to Rabbi Bleich the unborn fetus is to be considered "a person and is entitled to protection of society."[21] Under questioning he said that "an abortion could be performed in order to save the life of the mother."[22] The rationale for Orthodox Judaism is that in a life-threatening situation the fetus is considered an aggressor. The official Catholic teaching will not accept this solution because the fetus is considered innocent.

However, Paul Ramsey, Methodist ethicist at Princeton, rejects an analysis based on the innocence or guilt of the fetus. He compares the situation to that of the soldier who kills in self-defense. He is justified in killing his attacker. This is not because the attacker is guilty, but because that is the only way he can save his own life. If he could save his life by incapacitating the attacker, killing could not be justified. For Ramsey, it is the threat to the life of the mother and not the guilt or innocence of the fetus that justifies the abortion. Ramsey writes:

> Precisely the fact of the effect of the material aggression on life should be the main concern in our attempts to penetrate the meaning of the Christian life, not waiting to find a guilty aggressor before we are permitted ever to take one life in order to save another in mortal conflict of lives and values.[23]

Dr. Albert C. Outler, professor at Perkins School of Theology at Southern Methodist University, wrote to the committee:

> It is misleading to suppose that among Christian groups in the United States only the Roman Catholics, Mormons, etc. are the ones who are opposed to abortion on demand on moral and religious grounds....It is...my impression and belief that given an honest opportunity to vote for or against a responsible anti-abortion law (that is, one that disallows abortion on demand, but allows very cautiously for therapeutic abortion) a majority of United Methodists would vote for it. The case is even clearer with Southern Baptists, Lutherans, the black Churches, the Pentecostals, etc.[24]

Outler's conclusion is cautious:

> Abortion, therefore, may in all probability involve the killing of a defenseless human being. Its only conceivable justification therefore, would be to have the lesser of two evils, i.e., as some sort of therapeutic abortion defined *very, very* cautiously.[25]

There is, therefore, among other religious groups support for a public policy that could drastically reduce the number of legally approved abortions. Can Roman Catholics in conscience cooperate with the limited goals of these groups? Or must they adhere to the more restricted official Roman Catholic position that allows only indirect abortion as in the cases of the cancerous uterus and the tubal pregnancy?

A Gallup survey of 1983 showed that less than one-fifth of Catholics or Protestants thought that abortion should be "illegal in all circumstances." Andrew Greeley wrote in 1985 of a

> survey of American abortion attitudes in the early '70s. American Protestants and American Catholics in overwhelming majorities (more than nine-tenths) feel that abortion should be available when the mother's life is in danger or there is the chance of a seriously handicapped child. [Further] the Catholic attitude on abortion has not changed in the era after the Second Vatican Council...and is hard to distinguish from that of white Protestants.[26]

We may recall Grobstein's suggestion that there is a natural process in humans to screen out abnormal embryos. The screening is not complete, as evidenced by the significant frequency of various defects at birth. Can the abortion where there is the chance of a seriously handicapped child be seen as a correction where the natural process has failed?

An important goal of the Church leadership in this country is to influence public policy in order to preserve unborn life. In recent years, the American bishops have taken a very strong stand against legal abortion. The ability to change policy in a democracy depends on the state of public opinion. It is fair to ask: what effect has the bishops' teaching had on their own Catholic people?

The *New York Times*/CBS poll of 1986 on "What American Catholics Think" showed that only 15 percent of Catholics of all ages accepted the official Church teaching that opposed legal abortion; 26 percent favored legal abortion; 55 percent favored abortion only to save the life of the mother or in cases of rape and incest.

Gallup conducted a much more sophisticated poll in 1993. This had been a period in which the American bishops had been very active in their opposition to legal abortion. Although the question in the Gallup poll was worded differently, it is clear that Catholics moved significantly away from supporting their bishops and the official teaching.

The question in the new Gallup poll was: could you be a good Catholic without obeying the Church's teaching on abortion? The Gallup poll first gave the answer of all Catholics. For all Catholics the percentage who said yes, you could be a good Catholic, increased from 39 percent in 1987 to 56 percent in 1993. The poll then asked further questions to get the answers of highly committed Catholics. For the Catholics who considered the Church most important in their lives, the percentages who said you could be a good Catholic without obeying the Church's teaching on abortion went up from 26 percent in 1987 to 36 percent in 1993. For those who said they attended Mass at least once a week the increase was from 26 percent in 1987 to 40 percent in 1993. For those who said they would never leave the Church, the increase was from 34 percent in 1987 to 51 percent in 1993. In a period when the American bishops were taking a very strong public position against all abortion, highly committed American Catholics moved significantly away from support for the official Church teaching.

Should such findings influence official teaching? No one would propose that doctrine be determined by public opinion polls. Yet the Gallup poll was responsibly taken. Might this not indicate a growing conviction among Catholics of a need to rethink the Church's absolute prohibition of all direct abortions?

A majority of Catholic laity do not accept the official teaching. Moreover, some of the staunchest opponents of abortion among other religious traditions — Mormons, Missouri Synod Lutherans, Orthodox Jews — do not fully agree with the official Catholic position. This is especially true in the case of a threat to the life of the mother.

Catholic Theologians

How well do American Catholic theologians support the official teaching? The *National Catholic Reporter* for February 15, 1985, reported a survey of all the members of the Catholic Theological Society of America, the College Theology Society, and the Catholic Biblical Association. There were 498 responses, about one-fourth of the membership. This included a significant portion of U.S. theological scholars. Three out of five scholars who answered would not label every abortion "murder." They did not consider automatic excommunication an appropriate Church response to abortion. Asked whether abortion can ever be a morally acceptable option, they were almost evenly split, with 49 percent saying yes and 48 percent saying no.

This survey was anonymous. What of the publicly stated positions of theologians with national and even international reputations, and even of some bishops? There is "a cloud of witnesses" to the existence of responsible difference of opinion on the abortion issue within the Catholic community.

Charles E. Curran writes that many Catholic theologians would accept the opinion he had expressed in previous writings: that conflict situations in abortion cannot be resolved by observing the physical structure of the act. There must be a careful weighing of the human values involved. As reluctant as the Christian must be to take life,

> in the case of abortion there can arrive circumstances in which the abortion is justified for preserving the life of the mother or for some other value commensurate with life.

Curran cites Richard McCormick who

> after studying six different modifications of the concept of the direct effect also concludes that one cannot decisively decide the morality of the conflict situation on the basis of the physical structure of the act but ultimately on the basis of proportionate reason.

Curran then asks what constitutes proportionate reason in the abortion conflict. He shows that

> in other conflict situations in the past, especially in the case of unjust aggression, Catholic theology has been willing to equate other values with physical human life itself. [These included] bodily integrity, spiritual goods "of greater value than life or integrity" such as the use of reason or conservation of reputation in very important matters; and material goods of great value.

Using such a balancing of values Curran would justify abortion

> to save the life of the mother or to avert very grave psychological or physical harm to the mother with the realization that this must truly be grave harm that will perdure over some time and not just a temporary depression.[27]

In an article in *America*, "Rules for Abortion Debate," Richard McCormick contrasts traditional teaching with developments on the papal level. He points out that Pope Pius XI and Pope Pius XII both taught (and with them traditional Catholic ethical treatises on abortion) that direct abortion is never permissible, even to save the life of the mother.

As McCormick explains the Popes' teaching, "better two deaths than one murder." For a clear departure from the papal teaching McCormick quotes the Catholic bishop of Augsburg, Joseph Stimpfle, who stated:

> He who performs an abortion except to save the life of the mother sins gravely and burdens his conscience with the killing of human life.[28]

Or again the 1973 statement of all the Belgian bishops:

> The moral principle which ought to govern the intervention [in these rare and desperate conflict situations] can be formulated as follows: Since two lives are at stake, one will, while doing everything possible to save both, attempt to save one rather than allow two to perish.[29]

McCormick writes:

> Contemporary problems will always provoke doubts and questions and give rise to ambiguity. The Catholic tradition may well have some unfinished agenda and it would be counterproductive to the overall health of the position to leave this agenda unfinished or to sweep it under the carpet.[30]

The abortion issue is far from closed in the Roman Catholic Church. A vigorous discussion continues within the Catholic community. The diversity within the community can well be the basis for flexibility in dialogue with others in the abortion debate. The issue can be summed up in the words of Bernard Häring in his *Medical Ethics:*

> I am convinced that it is possible to persuade the decisive parts of society and the legislators about the necessity of protecting unborn human life if we observe the rules of respectful dialogue and avoid ... absolutizing abstract principles. Most decisive, however, is whether we give evidence that our commitment to protecting innocent life is a total one.[31]

Häring's call for a total commitment to life has been taken up in Cardinal Joseph L. Bernardin's "seamless garment," concern for all life from beginning to end. What of Häring's call for "respectful dialogue" not to be short-circuited by "absolutizing abstract principles"? The ongoing discussion on the principles within the Catholic theological community and the changing positions that have historically been accepted by the official Church show that not all of the "principles" are absolutes. Moreover, on at least one issue — the exception to save the life of the mother — the official Catholic teaching is at odds with the firmly held position of our closest allies in the abortion debate. We Catholics must make a choice: do we want to uphold abstract principles that can no longer be considered absolute or do we want to save unborn life? If our concern is to save unborn lives rather than uphold abstract principles we must be prepared to dialogue respectfully with all of the participants in the abortion debate.

Chapter 10

DEMOCRACY IN THE CHURCH
The Election of Bishops

He who governs all should be elected by all.
> —Pope St. Leo the Great

Democracy is the worst form of government except all those
other forms that have been tried from time to time.
> —Winston Churchill

In the preceding chapters I have discussed cases where official Roman Catholic teaching and discipline have caused suffering and
estrangement for many Catholics and are obstacles to reunion
with other Christian Churches. I have shown that Catholics —
faced with a rigid and authoritarian teaching authority — have
resources in their oldest tradition that allow freedom in decision-
making for individual Catholics and are helpful for dialogue with
other Christian Churches.

But a question arises: Does failure to respond to such important needs in these and other areas indicate a flaw in the Church's
contemporary institutional structure?

Compare the case of the birth control encyclical with reception
of Gentiles into the early Church. Before the birth control encyclical's promulgation, a crisis had developed among devout married
lay people because official teaching on contraception no longer
corresponded to their experience. A growing number of highly
respected theologians reached the conclusion that the teaching
could and should be changed. John XXIII established a commission on birth control but died before the commission met. At
Vatican II's fourth session three cardinals and a patriarch advocated change in the official teaching. By their applause the

assembled bishops made their support clear. Paul VI, however, immediately removed the issue from discussion at the council.

Pope Paul enlarged John's commission and stacked it in favor of the existing official teaching. After careful study, the commission voted overwhelmingly for change. Fourteen cardinals and bishops were added to the last session to bring their total number to sixteen. Why were the additional cardinals and bishops added? To turn the commission around. But of the sixteen, one appointee did not attend (the future John Paul II) and only three voted to keep the old teaching. After agonizing over the problem for over two years, Pope Paul VI came out with the birth control encyclical. There he reaffirmed the old prohibition of all use of artificial contraception.

The birth control encyclical has not been accepted in the Church, and at the 1980 Synod the bishops were rebuffed in their effort to reopen the case. John Paul II continues to demand the encyclical's acceptance. He insists that the issue is not open for discussion by theologians.

Contrast the handling of this crisis with the early Church's treatment of the reception of Gentiles. Thousands of Jews had been received into the young Church through baptism (Acts 2:41). The possibility of receiving uncircumcised Gentiles was never even considered. Peter had to be prepared for this drastic act by a special vision (Acts 10:9–16). Moreover, the Holy Spirit fell on the Gentile Cornelius and the members of his household before Peter had decided to accept them into the Church (Acts 10:44–48).

Peter was called to Jerusalem to explain his action. The question was raised again later when Paul and Barnabas also accepted Gentiles. Luke tells how the issue was settled at the so-called Council of Jerusalem. James, not one of the Twelve but "brother of the Lord,"[1] presided (Acts 15:13–21). The decisions were made by "the apostles and the elders, with *the whole Church*" (Acts 15:22).

The Vatican's handling of the birth control issue resembled the decision-making of a divine-right monarch. Pope Paul VI made the decision on his own. The way the decision was made at the Council of Jerusalem was like that at a New England town meeting. In the New Testament times democracy flourished in fact if not in name.

Certainly, an international institution like the Roman Catholic Church cannot operate like a town meeting. As the Church has grown in size and responsibilities, necessary changes in structure have occurred. New structures, however, must be faithful both to fundamental Gospel values and sensitive to special needs of the contemporary situation. The Church needs structures more responsive to the Spirit's voice at work among the People of God. I believe that democracy, with its openness and accountability, would be as fair and effective in the Church as it has been in secular government.

In what follows, I will show what I mean by democracy in the Church. I will also explore evidence for democracy in the Church's history. I will emphasize the ancient practice of popular election of bishops. We will then see how the people's right to elect their bishops was lost, first to the clergy, then to secular rulers. In the Investiture Struggle, from 1050 to 1300, the Church won back control over election of bishops from secular rulers only to have it become, at least in appearance, the privilege of the local clergy. Today, the Pope controls the appointment of bishops.

Through the centuries the Church has become highly centralized. Before the eleventh century, the Church was a collegial group of local Churches that made up the universal Church with the bishop of Rome described as "the first among equals." In this chapter we will see how the Popes tried but failed to gain control over the empire and the secular states. But during the long struggle they were able to centralize control over the Church, giving it the authoritarian character it has maintained to our day.

In the next chapter I will describe this struggle and present Brian Tierney's thesis that the constitutional principles and structures of modern democracy were developed by the Church's own great canon lawyers in the course of that struggle. With Tierney I propose that these principles and structures, which were developed within the Church's own tradition, should be adopted by the modern Church.

What Is Democracy?

To call the Church a democracy is not to say that the Church has been established by a contract among its members. No: the Church is God's congregation, the flock that God has gathered together.

God does not govern the Church directly, however, but through human beings. It is both legitimate and necessary to ask what type of government comes closest to realizing the New Testament ideal. Autocracy, in which the educated, privileged few teach and control the uneducated masses, the so-called simple faithful, probably never realized that ideal. Autocracy is particularly inappropriate in the modern world. The form of Church government that accords best with the Gospel spirit is democracy.

When we speak of democracy we do not limit it to the particular structures such as we have in the United States. Great Britain, the Netherlands, and the Scandinavian countries show that monarchy is compatible with genuine democracy. Opposition is not between democracy and monarchy, but between democracy and autocracy.

Brian Tierney's description of "constitutionalism" includes elements important in any discussion of democracy in the Church.[2] Constitutionalism involves such basic ideas as "government under law" and "government by consent." It means guarantee of due process of law. In democracy the law itself does not depend on an autocratic ruler's arbitrary will. It reflects the entire society's moral principles. It does not mean that a majority can force its will on a minority. Rather it means that machinery exists to develop an agreement that all citizens can be persuaded to accept, even if sometimes they are not all enthusiastic. This usually involves an elected representative assembly that makes laws and imposes taxes.

Such a system is usually called "constitutional democracy." It has also been called "participatory democracy." It is important for us to participate with our fellow citizens in the decisions affecting our lives. Cardinal Karol Wojtyła (nine years before his election as Pope John Paul II) wrote of the importance of participation.[3] Wojtyła said that by participation, by "acting with others," individuals reach personal maturity. They come to realize that being related to others is necessary for their own development and fulfillment. Moreover, "any authentic human community" is founded also on participation. He wrote of these two aspects of participation:

> The human community is strictly related to the experience of the person.... We find in it the reality of participation as that essential of the person which enables him to exist and act "together with

others" and thus to reach his own fulfillment. Simultaneously, participation as an essential of the person is a constitutive factor of any human community.

Wojtyła proposed two "authentic" attitudes for community: solidarity and opposition.

The attitude of solidarity is, so to speak, the natural consequence of the fact that human beings live and act together; it is the attitude of a community, in which the common good properly conditions and initiates participation, and participation in turn properly serves the common good, fosters it, and furthers its realization.[4]

Of "the attitude of opposition," Wojtyła wrote:

Opposition is not inconsistent with solidarity.... Far from rejecting the common good or the need of participation, it consists on the contrary in their confirmation.... Those who in this way stand up in opposition do not thereby cut themselves off from their community. On the contrary, they seek their own place and a constructive role within the community.[5]

In fact, society should be so structured that opposition can be expressed and operate in the society for the society's good. He continued:

More precisely, in order for opposition to be constructive, the structure, and beyond it the system of communities of a given society must be such as to allow the opposition that emerges from the soil of solidarity not only to *express* itself within the framework of the given community but also to *operate* for its benefit. The structure of a human community is correct only if it admits not just the presence of a justified opposition but also that practical effectiveness of opposition required by the common good and the right of participation.

Wojtyła then describes what he calls "a sense of dialogue."

The common good has to be conceived of dynamically and not statically.... In fact, it must liberate and support the attitude of solidarity but never to a degree such as to stifle opposition.... The principle of dialogue allows us to select and bring to light what in controversial situations is right and true, and helps to eliminate any partial, preconceived or subjective views and trends.[6]

To these ideas on constitutionalism and solidarity, I would add from Catholic social thought the important principle of subsidiarity. According to subsidiarity a social unit should never take over what an individual can decide and do. Nor should a higher social unit take over what a lower social unit can decide and do. This protects individual rights and prevents the absorption of smaller units of society by a monopolizing, central power. Subsidiarity safeguards freedom of action and participation throughout the various levels of society. Pius XI wrote in 1931:

> Just as it is gravely wrong to take from individuals what they can accomplish by their own initiative and industry and give it to the community, so also it is an injustice and at the same time a great evil and disturbance of right order to assign to a greater and higher association what lesser and subordinate organizations can do. For every social activity ought of its very nature furnish help to the members of the body social and never absorb them.[7]

In preparation for the 1985 extraordinary synod, almost all bishops' conferences referred explicitly or equivalently to the principle of subsidiarity. However, Cardinal Jean Jerome Hamer, apparently speaking for the Vatican, rejected the application of subsidiarity to the Church.[8]

I propose that principles of constitutional or participatory democracy and subsidiarity apply to the Church. The Church is a society, established by God but governed by human beings. All the norms recognized as essential to good government and authentic community in civil society apply equally to the Church.

Roots of Church Democracy

Democratic structures already exist in the Church. Vatican Council II was an example of democracy in action. Opinion had been widespread that, with the definition of papal infallibility, councils would no longer be needed or held. After Vatican I, it seemed that the Pope would function as the Church's sole teacher. Vatican II, however, showed what could be accomplished in the Church when all the bishops worked together. There was significant input from theologians (some formerly silenced). Protestant observers made an important contribution. Above all, because of the press, input came from the Church at large. The press kept the laity informed about what was happening in the council. The laity made their concerns known to the bishops.

Actions of the council made it clear that the Church is wider than just the Pope and bishops. Here is an important example. The original document on the Church presented to the bishops for their approval had three opening chapters. The first chapter was about the "Mystery of the Church" in its relation to Jesus Christ. The second was about leadership in the Church, the Pope and the bishops. Only after that was there a chapter about the "People of God." Obviously, these chapters were presented in what was considered the order of their importance. The bishops at Vatican II deliberately turned the second and third chapters around. They placed the chapter on the Church as "People of God" ahead of the chapter on the official leadership.

The council took into consideration the "mind of the faithful." It recognized that the Holy Spirit was at work throughout the Church, not just among the leaders. The council also taught that the infallibility of the Pope and bishops has meaning only within the infallibility of the Church as a whole.

These democratic tendencies at Vatican II have deep roots. They go back to the New Testament Church, with its high level of community participation. The election of Matthias (Acts 1:12–26) and of the seven (Acts 6:1–6) is by the community. Of the Council of Jerusalem (Acts 15), Myles Bourke wrote that, although leaders' roles were important, it is clear that the entire community took part in the discussion.[9] To meet the standards set at Jerusalem, any Church assembly in our day would have to involve the laity in an active role.

So uncertain are structures in the New Testament period that it is not possible to distinguish between presbyters (elders) and bishops (overseers). It is more accurate to speak of presbyter-bishops. It is true that Barnabas and Paul appointed elders in Churches they founded (Acts 14:23) and Titus was instructed to "appoint elders in every town" (Titus 1:5). But the rest of the New Testament evidence about choosing leaders and about decision-making is not clear.

Further, Bourke points to the importance of teachers (*didaskaloi*) in the decision-making process. Paul ranked them third, after apostles and prophets (1 Cor. 12:28). Bourke thinks that in the Church today theologians would be the equivalent of the teachers that Paul lists. He suggests that if the "whole Church" is to have a role in the making of decisions in matters of faith, then

Democracy in the Church

the authority of theologians should be given much greater weight than is often the case today.

After looking at all the related biblical texts, Patrick Granfield of Catholic University concluded that decision-making in the New Testament Church had two important democratic characteristics. First, it involved majority rule. Second, it was decentralized. He especially noted absence of heavy handed use of authority and the open atmosphere that promoted free discussion of important issues. New Testament evidence, therefore, would suggest that the laity should have an active role in every Church assembly when matters that concern them are discussed.

Ignatius of Antioch, in his letter written to the Smyrneans between 108 and 117, described the Church with its bishop surrounded by his presbyters and deacons.[10] For many centuries, Ignatius's description of local Church structure, a single bishop surrounded by his presbyters and deacons, was thought to fit all of the local Churches in the entire early second-century Church. In his letters to the Churches in Asia Minor Ignatius always addresses the local bishop. So this seems to have been the pattern in Asia Minor. But in his letter to the Romans he doesn't address the bishop. Apparently, he doesn't address a ruling bishop in Rome because there wasn't one. Here, the evidence in the letters of Ignatius and also in the *Shepherd of Hermes* would indicate that the Roman Church was governed by a small group of presbyter-bishops. A single bishop at the head was true in the Churches of Asia Minor. However, it does not seem to have developed in Rome until mid-second century. Moreover, according to many historians, the commonly held view that Peter was bishop in Rome is not supported by the evidence.[11]

Witnesses of the earliest period point to variety rather than uniformity in Church structure.[12]

The People's Bishop

A review of the first centuries shows important democratic elements in the life of the early Church.[13] In the third century in the West, it was considered important that the people elect their bishops. The *Apostolic Tradition* of Hippolytus (from around 230) stated:

Let the bishop be ordained after he has been chosen by all the people. When he has been named and shall please all, let him, with the presbytery and such bishops as may be present, assemble with the people on a Sunday. While all give their consent, the bishops shall lay their hands upon him, and the presbyters shall stand by in silence.[14]

Cyprian of Carthage, writing to an African council in Spain in 254, warned the people to separate themselves from a sinful leader,

especially since they themselves have the power either of electing worthy bishops or of rejecting the unworthy. We see that this very fact also comes from divine authority that a bishop be chosen in the presence of the people before the eyes of all and that he be approved as worthy and fit by public judgment and testimony.[15]

About the same time, Cyprian showed that he wanted to share responsibility. In a letter to his priests and deacons, he wrote:

From the beginning of my episcopate I decided to do nothing of my own opinion privately without your advice and the consent of the people.[16]

In Cyprian's election the people had prevailed against the local clergy. In the case of Martin of Tours in 371, they prevailed over neighboring bishops.[17]

In the election of Ambrose in Milan in the fourth century, the people gathered in the cathedral to choose a new bishop. Feelings ran high between the Arian heretics, who had controlled the bishopric, and the Catholics, who hoped to gain control. Ambrose was preparing for baptism at the time. As governor of the province, he went to the Church during the election to prevent a disturbance. When he spoke soothing words, a voice (said to have been that of a child) called out: "Ambrose for bishop!" The whole congregation, Arians and Catholics alike, took up the cry. Ambrose made a serious attempt to avoid the office. He was finally baptized, ordained to the various degrees of the ministry in six days, and consecrated bishop on December 1 in 373.

F. Homes Dudden observes that although the people's choice of a bishop was approved by a majority of the clergy, the chief factor in Ambrose's election was the call by the people. It was the Western custom, he claims, that the people elected, the clergy concurred, and the neighboring bishops examined, approved, and consecrated. If the parties were divided, the people's will usually prevailed. Dudden's description may oversimplify a complicated pattern. Nevertheless, the influence of the people was normally significant.

A letter of Pope Julius (337–52) gives a very good example of respect for local feelings and the rights of the people. Athanasius, the famous Greek Church father, had been arbitrarily replaced in the Church of Alexandria by someone named Gregory. Julius wrote:

> For what canon of the Church, or what Apostolical tradition warrants this, that when a Church is at peace...Gregory should be sent thither, a stranger to the city, not having been baptized there, not known to the general body, and desired neither by Presbyters, nor Bishops, nor Laity?[18]

Subordination of the Laity

However, a tendency to ignore the rights of the people had already begun earlier, at the Council of Nicaea (325). Here is the fourth canon of Nicaea that limits the appointment of the bishop to the local bishops:

> It is by all means desirable that a bishop should be appointed by all of the bishops of the province. But if this is difficult because of some pressing necessity or the length of the journey involved, let at least three come together and perform the ordination, but only after the absent bishops have taken part in the vote and given their written consent. But in each province the right of confirming the proceedings belongs to the metropolitan bishop.[19]

The action of Nicaea was repeated by the Councils of Antioch (341), Sardica (343), and Laodicea (c. 360). They ordered that the bishops of the local province must be present at episcopal elections.

What is behind this radical change from election by people and clergy to election by the bishops of the province with control by the metropolitan bishop? It will be recalled that we are at the period of the Church when the Emperor Constantine had become a Christian. Now in the pagan Roman Empire the emperor had been the *Pontifex maximus*, head of the state religion. In fact, Nicaea had been called and presided over by Constantine. Was this change in the method of choosing bishops part of a move by the emperor to take control over the Christian Church, just as he had controlled pagan worship? It would be much easier for him to control metropolitans and the local bishops under them than to control the laity and clergy in the cities and towns.

However, election by the local bishops was not yet practiced everywhere. Pope Siricius (384–99) in the West still spoke of presbyters and bishops being elected and chosen by the clergy and people.[20] He only insisted that there be no election in rural Italy without knowledge of Rome.[21]

By the fifth century, the bishops of the province were primarily responsible for the election of new bishops. But the consent of clergy and people was still required. Pope Celestine I (422–32) wrote:

> A bishop should not be given to those who are unwilling [to receive him]. The consent and the wishes of the clergy, the people, and the nobility are required.[22]

The statement of Pope Leo I (440–61) is frequently quoted: "He who governs all should be *elected* by all."[23] But in a letter written probably a year or so before, Leo seemed to distinguish between election by the clergy and the people's request:

> It would be unreasonable to count among the bishops those who were not *elected* by the clergy, *requested* by the people, or consecrated by the bishops of the province with the approval of the metropolitan.[24]

In 446, Leo gave a practical reason for the people's approval:

> No one, of course, is to be consecrated against the wishes of the people and without their *requesting* it. Otherwise, the citizens will despise or hate the bishop they do not want and thus become less religious than they should, on the grounds that they were not permitted to have a man of their choice.[25]

In the fifth century "elected" could mean "elect" in a narrow sense. It could be used to signify choice, preference, or approval. Leo himself could speak at one time of election by clergy and laity alike. At another time he could speak of the clergy's election and people's request. In practice as well as in theory, the fifth-century papacy generally distinguished differing parts played by clergy and laity. The clergy's election was more important than the people's request.[26]

Meaningful election by those to be governed continued in the Church a century later in the Rule of St. Benedict (529). Benedict provided for the abbot's election by the monastic community.[27] Moreover, democracy in the monastery did not end with election. Benedict provided for a high level of consultation by the abbot. For lesser matters, he was to consult a council of seniors. For more important matters, the whole community was to be consulted. Benedict also insisted that age should not determine rank in the community: "Remember that Samuel and Daniel were still boys when they judged their elders (1 Sam. 3; Dan. 13:44–62)."

It is true that, according to the Rule, the abbot, after listening to all, makes the final decisions. It is possible that Benedict was influenced by the autocratic forms of civil government of his day in leaving it to the abbot to make the final decisions. But I suggest that the abbot's role in making the final decision should not be seen as an exercise of autocratic power. His role is to achieve and then to implement a consensus.

Secular Control

The people's loss of involvement in the Western Church came with the fall of the Roman Empire, usually dated 476, and the collapse of civilization in the West. Struggles between military factions, widespread disease and famine, and serious poverty in the preceding century left the empire powerless before the invading Germanic tribes. Western Europe underwent a period of steep cultural decline that lasted until around the year 1000.

Because of the moral and educational decline of clergy and laity during the Germanic invasions and abuses in the election process in this period of turmoil, the people lost the right to elect their bishops. With the breakdown of civil government, many bishops, the only educated and competent personnel available, became heavily involved in civil government. Under the feudal system, bishops were both secular and ecclesiastical rulers of their dioceses. As civil rulers they were appointed by the king or the emperor. These, of course, were laymen. Their choices weren't likely to consider the spiritual needs of the people or of the Church.

Before the beginning of the reform under Pope Gregory VII (1073–85), monarchs normally appointed bishops and invested them with ring and crosier, symbols of their office. This gave enormous control over Church affairs to the rulers who chose the bishops. The bishops were usually not selected because of their religious qualifications.

The drastic need for reform can be seen in the Church in Rome. The bishop of Rome, by his election, automatically became Pope. In theory he was elected by the clergy and people of the city. But serious abuses, involving contending factions of the Roman nobility and interference by Holy Roman emperors, had devastating consequences. In the century and a half before the beginning of reform under Pope Leo IX (1048–54), there were thirty-six Popes. Compare this to eleven in the last 150 years in our own time. Beginning early in the tenth century one woman, Marozia, and her son, Alberic II, members of the Roman nobility, controlled the papacy for thirty-six years. According to the official records, Marozia was Pope Sergius III's mistress. She controlled selection of Popes from 928 to 932. One of her appointees was her twenty-nine-year-old son, probably by Sergius. He became Pope John XI. From 936 to his death in 954, Alberic II controlled the papacy. Before his death he arranged for his illegitimate son to become Pope John XII (d. 964).

With John XII, control of the papacy shifted to the Holy Roman emperors. In 962, John XII crowned Otto I emperor. Otto promised John XII temporal control over almost three-fourths of Italy. In exchange, Otto made John XII recognize imperial rule over the Papal States and made him agree that future Popes could not be consecrated until they had taken an oath of loyalty to the emperor as their overlords. Later, John XII tried unsuccessfully to revolt against imperial control.

Except for a short period from 1003 to 1012, emperors controlled the election of Popes until the electoral reform of Pope Nicholas II in 1059. Popes crowned emperors and emperors appointed Popes. Approval of the emperor was sought in every election until that of Stephen XI in 1057. Even St. Leo IX, under whom the Gregorian reform began, was appointed Pope in 1048 by his cousin, Emperor Henry III. A decree of Pope Nicholas II in 1059 finally limited papal elections to the college of cardinals. These were the pastors of the principal, or cardinal, churches of the city of Rome. Until this day the cardinals, at least in name, are considered pastors of parish churches in Rome.

Clerical Control Regained

One of the great, but short-lived, triumphs of the Gregorian reform was the restoration of the ancient ideal of the election of bishops by clergy and people. At the beginning of reform under Leo IX, the Synod of Reims (1049) decreed: "Without the election of the clergy and the people, no one may be advanced to an ecclesiastical office."[28]

Cardinal Humbert (1054–58), in contrast, prepared for reduction of the people's role. He insisted that

> according to the decrees of the holy fathers anyone who is consecrated as a bishop is first elected by the clergy, then requested by the people and finally consecrated by the bishops of the province with the approval of the metropolitan.[29]

The issue was far from settled. At the beginning of the next century Hugh of Fleury could say that a king, inspired by the Holy Spirit, could appoint a pious cleric to the honor of being bishop. However, he continued:

> If, indeed, a bishop has been elected by clergy and people reasonably and according to ecclesiastical custom the king ought not to use force against the electors tyrannically or harass them but should lawfully give his consent to the ordination.[30]

The Popes' struggle to take control of episcopal appointments away from the emperors lasted half a century. It ended with a compromise in the Concordat of Worms (1122). The emperor could no longer appoint bishops and abbots. They were to be elected in the emperor's presence but according to the laws of the Church. Only after election did the emperor grant the control over civil, political matters for which the bishop was to "perform his lawful duties" as the emperor's vassal.

The early period saw great variety in the composition of the assemblies gathered to elect bishops. For an election in Angers in 1102, the summons included "neighboring bishops and abbots, and religious men."[31] A high point in the restoration of the ancient ideal came in canon 28 of the Second Lateran Council in 1139.

First they placed a solemn curse on those who would delay the appointment of a bishop for more than three months. The council then provided for the inclusion of religious men. The phrase "religious men" could refer to abbots and other priests who did not belong to the cathedral chapter. In this early period, it could also include lay nobles and important laymen. If the election was done "without their consent and participation it would be null and void."[32] Only the lower levels of lay society seem always to have been excluded.[33]

The end of the people's role was in sight. In his famous collection, Gratian wrote on election of bishops:

> It is commanded that the people be summoned not to perform the election, but rather to give consent to the election. For election... belongs to priests, and the duty of the faithful people is to consent humbly.[34]

They were to show this "humble consent" by acclaiming the bishop whom the priests had just elected.[35]

In fact, Gratian himself was not above manipulating evidence to fit his desired conclusion. Immediately after this "saying," he quoted a short form of Celestine I's statement: "The consent and the wishes of the clergy, and the people, are required."[36] But Gratian introduced this quotation from Celestine with the statement: "It is not for the people to elect, but to consent to the election." Anyone who has attended the ordination of a bishop or priest since Vatican II may have taken part in this now optional symbolic gesture. The laity present, his family and friends, show their consent by their applause.

In the 1170s, Pope Alexander III still acknowledged that "the favor and consent of the prince should be requested." He added:

> Nevertheless laymen must not be admitted to an election.... If, therefore, laymen wish to meddle in such matters, you should be mindful of that decree in which it is said, "The people should be taught, not obeyed." When they have been excluded, you should proceed in the election harmoniously and canonically.[37]

The first great canon lawyer to become Pope, Alexander III, insisted that there could be no harmonious, legal election of a bishop if the laity were present.

The Popes Begin to Take Over

A century before this action by Alexander III, Gregory VII (1075–83) had already added a new element that pointed to future papal control of the choice of bishops. Instead of confirmation by the metropolitan of an election, he offered papal confirmation. In an invalid election, Gregory provided that an appointment would be made by the Pope or metropolitan.

In the twelfth century, a radically new interpretation of the effect of confirmation added a powerful tool to increasing papal control of the episcopacy. In the making of a bishop, there were essentially three stages: election, confirmation, and consecration. In the earlier period, consecration had been considered the source of all of a bishop's powers. A bishop-elect could not function until he had been consecrated. A series of discussions by canonists led to the conclusion that "power of administration," or jurisdiction, did not come from either election or consecration. The newly elected bishop got the power to run things as soon as the election was confirmed. This new understanding of the effect of confirmation reduced the clergy's role to little more than proposing a candidate for the metropolitan, by now called an archbishop, to approve. This significantly increased a bishop's dependence on the archbishop. However, the archbishop's power was only temporarily increased.

In the thirteenth century, the Popes moved to control archbishops. Canonists accepted a model of the Church as being like a pyramid. The Church on earth was said to be like ranks of heavenly spirits where the inferior spirits joyfully and humbly obeyed the higher ranks. Canonists applied this same arrangement to the Church, with the Pope at the top of the pyramid. If archbishops could control ordinary bishops by confirmation, then Popes could control archbishops by confirmation. So the lawyers said:

> Just as the consent of the archbishop is necessary in the confirmation of the bishop...in the same way the consent of the supreme pontiff is needed in the confirmation of the archbishop.[38]

It seems that confirmation by the Pope was introduced in the twelfth century to increase power by centralizing control. But in the following century, the Pope expected a large "voluntary" gift for confirming a newly elected bishop. This became an important source of papal revenue and a heavy burden on the newly elected bishops.

A man temperamentally and intellectually capable of taking advantage of the developing situation was elected Pope at the beginning of the thirteenth century. Innocent III (1198–1216) is often described as the greatest medieval Pope. More than any other Pope, Innocent III pushed papal monarchy toward absolute control.[39]

Innocent III saw control over resignation, deposition, and transferring of bishops as a way to gain power. Until the end of the twelfth century, there were no consistent rules governing transfer of bishops from one diocese to another. Certainly it did not require papal approval and authorization. Innocent changed that. To do so, he used a commonly held idea of the time that bishops were married to their Churches. On this basis, he claimed that as only God could break the bond of a marriage, so only God could dissolve the bond between the bishop and his Church. But, according to Innocent, Christ had granted a special privilege to Peter and his successors to dissolve unconsummated lay marriages, and hence also marriages between bishops and their Churches. Innocent wrote:

> God, not man, separates a bishop from his Church because the Roman pontiff dissolves the bond between them by divine rather than by human authority, carefully considering the need and usefulness of each translation. The Pope has this authority because he does not exercise the office of man, but of the true God on earth.[40]

Innocent III held that he, as Peter's successor, was the head of the Church. According to him, divine law required that important cases in the Church be referred to the Pope. As head of the Church the Pope had "fullness of power" (*plenitudinem potestatis*).

Control of benefices shows how Innocent III centralized power in the papal office. Benefices were offices in the Church to which a financial endowment was attached to support the person who held the office. Normally the bishop appointed clergymen to these financially endowed offices. In the medieval period bishops frequently gave them to unworthy persons. By the end of his pontificate, Innocent had established the Pope's legal right to bestow benefices in *any* Church.

Earlier canonists had justified use of "fullness of papal power" only in extraordinarily important matters. Innocent IV (1243–54) explicitly claimed that the right to control benefices was based on the "fullness of papal power." He used it to justify interference in relatively unimportant diocesan affairs. Under Innocent IV the Pope's power as an absolute monarch was significantly extended.

In the secular sphere, kings had increased control over their realms and gained important sources of revenue by providing satisfactory justice in their courts.[41] For similar reasons, bishops, abbots, and other litigants showed themselves more than willing to appeal cases to the Pope's courts.[42] Appeal to papal courts thus increased the Popes' control.

Confirming bishops, approving transfers to better dioceses, conferring benefices,[43] and offering justice in their courts, all became sources of revenue, which in itself increased the Popes' prestige and power. Frequently the Pope quashed an election and then immediately appointed to the office the one who had just been elected. Of course, the usual "voluntary" gift was expected.[44]

In the centuries that followed, Catholic rulers regained much influence in the appointment of bishops. Beginning in the sixteenth century, in exchange for financial considerations, Rome granted Catholic monarchs the right to appoint bishops to dioceses that had been reserved to Rome itself.[45] These arrangements continued through a series of concordats (treaties) entered into at the beginning of the nineteenth century between Pius VII and various Catholic rulers.[46] When rulers in Protestant countries sought to control episcopal appointments, Rome agreed to accept recommendations by cathedral chapters, that is, the priests connected with the cathedral. As late as 1829, Popes appointed only a limited number of bishops outside the Papal States. The two principal methods for choosing candidates to become bishops were election by cathedral chapters and naming by Catholic kings or emperors.

An unusual situation in the United States led to worldwide appointment of bishops by Rome. In missionary countries governed by Catholic Spain and Portugal, control of appointment remained in force and missionary bishops were appointed by the king. But the American colonies had been founded from Protestant England. Moreover, no cathedral chapters existed to elect bishops and separation of Church and state prevented any interference by the American government. The first bishop, John Carroll, had been elected by twenty-six active priests in the United States, and

Pius VI accepted their choice. Afterward, Pius VII accepted five candidates elected by American priests and bishops. However, he appointed four other bishops without any consultation in the United States. In one case he rejected their choice. (While the American Church favored French bishops, Rome imposed Irish bishops on it.)

In 1810, the American bishops requested that the right to nominate future bishops be granted to the archbishop of Baltimore and the other bishops in that archdiocese. Their request was refused. A decision was made that American bishops could only recommend possible appointees. The Pope could freely accept or reject their recommendations. This procedure was gradually adopted for the whole Church.[47]

When the Catholic countries in Europe became secularized in the twentieth century, the Church recovered control over appointment of bishops in those countries. Instead of restoring the right of election to cathedral chapters, however, appointment was reserved to Rome.[48] The 1917 Code claimed that the bishop of Rome "freely appoints" the other bishops and that the right of any others to appoint is a concession.[49] At that time, only about half the world's bishops were appointed by Rome. Today, at least in the Latin rite, Roman control of episcopal appointments is almost complete.[50]

At Vatican II, Patriarch Maximos IV Saigh insisted that "appointment of bishops is not restricted by divine right to the Roman Pontiff." He urged that this merely historical development in the Western Church should not be made a rule of law for the entire world.[51]

The 1983 Code ignored this call to broaden the method of choosing bishops. It states: "The Supreme Pontiff freely appoints bishops or confirms those who have been legitimately elected."[52] The Code makes it clear: those who may be consulted to find suitable candidates for bishop have no right of election. It provides a long and strictly secret process for obtaining names of suitable candidates for the office:

> the pontifical legate is to hear some members of the college of consultors, and of the Cathedral chapter, and *if he judges it expedient*, he shall also obtain, *individually and in secret*, the opinion of other members of the secular and religious clergy as well as of the laity who are outstanding for their wisdom.[53] (emphasis added)

Democracy in the Church

The clergy and laity *may* be asked, but it isn't required. They are not to be consulted "collectively." That might give them the impression that they are involved in actually choosing their future bishops.

From Popular Election to Papal Appointment

It has been a long journey: from election of bishops by the people, to election by people and clergy, to election by clergy with the people's approval, to election by the synod of bishops with the archbishop's approval, to loss of control to secular rulers, to control regained by the Church with election by cathedral chapters, to control by the papacy in the thirteenth century through power to confirm. The long and involved story came to a climax with the claim of the 1917 Code of Canon Law that the bishop of Rome "freely appoints" other bishops and that the right of any others to appoint is a concession.

The original reasons for the people's election of their bishops remain valid today. Leo the Great's assertion — "He who governs all should be elected by all" — still holds. Election of their bishops by clergy and people has deep roots in the democratic nature of a Church whose leaders are called to serve and not to be served.

The popular election of bishops, with necessary safeguards, is seriously needed. Only such a structural reform can reduce damaging autocratic use of authority. It can lead to the harmonious relations between the People of God and their leaders needed for the Church and its mission. Moreover, without this change there will be no reunion with the other Christian Churches.

Another democratic change can be made while we wait for the election of bishops. Rome can begin to put into practice the principle of subsidiarity. We have already seen the endorsement of that principle in an encyclical of Pius XI. Here is the key sentence:

> Just as it is gravely wrong to take from individuals what they can accomplish by their own initiative and industry and give it to the community, so also it is an injustice and at the same time a great evil and disturbance of right order to assign to a greater and higher association what lesser and subordinate organizations can do.[54]

There have been several recent violations of that principle. One in particular attracted a great deal of attention. This was the Vatican's rejection of the American translation of the *Catechism of the Catholic Church* because of its inclusive language.

Then there was the rejection by the Congregation for the Doctrine of the Faith (CFD) of use in Mass of the *New Revised Standard Version* (NRSV) of the Bible. This had been strongly approved by the American and Canadian bishops because of its suitability for English-speaking Catholics. It was then approved by the Congregation for Sacred Worship in Rome. Afterward the higher ranking CFD rejected its use. By this time, the Canadians already had liturgical books using the NRSV just off the press. Their bishops had to go to Rome to get special permission to go ahead and use the books, which had already been printed at great cost.

What about the general permission for an alcoholic priest to use grape juice in Mass? This was later changed so that each priest had to get special permission from Rome. Those of us who respect the principle of subsidiarity may have wondered why a general permission was needed in the first place. It would have been quite enough if the proper theological experts in Rome had said that grape juice was "valid matter" and could certainly be used in justifiable circumstances. Each alcoholic priest could then decide if he wanted to use that information. To then take back the general permission and demand that each priest apply to Rome for special permission...?

Intercommunion: Who Decides?

I would like to consider another example where subsidiarity should apply. This is the problem of intercommunion. Catholics who live in countries where most inhabitants have been baptized into the Roman Catholic Church probably find it difficult to understand its practical significance. The issue affects the many Catholics in mixed marriages. It also affects those involved in ecumenical dialogue.

Following the Decree on Ecumenism of Vatican II the *Directory for the Application of Principles and Norms on Ecumenism* speaks of two basic principles. First, sacraments are signs of an existing unity. Second, however, they are means for building up unity, especially the sacrament of the Eucharist.

In the light of the first principle the Church would normally allow the Eucharist, the sacrament of penance, and the anointing of the sick only for its own members. However, under the second principle, it permits or even recommends that these sacraments, under limited circumstances, may be given to "Christians of other Churches and ecclesial Communities."[55]

The implementation of these principles is left to local hierarchies. The American bishops have ordered that "Guidelines for Receiving Communion" should be placed in all missalettes. These guidelines ignore the second principle, that the Eucharist is a means for building up the spiritual life and unity of the Christian community. Present discipline is harsh: no communion for Catholics in non-Catholic Churches and communion for non-Catholics in Catholic Churches only, if in grave spiritual need, there is no opportunity to receive it in their own Churches. This is often a source of embarrassment and division in family life. It is frustrating for groups gathered to promote Christian unity.

Contrast this narrow official approval of what can be allowed on the local level with the agreement now achieved among theologians on national and international levels. Roman Catholics have joined theologians from "virtually all confessional traditions" to produce the Lima statement. Here there is "significant theological convergence . . . in doctrine and practice on baptism, Eucharist and ministry."[56]

Vatican II opened the way for eucharistic reciprocity. However, in its encouragement of intercommunion, the council discriminated between separated Churches of East and West. But their distinction was based on a too restrictive, although traditional, understanding of apostolic succession. This teaching was that Jesus had ordained the first apostles at the Last Supper. They in turn had ordained their successors as the first bishops of the Church by laying on of hands. Through the centuries, all later bishops were ordained, in a chain of succession, by physical imposition of hands. The Orthodox are said to have kept the chain unbroken. In the case of Christians of the Western Churches the chain is said to have been broken. However, as Raymond Brown has written, the theory about the passing on of powers through ordination faces the serious obstacle that the [New Testament] does not show the Twelve laying hands on bishops either as successors or as auxiliaries in administering sacraments.[57]

Of the Eastern Churches, the Decree on Ecumenism affirmed that because

> they possess true sacraments, above all — by apostolic succession — the priesthood and the Eucharist...*some worship in common* [*communicato in sacris*, which involves penance and anointing as well as the Eucharist] is not only possible but is recommended.[58]

According to the Code of Canon Law, general norms for mutual intercommunion in this and comparable situations are to be enacted only "after consultation with at least the local competent authority of the interested non-Catholic Church or community."[59] The Standing Conference of the American Orthodox Bishops has rejected the possibility of intercommunion with Roman Catholics.

Of the separated Western Churches, the Decree on Ecumenism asserted that "because of the lack of the sacrament of orders they have not preserved the genuine and total reality of the eucharistic mystery."[60] Therefore, permission to share the Eucharist in one another's Churches is not allowed. All that is allowed is for Christians of other Western Churches to receive communion individually in the Roman Catholic Church in cases of grave spiritual need.

Further studies in history and Scripture have seriously eroded the basis for this distinction between the separated Churches of East and West. The Roman Catholics in the national Lutheran-Catholic dialogue stated that they found serious defects in the arguments against validity of the eucharistic ministry in Lutheran Churches. They said,

> we see no persuasive reason to deny the possibility of the Roman Catholic Church recognizing the validity of this Ministry...and, correspondingly the presence of the body and blood of Christ in the Eucharistic celebrations of the Lutheran Churches.[61]

What of the Eucharist in Churches that celebrate the Lord's Supper but do not claim a tradition of tactile succession or whose claim is rejected by Rome? Their members are baptized members of the body of Christ. Their coming together to celebrate the Lord's Supper must be seen as a response to a divine call to

170

gather for this particular act of worship. Christ is truly present, as the Council stated, "for He promised 'Where two or three are gathered together for my sake, there am I in the midst of them.'" Their intention is to carry out his command, "Do this in remembrance of me." Is not Christ, therefore, the One who through their minister is acting in their celebration? If it is Christ who baptizes when pagans baptize, will Christ not likewise become present to feed with his body and blood a Christian community gathered under the leadership of its minister to celebrate his Supper? Brown wrote:

> The likelihood that in Paul's lifetime some of his Churches that had no bishops lived in fellowship with Churches that had bishops suggests the possibility of two such Churches living in union today. The probability that not all the presbyter-bishops of the years 80–110 could trace their position back to appointment or ordination by an apostle suggests the possibility of our openness to Churches with an episcopate that (by our standards) is not in historical succession to the apostles.[62]

His argument encouraging the possibility of Church union under these circumstances would apply equally well to intercommunion with Churches that share apostolic faith, especially when they agree on the essential meaning of the Eucharist.

Current biblical studies undermine the theory of a chain of imposition of hands in ordination that goes back to Jesus and the apostles. A beginning for the chain is missing. No evidence exists acceptable to reputable Scripture scholars that Jesus ordained anyone or that the "Twelve" who were present at the Last Supper appointed and ordained their successors.[63] In light of the teaching of Vatican II on ecclesiology, baptism, presence theology, and the Church's teaching on extraordinary ministers, a strong case exists for the presence of Christ in eucharistic celebrations of Churches with no claim to a tactile succession.[64] To justify intercommunion there is no sound basis for a distinction between the Orthodox and the other separated Churches.

At the 1980 Synod on the Family, Cardinal Johannes Willebrands, president of the Vatican Secretariat for Promoting Christian Unity, suggested that to promote unity in the family the time had come to study the possibility of mutual eucharistic sharing, Catholic and non-Catholic spouses being allowed to receive communion in one another's Churches.[65] His suggestion, however, was ignored.

Five years later Pope John Paul II rejected the request for inter-communion made by nine U.S. Lutheran bishops visiting the Vatican:

> There is joy and hope, because the Lutheran-Catholic dialogue over the last 20 years has made us increasingly aware of how close we are to each other in many things that are basic. We experience sorrow, too, because there are important issues which still divide us in the profession of faith, preventing us from celebrating the Eucharist together.[66]

Willebrands seems not to have considered these "important is-sues" as obstacles to reciprocity for the good of family unity.

In his history of paragraph 8 of the Decree on Ecumenism, the late George Tavard, a member of Vatican II's Theological Commis-sion, noted that the text, "in keeping with the present structure of authority in the Catholic Church," refers the decision on appro-priateness of intercommunion to the local bishop, the episcopal conference, and the bishop of Rome.[67]

Is only the hierarchy qualified to make a judgment in this matter? Is this not an area in which the "mind of the faithful," is as significant as that of the hierarchy? Here again do we not see the Roman magisterium imposing its view as if it were the only legitimate position — notwithstanding solid opinion to the contrary?

Many Catholics, intelligent and deeply committed, have be-gun to practice intercommunion in spite of clear prohibitions. For them, this is not a matter of indifferentism, so much feared by the official leadership. These Catholics are convinced that this is the way the Spirit is at work in the Church. They are aware of the high level of agreement reached among Christian Churches in offi-cial discussions. They sense that remaining differences with other Christians are not sufficient to justify present radical institu-tional divisions. They certainly do not consider these differences important enough to cause division at the Lord's table.

Certainly, many who practice intercommunion see it as a means of strengthening the bonds within their families. In ad-dition, they find that it helps break down unnecessary barriers to the union among the Churches for which the Lord of the Church prayed.

172   *Democracy in the Church*

There is a well-known story about two Australian bishops discussing situations they had been involved in. One bishop described the large ecumenical meeting that he had allowed one Saturday afternoon in the cathedral. At the end of the meeting he announced that he would offer Mass. The Catholics who stayed would fulfill their Sunday obligation. He was quite edified that no one got up to leave. Then at communion time everyone stood up to come forward.

"What did you do?" asked the other bishop.

"I didn't know what to do. I didn't know who was Catholic and who was Protestant."

"What *did* you do?" repeated the other bishop.

"I didn't know what to do. I asked myself, 'What would Jesus do?' "

"You didn't do it, did you?"

The story fits many other situations.

Chapter 11

DEMOCRACY IN THE CHURCH
The Struggle for Control

A dispute also arose among them as to which one of them was to be regarded as the greatest. But he said to them, "The kings of the Gentiles exercise lordship over them; and those in authority over them are called benefactors. But not so with you; rather let the greatest among you become as the youngest, and the leader as one who serves. For who is the greater, the one who is at the table or the one who serves? Is it not the one at the table? But I am among you as one who serves."

—Luke 22:24–27

In his column "Q.E.D." in *The Critic*, John L. McKenzie wrote: "The infallibility syndrome is a symptom, not a disease. The disease is the compulsion to impose doctrine upon the faithful, to control thinking and expression." Speaking of the Roman bureaucracy he asked:

Yet it seeks to impose — what? Not faith and morals, certainly. What is sought is power; and the lust for power needs no explanation which would be different from an explanation elsewhere. It is pleasant to have power, and no one needs to explain why he wants it.

We have just seen how the Church's leaders have attempted to control the lives of its members on birth control, divorce and remarriage, and abortion. This struggle for control is not new in the Church. There is evidence in the New Testament that the problem was already present from the earliest years. All the Gospels warn against seeking authority over others.[1] We now realize that such warnings usually show concern for a problem that exists in the Churches where the Gospels were written. In chapter 23:1–12

174

Matthew condemns a different style of dress and places of honor for leaders. Certainly leaders are needed in a Church. But is Matthew's concern that "a good and necessary leadership role will turn into domination, monopoly, and 'clericalism' "?[2]

An early example of monopoly and domination is found in the letter of Ignatius of Antioch to the Smyrneans written between 108 and 117. He wrote:

> No one is to do anything with reference to the Church without the bishop. That Eucharist is to be considered valid which is [celebrated] by the bishop or by a person he permits [to celebrate]. Wherever the bishop appears, there the assembly is to be, just as wherever Jesus Christ is, there is the catholic Church. Apart from the bishop it is not lawful either to baptize or to hold the sacred meal [agapē]. But whatever he approves is likewise acceptable to God. (8:1–2)

In chapter 5, we saw Laeuchli's thesis that anti-sexual legislation at the Council of Elvira (c. 309) was part of a clerical effort to gain control over the laity. I have suggested that the same desire for power may have subconsciously motivated retention of the prohibition of contraception and imposition of a rigid discipline on divorce and remarriage.

The Investiture Struggle

The papal will to power reached a climax in the Investiture Struggle (1050–1300). This was a conflict between the Popes on one side and the secular rulers, that is, the emperors and various kings in western Europe, on the other side. For their part the secular rulers tried to gain control over the Church. On the other side the Popes tried to gain political control over all western Europe. The Popes' will to power extended far beyond their desire to keep emperors and kings from ruling the Church. They wanted to establish a priestly rule over all Europe under the Popes.

Near the beginning of the Investiture Struggle stood a great reforming Pope, Gregory VII (1073–85). A year after his election, Gregory wrote a letter to Solomon, king of Hungary. In it Gregory made it clear that he didn't intend to give up any of the power to rule in civil affairs that the Roman Church had gained earlier. A year later (1075), the *Edicts of the Pope* were put into Gregory's official register. Apart from claims concerning papal authority within the Church, these are his claims in the civil realm:

8. That he [the Pope] alone may use the imperial insignia.

9. That the Pope is the only one whose feet are to be kissed by all princes.

12. That he may depose emperors.

17. That the Pope may absolve subjects of unjust men from their fealty.

Gregory's best-known display of power was to bring the Holy Roman Emperor Henry IV to his knees in the snows at Canossa in January 1077.

Historians disagree in their assessment of Gregory. Was he a worldly Pope obsessed with desire to dominate Europe or a saintly servant of the Church concerned only for the Church's liberty and ecclesiastical reform? Brian Tierney suggests that both may be true. Someone moved by an irresistible drive for power could be utterly convinced that everything he did was entirely for a cause greater than himself.[3] Perhaps the same judgment can be applied to other Popes whose search for power we will discuss.

The papal struggle to prevent lay rulers from controlling the Church continued in the conflict between the papacy and Holy Roman emperors. Popes after Gregory VII also sought to establish jurisdiction over secular rulers. A highly symbolic earlier event had been Leo III's crowning of Charlemagne as emperor of the Romans on Christmas day in 800. Since the Pope had crowned them as emperors of Rome, it could hardly be denied that emperors should have some kind of authority in Rome. The Popes, however, were not about to acknowledge that the Church of Rome was a diocese to be controlled by the emperor.

The Popes tried to establish their authority by claiming that any rights the emperor possessed as Roman emperor came from the Pope as the emperor's overlord. All through the twelfth century, Popes tried to establish their power over emperors. In fact, in 1133, the Emperor Lothar III, when he was crowned, did homage to the Pope for some disputed land in Italy.

When Frederick Barbarossa was crowned emperor by Pope Hadrian IV in 1155, he made it clear that he claimed the imperial

Democracy in the Church

crown by right of conquest. Two years later, Hadrian wrote a letter to Frederick. In it he seemed to claim that the Pope was the emperor's overlord. Frederick reacted by threatening to invade Italy. Hadrian insisted that he had been misunderstood. Hadrian probably claimed lordship in deliberately unclear language. If his claim had gone unchallenged, it would have established a precedent. At the worst, his words could be explained away without too much loss of face.

There was nothing unclear, however, in the claims of Popes Innocent III (1198–1216) and Innocent IV (1243–54). They claimed both kingly and priestly power. They based their case on belief that Peter, the first Pope, had received *all power* on earth from the Lord who was both king and priest. Innocent III insisted that Christ had established Peter and his successors as his vicars on earth. Therefore the Pope should be the final court of appeal in all civil cases.

The Pope, however, had no army or other resources to enforce such a claim. So Innocent introduced a useful face-saving distinction. He said that the Pope was civil overlord of all kings according to law but not in fact.[4] Innocent held that in an ideal world Popes would be overlords of all kings both in law and in fact. If history worked out as it should, eventually they would be. But meanwhile Popes could exercise rightful control only over those kings who acknowledged their overlordship. John Lackland, king of England, accepted his kingdom from the Pope. Philip of France did not.

Exercise of such claims against the emperors reached a climax when Pope Innocent IV deposed the Holy Roman Emperor Frederic II at the Council of Lyons (1245). The rule of the empire by Frederic's family was destroyed and with it the dream of a universal secular empire.

A United Christendom Ruled by the Pope Fails

This set the stage for the Popes' next battle in their search for control over European political life. The struggle came between Philip IV, king of France, a rising national state, and Pope Boniface VIII.

The clergy in France had been exempt from paying royal taxes.

In 1297, Philip forced Boniface to back down and allow the king to tax the clergy. Four years later, Philip acted again to prove his control in his own kingdom. In a deliberately provocative act, Philip ordered the arrest of a French bishop. He had the bishop tried in his own presence and imprisoned on charges of blasphemy, heresy, and treason. Boniface was not concerned that the charges were false. He challenged the king's gross presumption even to touch a bishop.

Boniface ordered all the French bishops to attend a council in Rome to consider the state of religion in France. Philip forbade the bishops to attend. Thanks to the king's prohibition only thirty-six out of seventy-eight French bishops went to Rome at the Pope's command. A majority obeyed the king rather than the Pope.

Boniface considered this an attack on the Church's unity. He issued what became the best-known medieval document on spiritual and temporal power. It concluded with the famous statement:

> We declare, state, and define that it is altogether necessary for salvation for every human creature to be subject to the Roman Pontiff.[5]

This papal document is a long theological treatise on the Church's unity. Boniface saw clearly the threat to that unity when bishops of a national hierarchy hesitated between allegiance to their king and obedience to the Pope.[6]

So much of the document dealt with Church unity that some modern commentators deny that it had political significance. Tierney is convinced, however, that there are passages where Boniface claimed that the Pope gave kings their power to rule. Boniface's claims about papal authority probably didn't differ from those of the Popes before him. But these claims had now been stated clearly. A Pope had solemnly stated that "it is altogether necessary for salvation for every human creature to be subject to the Roman Pontiff." This strong religious statement could easily be interpreted as a political claim.

Philip's response was brutal. Nogaret, the king's minister, left for Italy to settle the issue by force. The old Pope, Boniface VIII, was held prisoner and abused for three days in his palace in Agani. He was finally rescued by the townspeople. He died a few weeks later. In France, there seems to have been no wave of indignation, even among the clergy. Boniface was succeeded after a very short period by Pope Clement V (1305–14). He was French and completely dominated by Philip. Clement denied that anything in Boniface's document was prejudicial to the French king or his kingdom. He wrote later that Philip and Boniface's other opponents were guiltless and had "acted out of an estimable, just and sincere zeal and from fervor of their Catholic faith."[7]

In previous centuries, when emperors tried unsuccessfully to control the Church, visions of a universal empire under the ideal emperor had failed. Now Boniface failed to realize Innocent III's dream of a universal society of peace and concord in a united Christendom, ruled by the Pope. Boniface's impatient and irascible disposition and his preoccupation with his own family's fortunes were certainly obstacles to attaining his goals. But would a saintly Pope have been more successful? Boniface didn't recognize that history had passed him by. During the Investiture Struggle new national states arose and principles of constitutional government developed. The national states and principles of constitutional government were incompatible with a united Europe under the rule of the Pope. Thus, the Popes of the thirteenth century, successful at increasing autocratic, centralized control over the Church, didn't succeed in enforcing their claims in the secular sphere.

Canon Lawyers and Constitutional Democracy

The newly developing national states became the constitutional democracies of the modern world. During the Investiture Struggle, the Church's lawyers developed constitutional principles that became important for democratic government.

Historically, democracy has not been the customary way to organize political societies. Most past societies solved problems of maintaining order and unity in large and heterogeneous groups by concentrating spiritual and temporal power in one sacred ruler. Egyptian Pharaohs, Peruvian Incas, and, until recently, Japanese emperors were all revered as divine beings. Roman emperors bore the title *Pontifex maximus* (high priest). The early Christian martyrs paid with their lives for refusing to offer them incense. In the Eastern Roman Empire, Christian emperors came close to achieving a similar spiritual role. They not only summoned the first great ecumenical Church councils, but also completely dominated the Church in their territories.

Tierney contends that a similar all-encompassing rule by one sacred ruler didn't develop in the West because the Middle Ages always had at least two claimants to the role. On one side, an emperor or king claimed to rule as minister of God's authority on earth. On the other side, the Pope made the same claim as "vicar of Christ," one who takes Christ's place as both priest and king. Each opposing claimant possessed a formidable apparatus of government. For several centuries neither could dominate the other completely. In daily life, people had to make decisions in conscience, or in self-interest, between these two conflicting appeals to their loyalty. The possibilities for human freedom were greatly increased when there were two opposing power structures, each demanding allegiance and neither able to dominate the other.

Medieval canonists struggled with these conflicting claims of authority for obedience and loyalty. They combined (1) the Church's own principles and traditions, (2) the customary ideas of law from their Teutonic background, and (3) the newly recovered Roman law. From these three sources they developed the constitutional ideas that are the foundation of contemporary democracies. Lord Acton wrote: "To that conflict of four hundred years we owe the rise of civil liberty."[8]

To understand how ideas of canon lawyers could so profoundly influence developments in secular government, we have to realize how closely ecclesiastical and secular systems intertwined. A comparison with conflicts between Church and state in the modern world gives a false picture of medieval conflicts. In the Church's struggle with totalitarian regimes in our time, the leadership and bureaucracies in state and Church are separate and opposed. By contrast in the medieval period, the personnel constantly changed back and forth. In England, the king's chancellor was usually a bishop. When a historian like Strayer writes of the professionalism of chancery clerks and their essential role in building up medieval states, we have to realize that these clerks were "clerics." Many were supported by benefices granted by the Church. Indeed, churchmen were so deeply involved in secular politics that their political ideas and administrative techniques directly influenced lay governments. The interchange was especially important for development of constitutional ideas on

Democracy in the Church

representation and consent. These ideas usually emerged first in writings of canon lawyers, who served in both royal chanceries and in the Church's bureaucracy.

Roman Law and the Need for Consent

The importance of the revival of Roman law at Bologna around the year 1100 and the appearance of Gratian's collection around 1140 have been widely recognized.

Nothing is known about Gratian except that he produced his *Concord of Discordant Canons,* usually known as the *Decretum.* This is a collection of ideas, Church laws, and Church practices from a thousand years of the Church's history. We will refer to it simply as "Gratian." In it Gratian tried to reconcile contradictory evidence of the preceding centuries.

Gratian had special importance in the development we are describing. Into the fragmented feudal world, Roman law introduced ideas of strong government capable of legislating and taxing for the common good. In the law school that developed in Bologna, writers in their influential commentaries on Gratian merged orderly principles of Roman law with complex and often contradictory evidence from Church tradition. In it all, they were influenced by Teutonic customary law. This tended to see law, not just as a ruler's command, but as an expression of a people's life. These legal writers sought to provide a legal basis for the ancient teaching that the Church is the People of God. It is an ordered community of believers.[9]

If revived Roman law exalted the prince's authority and seemed to justify autocracy in the Church, Gratian recovered many democratic elements in the Church's past. Texts revealed not only beliefs, but a community. Early Christian life was filled with community meetings, community sharing, community participation in decision-making, and community elections. Above all there was a strong conviction that agreement among the Christian people came from the active presence of the Holy Spirit.

Indeed, despite centralized ecclesiastical power in Gratian's day, the Church retained a structure of elected offices. Popes were elected by cardinals, and officials were elected in monasteries, cathedral chapters, collegiate Churches, confraternities, universities, and the new religious orders. The Dominicans' constitution was particularly important.

The nature of Gratian's collection of "discordant canons" protected the canonists from a conviction that things have always been as they are now and can't be changed. It revealed conflicting teachings, laws, and customs and showed a thousand years of the Church's history, defects and all.

The canonists may have described the Pope the way Roman law described a sovereign emperor. But they did so with examples of Popes who had sinned and even fallen into heresy. A text of Gratian said that all Popes were to be considered holy. Johannes Teutonicus wrote around 1216: "Note, it does not say that they are holy but that they are presumed to be holy... which means until the contrary becomes apparent."[10]

The highly organized and centralized worldview of Roman law contrasted sharply with the canonists' own feuding, chaotic world. This led them to face a perennial problem. They had to allow the ruler enough power to rule effectively, while safeguarding the community's right to protect itself against abuse of power. This was a problem in civil government. It was also a problem in the Church. The canonists often wrote about the Pope's increasingly unjust commands and financial demands. So even as canonists continued to exalt papal powers, they sought principles to temper papal authority. Writings of lawyers from the age of Innocent III contain the expected passages exalting the Pope's power. But they also have sophisticated discussions of constitutional concepts. They write about representation and consent. They discuss necessary limits on lawful authority, including the Pope's authority.

The canonists found their solution to the problem of papal authority, and its potential abuse, in the consensus of the entire Christian community. The Holy Spirit helped Christians establish guidelines of faith and order that could define the limits of papal legislative and judicial powers.

Gratian had supplied a basis for their thinking with a text from Gregory the Great. Gregory taught that canons of the Church's first four general councils were to be kept inviolate, because they had been established "by universal consent." Canonists built on the word "consent." They quoted phrases like, "What touches all should be approved by all." On such notions, they based right of lay representation at the general councils that dealt with matters of faith. It was commonly held around 1200 that canons from general councils bound Popes "in matters pertaining to faith and the general state of the Church."

Since Popes usually presided at councils, this didn't create a conflict between Pope and council. An English canonist expressed the view "that the authority of a Pope with a council is greater than that of a Pope without one."[11] So the Pope, acting with representatives from the whole Church, was seen to have more authority than the Pope acting alone.

Contrast this perception with a question raised on the birth control issue after Vatican II. Was Paul VI bound by the decrees of Vatican II, which he had signed, or, as Archbishop Parente said to Häring, was he totally free to return to the teaching of Pius XI?

A clear statement on the importance of consent came from Hervaeus Natalis, professor of theology at the University of Paris and Dominican master-general. He wrote around 1315 on the origin of jurisdiction. To the question: How is jurisdiction acquired? Hervaeus answered: "Only by the consent of the people....No community can be justly obliged except by its own consent or command of one having overlordship over it." Overlordship was *just*, however, only if the one who commanded had been justly appointed. Eventually it would be necessary to get back to someone whose authority was based on consent.[12]

But is not God the source of all authority? Paul wrote: "There is no authority except from God, and those authorities that exist have been instituted by God" (Rom. 13:1–2). But the practical problem is: how is God's authority transmitted? A solid theological tradition supports what is called the transmission theory.[13] According to this theory, God is the ultimate source of all authority. God's authority, however, is not transmitted directly to rulers, but indirectly through the people. Aquinas had already strongly implied this when he wrote:

> The chief and main concern of law properly so called is the plan for the common good. The planning is the business of the whole people or of their vicegerent [representative].[14]

The transmission theory was developed among Catholic theologians by Cajetan (d. 1534), Robert Bellarmine (d. 1621), and Francisco Suárez (d. 1617). Suárez is noted in the history of political theory for his opposition to James I of England's claim to the "divine right of kings." The theory of the transmission of authority from God through the people is now accepted for every form of legitimate *civil* government.

But official Church teaching rejects the transmission theory for Church offices. It insists that sacred power and a mandate for exercising it comes to the hierarchy from God and not through the people. Such a claim could be made for the Old Testament. There God was said to have sent his prophets to choose and advise kings like Saul and David. However, from the New Testament to our day there is no evidence for such direct intervention by God.

Hervaeus would have agreed, even for the office of the Pope. He would allow that God had established the papal office. But God didn't directly choose the officeholder. According to Hervaeus, the papacy was an elective office. The Pope obtained his authority through election by the cardinals, and the cardinals acted for the entire Christian people, who had entrusted to them the function of election. So the Pope also ruled by consent.[15] This was no revolutionary theory. It is an application to the fourteenth century papacy of the ancient teaching of Leo I: "He who governs all should be elected by all." A twelfth-century canonist-bishop expressed it neatly: "In these matters God is the bestower; we are His instruments."[16]

The Conscience of the People

Obedience, even to the Pope, was always ruled by conscience. The great thirteenth-century canonist Hostiensis wrote:

> If the subject cannot bring his conscience into conformity with his prelate's [which implicitly included the Pope], then he should follow his conscience and not obey...even if his conscience is wrong.[17]

A famous case related to this issue involved the canon lawyer Pope Innocent IV and Robert Grosseteste, bishop of Lincoln in England. In 1253, Grosseteste refused to confer a richly endowed office on the Pope's nephew. For Grosseteste, the many abuses in the bestowal of benefices were a Churchwide scandal. By his refusal he obviously meant to make a public statement. He based his action on accepted canonical opinion of his day that no exercise

Democracy in the Church

of papal power should be endured that threatened the Church's well-being. Canonists described such actions as "against the general state of the Church." Grosseteste claimed, adapting Paul's words in 2 Corinthians 10:8, that the Pope's command had been, not for building up the Church, but for its destruction.[18] Innocent IV's own writings contained justification for Grosseteste's action. Innocent had indeed written that unjust papal commands must be obeyed, but Innocent himself then added a significant reservation: "unless the unjust command would vehemently disturb the state of the Church [peace and order], or perhaps give rise to other difficulties."[19]

Let me suggest several present-day issues that seem to be more serious for the "state of the Church" than awarding a rich benefice to the Pope's nephew. What of depriving millions of sharing the Sunday Eucharist in order to maintain the thousand-year-old Latin-rite discipline of celibacy? What of muzzling all those who seek to discuss ordination of women? What of the imposition of doubtful moral demands, as in the condemnation of all use of artificial contraceptives or the rigid discipline for the divorced and remarried? What of silencing theologians who try to discuss such issues for the good of "the general state of the Church?"

Many of the constitutional principles underlying contemporary democracies come from the Church's own traditions. They come from democratic elements in the Church's past. They were developed by the Church's own canonists. To adopt such constitutional practices into its own structure would not be to embrace an alien system. It would be a return to a tradition that the Church's great lawyers initially drew from the Church's own practice.[20]

I contend that such structural changes are especially appropriate for a Church in which all members receive the gifts of the Spirit and in which the guarantee of infallibility is to the whole Church.[21] One of those gifts is the mind of the faithful, "a faculty of perceiving the truth of the faith and of discerning anything opposed to it."[22] The People of God should be a primary source of "what the Spirit is saying" to the Church. Structures of constitutional democracy are best suited to make that source available to leaders in the Church.

A Modern Parallel

We have studied the struggle for control between Popes and secular rulers during which the Church's lawyers developed the constitutional principles that were gradually adopted in the democratic states of the West. I would like to use a modern comparison to show the social and cultural context in which these events occurred.

The economist John Kenneth Galbraith shows how the situation of dictatorships in undeveloped countries today resembles the situation in Europe in the Early Middle Ages.

> People who are subject in their daily lives to the personal authority or economic power of tribal leaders, large landowners or primal capitalists or the weight of economic depression are not especially sensitive to the authority of some civilian or military dictator or junta in some remote capital. Their freedom of expression is sufficiently circumscribed by the local talent, as also by poverty and an all-embracing struggle to survive. Mass illiteracy also contributes greatly to political docility.[23]

In Europe the barbarian invasions had brought an almost total collapse of Western society. Most people were preoccupied with sheer physical survival. In fact "medieval conditions were essentially similar to those of an 'underdeveloped' society nowadays."[24] As Galbraith points out, in undeveloped societies in the modern world

> All of this changes with economic and industrial development. The controlling circumstance then is simply that a very large number of people, individually and in organizations, insist on being heard. Poverty and ignorance have sufficiently released their grip so as to allow the luxury — in fact the imperative — of self-expression.

In the Early Middle Ages, chaotic conditions were gradually reversed at the end of the barbarian invasions. With return to some kind of order, commerce revived and town life was restored. Traders and craftsmen obtained the personal freedom that they had not had as serfs attached to the soil. In towns, they organized themselves into guilds and sought the right to manage their own financial and judicial affairs. They often developed enough capital to offer money as revenue to their lord in exchange for the privileges they wanted. Towns in the empire obtained charters that freed them from the control of their local overlords. In other areas, they freed themselves from the control exercised by their local bishops.

Growth of towns created a market for agricultural products. That brought slow but significant changes in the life of the peasants still on the land. Serfs could sell their surplus and offer their lords tempting money payments for their freedom, or they could escape to the towns. Town charters often provided that a runaway serf who fled to a town and escaped capture for a year and a day had won freedom. In this same period, guilds of scholars developed into the first universities. These became the source of a growing educated class. Like merchant and craft guilds, the universities struggled to become independent of both Church and secular authorities.

A development anticipating the feminist movement by many centuries was the founding of the Beguines in the late twelfth and early thirteenth centuries. These were religious communities in which unmarried women, mostly middle and upper class, found an outlet for their idealism and emotional and social needs. In addition to their religious exercises, they sewed for the poor, did baby-sitting, and nursed the sick and needy. Membership in beguinages released them from the usual inferior status of women. Some beguinages taught that women were spiritual equals of men. They allowed them to share religious authority and responsibility.[25] As James Brundage points out: "The reaction of the papacy was predictable: strenuous efforts to suppress the dissident women, accusations of heresy, intimations of sexual temptations and indiscretions and a strong papal injunction (from Boniface VIII) that all religious women must remain permanently cloistered."[26]

Release of important elements of the population from the grip of poverty and ignorance brought a widespread demand for freedom from arbitrary control. The invention of moveable type in the middle of the fifteenth century made cheap reading material available. This furthered reduction of illiteracy and increased the spread of knowledge and ideas.

In medieval Europe an inflexible and often corrupt Church leadership failed to respond to the new atmosphere. The Reformation and the Enlightenment must be seen, in some measure, as results.

The Church in eighteenth-century France failed to read "the

signs of the times." Against a rising tide of democratic aspirations, the upper clergy continued their alliance with the old Catholic nobility. This helped prepare for the French Revolution. The Church failed to recognize that the motto of the Revolution, "Liberty, equality, fraternity," represented Gospel values.

Joseph Komonchak has an excellent description of official Catholic reaction to the Revolution and the Napoleonic upheaval. He describes the building

> of a new form of Catholicism as a counter-society, autonomous and sovereign, centralized and bureaucratized, prizing clarity, order, and unity. The whole purpose of this new construction was anti-modern, designed to legitimate and render plausible a Catholic counterculture whose devotion and dogmas were an antidote to the spread of liberalism in economics, society, politics, and culture.[27]

The definition of papal infallibility in 1870 at Vatican I, biblical decrees and the anti-modernist crusade of Pius X (1903–14), the restrictive encyclical letter of Pius XII, *Humani generis* (1950), and the silencing of theologians, are all part of an effort to maintain tight control over thought and conduct in the Church. But, as Galbraith pointed out in the political sphere, such a condition cannot be maintained with an increasingly literate and economically liberated laity. Galbraith contends that the movement toward democratization is historically inevitable in civil society.

With the distribution of special graces among the faithful of every rank, the movement toward democratization should develop even more inevitably in the Church. Democratic structures are needed if the Church is to utilize the gift of the mind of the faithful as a source of theological insights. Vatican II taught: "The universal body of the faithful who have received the anointing of the holy one cannot be mistaken in belief."[28] Bishop Butler even suggested that when the People of God do not accept what was intended as a solemnly defined teaching, that would itself be sufficient evidence that the stringent conditions for infallible teaching had not been met.[29]

However, more than passive acceptance by the laity is involved. The laity must be heard because the Holy Spirit also speaks through them. At the 1980 Synod on the Family, Cardinal Hume spoke of the importance of listening to the married people, the ones who confer the sacrament of matrimony and also the ones who experience its reality. But the laity have significant experience in many areas of life other than marriage. In his early condemnation of liberation theology, Cardinal Ratzinger attempted to establish a radical opposition between the secular and the "religious."[30] But no aspect of reality is separated from the dominion of God, and in many areas of that reality, the laity have the experience and the insight.

As Vatican II teaches, "The holy people of God has a share, too, in the prophetic role of Christ."[31] Therefore the laity must be recognized as part of the teaching Church as well as part of the learning Church. Many bishops have come to recognize this, as shown by the American bishops' wide consultation for their pastoral letters on nuclear weapons, economics, and women's concerns in Church and society. At the Synod of the Family many bishops presented points of view of the laity whom they had consulted. But consultation is not enough. The laity should be included as full-fledged members of Church bodies that make these decisions. "What touches all should be approved by all." In the medieval period the laity were present as active voting members of councils. A Synod on the Laity without fully active lay participants is a contradiction.

The Spirit's gift of newness usually manifests itself first at the grassroots, in the mind of the faithful. The hierarchy's usual role is "to distinguish between spirits" (1 Cor. 12:10), without quenching the Spirit (1 Thess. 5:19).

"The voice of the people, the voice of God." For issues in the Church this "voice of God" would be made manifest through the mind of the faithful. That mind of the faithful may have been difficult to determine in past ages with poor means of communication. In our day, however, reliable and competently conducted surveys can inform us about what the faithful believe and what they reject as contrary to their faith experience. It is not a question of governing the Church by polls, but of using polls to help determine "what the Spirit is saying to the Churches" (Rev. 2:7, 11, 17, 29; 3:6, 13, 22). A wise Church leadership will use carefully conducted polls as tools for guidance.

The American Contribution

If democracy is the future of the Church, do American Catholics with their experience of democracy and pluralism have a special role to play in the Church? In his address to Pope John Paul II at the meeting with the American bishops in Los Angeles, Cardinal Bernardin said:

> The Church in the United States has much to contribute to the universal Church. I am thinking, for example, of our role in the development of the documents on religious liberty and ecumenism of the Second Vatican Council.[32]

It is widely recognized that John Courtney Murray's American background played a major part in his important contribution to Vatican II's *Declaration on Religious Freedom.*

Democracy and pluralism will be essential in a united Church of the future. The Churches of the East have always recognized the bishop of Rome as the first among equals. Lutherans and Anglicans in official dialogues recognize the need for a ministry for the unity of the whole Church. They acknowledge that the bishop of Rome has traditionally held that position in the Church. But reunion is not possible as long as they perceive the style of governing in Rome to be contrary to the spirit of the Gospel.

A united Church of the future should be democratic, and it will have to be a community of very diverse Churches. Rome's experience with the Eastern rites within the Roman Catholic Church is enlightening. There was a serious move to Latinize these Churches as part of an effort to construct, in Komonchak's words, "a new form of Catholicism as a counter-society autonomous and sovereign, centralized and bureaucratized, prizing clarity, order, and unity." Abandonment of that tragic effort is a good omen for the future.

Galbraith says that "we have heard too little of [democracy's] practical utility, and, more especially, given the relevant circumstances, of its historical inevitability." If democracy is both useful and inevitable, then the experience of how to live democratically in a pluralistic society may be the special contribution of the American Church to the Church of the future.

For individual believers, one's conscience is, in Newman's words, "a sacred and sovereign monitor." In the formation of their consciences Catholics have a duty, as Häring has said, "to accept other information in the Church" than that given in official teaching. If they have such a duty then they have a right to know of the existence of options on issues like those we have examined here. To deny them that right is immoral.

It will be said that the attempt to close ranks by imposing doubtful teaching is done in good faith for God's honor and the preservation of holy Church. This good faith produced the Syllabus of Errors of Pius IX, biblical decrees of Pius X, the silencing of scholars such as Teilhard de Chardin, John Courtney Murray, Yves Congar, and others for their teaching on such subjects as evolution, freedom of conscience, and the separation of Church and state. To that list must now be added such scholars as Hans Küng, Leonardo Boff, and Charles E. Curran, who, among American theologians, led the original criticism of the birth control encyclical.

Harm done by an autocratic official teaching, where decisions of conscience are involved, is especially serious. It imposes excessive moral burdens on those trying to please God. It causes guilt among those unable to meet the rigorous demands of what are essentially doubtful laws. It causes many to believe that they can no longer remain in the Church. It places serious obstacles in the way of the reunion of the Churches. It undermines the credibility of a teaching authority to which Catholics should be able to listen with reverent confidence. In our day of mass communications and a well-educated laity, only a voice that is recognized as completely open and honest will be trusted. That trusted voice will not be autocratic and authoritarian. It will relish a diversity of sound, sincere, differing opinions because it knows that the many voices of the people can only help the magisterium. As Cardinal Karol Wojtyła wrote in 1969:

> The structure of a human community is correct only if it admits not just the presence of a justified opposition but also that practical effectiveness of opposition required by the common good and the right of participation.[33]

And the Catholic who obeys a sincerely informed conscience, even if it is opposed to official teaching...remains a faithful Catholic.

Notes

Abbreviations

AAS	Acta Apostolicae Sedis
CCSL	*Corpus Christianorum, Series Latina.* Tournhold: Brepols, 1954.
CSEL	*Corpus Scriptorum ecclesiasticorum Latinorum.* Vienna: F. Tempsky, 1866–.
D	Denzinger, H. J. *Enchiridion Symbolorum, definitiorum et declarationum.* Freiburg: Herder, 1953.
DS	Denzinger, H. J., and A. Schonmetzer. *Enchiridion Symbolorum et Definitionem.* Barcelona: Herder, 1965.
GCS	*Die greichischen christlichen Schriftsteller der Ersten Drie Jahrhunderte.* Leipzig: J. C. Hinrichs, 1897–.
Mansi	*Sacrorum conciliorum nova et amplissima collectio.* Ed. Giovanni Domenico Mansi. 60 vols. Paris: Hubert Welter, 1901–27.
PG	*Patrologiae cursus completus...series Graeca.* Ed. J. P. Migne. 167 vols. Paris: J. P. Migne, 1844–64.
PL	*Patrologiae cursus completus...series Latina.* Ed. J. P. Migne. 221 vols. Paris: J. P. Migne, 1844–64.

Preface

1. *Human Life in Our Day,* a collective pastoral letter of the American hierarchy, issued on November 15, 1968, at their annual meeting in Washington, D.C., 43.

2. Karl Rahner, "Open Questions in Dogma Considered by the Institutional Church as Definitively Answered," *Journal of Ecumenical Studies* 15, no. 2 (Spring 1978): 212.

3. *America* 156, no. 17 (May 2, 1987): 362.

4. Bernard Häring, *General Moral Theology,* vol. 1: *Free and Faithful in Christ: Moral Theology for Clergy and Laity* (New York: Seabury, 1978), 263.

5. "Open Questions in Dogma Considered by the Institutional Church as Definitively Answered," 221.

Introduction

1. *New Catholic Encyclopedia* (New York: McGraw-Hill, 1967), 5:685.
2. All references to the *Catechism* are identified by the paragraph numbers.
3. *Divino afflante Spiritu*, 1943.
4. *Catechism* §283.

Chapter 1 / Conscience

1. *Gaudium et spes.* All quotations from conciliar documents are from Norman P. Tanner, S.J., ed., *Decrees of the Ecumenical Councils*, 2 vols. (Washington, D.C.: Georgetown University Press, 1990).
2. *Council Daybook* Vatican II, Session 3 (Washington, D.C.: National Catholic Welfare Conference, 1965), 203ff.
3. *National Catholic Reporter* (April 19, 1967), and *The Tablet* (London, April 22, 1967).
4. "Intrinsice inhonestum," *Humanae vitae* §14.
5. See Robert Blair Kaiser, *The Politics of Sex and Religion: A Case History in the Development of the Doctrine, 1962–1984* (Kansas City: Leaven Press, 1985), 197–98.
6. Charles E. Curran, Robert E. Hunt, et al., *Dissent in and for the Church: Theologians and Humanae Vitae* (New York: Sheed & Ward, 1969), 5–8.
7. *America* 119, no. 94 (August 17, 1968).
8. "An Alternative Proposal: 'The Pope Has Taught Bad Morality,'" *Commonweal* 88, no. 559 (August 23, 1968).
9. *Human Life in Our Day*, pastoral letter of the American hierarchy issued November 15, 1968, 14.
10. *Summa theologiae*, I, 79, 13.
11. James Q. Wilson, *The Moral Sense* (New York: The Free Press, 1993).
12. Robert Wright, *The Moral Animal: The New Science of Evolutionary Psychology* (New York: Pantheon Books, 1994), 8ff.
13. Wilson, *The Moral Sense*, 165–66.
14. Quoted in Wright, *The Moral Animal*, 242.
15. Ibid., 242.
16. Clifford Grobstein, *Science and the Unborn: Choosing Human Futures* (New York: Basic Books, 1988), 137–38.
17. Wright, *The Moral Animal*, 242.
18. Sidney Callahan, *In Good Conscience: Reason and Emotion in Moral Decision Making* (San Francisco: Harper, 1991), 177.

19. *Summa theologiae*, I, 79, 12.

20. Wright, *The Moral Animal*, 12.

21. Ibid., 9.

22. "Mental Development in Children Exposed to Alcohol in Utero," *American Family Physician* 46, no. 5 (November 1992): 1544; Paul Cotton, "Smoking Cigarettes May Do Developing Fetus More Harm Than Ingesting Cocaine, Some Experts Say," *JAMA, The Journal of the American Medical Association* 271, no. 8 (February 23, 1994): 576. To put a human face on the Fetal Alcohol Effect (FAE) see Michael Dorris, *The Broken Cord* (New York: Harper & Row, 1989).

23. Callahan, *In Good Conscience*, 200.

24. Ibid., 201.

25. *Catechism* §1869.

26. David Chanoff, "Street Redeemer, James Galipeau: A Former Gang Member Turned Law Officer Uses a Dying Art — One-on-one Probation — to Save the Unsaveable," *New York Times Magazine*, November 13, 1994, 44–47. See also "Who Will Help the Black Man?: A Symposium Moderated by Bob Herbert," *New York Times Magazine*, December 4, 1994.

27. See Linda Mealey, "The Sociobiology of Sociopathy: An Integrated Evolutionary Model," *Behavioral and Brain Sciences* (December 1995): 35.

28. *Catechism* §1735.

29. Ibid., §198.

30. Ibid., §389.

31. Ibid., §375.

32. Ibid., §390. For Augustine's role in the development of ideas about Adam's role on the basis of an incorrect reading of Romans 5:12, see John Mahoney, *The Making of Moral Theology: A Study of the Roman Catholic Tradition* (Oxford: Clarendon Press, 1987), 60, n. 74.

33. Bruce Vawter, *On Genesis: A New Reading* (New York: Doubleday, 1977), 89.

34. *Catechism* §283.

35. *Human Life in Our Day*, 14.

36. *Summa theologiae*, I–II, 94, 4.

37. John Langan, S.J., "Beatitude and Moral Law in St. Thomas," *Journal of Religious Ethics* 5, no. 2 (Fall 1977): 1895–90, and Timothy C. Potts, *Conscience in Medieval Philosophy* (Cambridge: Cambridge University, 1980), 60.

38. *Summa theologiae*, I–II, 94, 5.

39. Ibid., 100, 8.

40. *Absolutus, absolutê.*

41. *Absolutê,* or *malum in se.*

42. *Aliquid autem potest esse in prima sui consideratione, secundum quod absolute consideratur, bonum vel malum, quod tamen prout cum aliquo adjuncto consideratur, quae est consequens consideratio ejus, e contrario se habet....* (*Summa theologiae*, 1, 19, 6, 1.), quoted in Albert R. Jonsen

and Stephen Toulmin, *The Abuse of Casuistry: History of Moral Reasoning* (Berkeley: University of California Press, 1988), 109.

43. Mahoney, *The Making of Moral Theology*, 80.

44. *Humanae vitae* §14.

45. "Intrinsice inhonestum," *Humanae vitae* §14.

46. *Human Life in Our Day*, 10.

47. *Veritatis splendor* §§56, 67, 78 (heading for §79), §80 (twice), §81 (three times), §83 (twice), §§90, 95, 96, 110, 115.

48. "Letter to the Duke of Norfolk," quoted in *Human Life in Our Day*, 14–15.

49. *The Code of Canon Law: A Text and Commentary Commissioned by the Canon Law Society of America*, ed. James A. Coriden, Thomas J. Green, and Donald E. Heintschel (New York: Paulist Press, 1985), 548.

Chapter 2 / Teaching Infallibly in the Church

1. Charles E. Curran, *Faithful Dissent* (Kansas City: Sheed & Ward, 1986), 46.

2. Robert Suro, *New York Times*, August 20, 1986.

3. According to John Mahoney this use of the word "morals" in the phrase *fides et mores* first appeared in a major Church document at the Council of Trent. At Trent *mores* did not refer to Christian morality but to "customs." It was about the traditional religious practices being attacked by the Protestants. In his study of Vatican I Mahoney concludes that the council's treatment of "morals" was hurried and ambiguous. See John Mahoney, *The Making of Moral Theology: A Study of the Roman Catholic Tradition* (Oxford: Clarendon Press, 1987), 120–56.

4. Francis A. Sullivan, S.J., *Magisterium: Teaching Authority in the Catholic Church* (New York: Paulist Press, 1983), 25.

5. *The Code of Canon Law: A Text and Commentary Commissioned by the Canon Law Society of America*, ed. James A. Coriden, Thomas J. Green, and Donald E. Heintschel (New York: Paulist, 1985), 548.

6. Acta Synodalia Conc. Vat. II, III/1, 251 quoted in Sullivan, *Magisterium*, 132.

7. *Lumen gentium* §12.

8. Ibid., §25.

9. Brian Tierney, *Origins of Papal Infallibility, 1150–1350: A Study on the Concepts of Infallibility, Sovereignty and Tradition in the Middle Ages* (Leiden: E. J. Brill, 1972), 93–130.

10. Vatican I, *Pastor aeternus*, chapter 4 "On the Infallible Teaching Authority of the Roman Pontiff," Norman P. Tanner, S.J., ed., *Decrees of the Ecumenical Councils* (Washington, D.C.: Georgetown University Press, 1990), 815–16.

11. *DS* 2803.

12. Session 22, can. 9; Tanner, *Decrees of the Ecumenical Councils*, 736.

13. *Bulla unionis Armenorum* in Tanner, *Decrees of the Ecumenical Councils*, 1:549.

14. Joseph Pohle, *The Sacraments: A Dogmatic Treatise*, trans. Arthur Preuss (St. Louis: Herder, 1917), 4:62–70.

15. Pius XII, "Apostolic Constitution on the Sacred Orders of Diaconate, Priesthood and the Episcopate," November 30, 1947: *AAS* 40: 5–7, in *Homiletic and Pastoral Review* 48, no. 7 (April 1948): 691–95.

16. See Avery Dulles, *The Survival of Dogma* (New York: Doubleday, 1971), 146–47.

17. Ferdinando Lambruschini, "Statement Accompanying Encyclical on the Regulation of Birth," *Catholic Mind* 66, no. 1225 (September 1968): 54–55.

18. *DS* 2803–4.

19. Ibid., 3903–4.

20. John P. Boyle, "The Ordinary Magisterium: Towards a History of the Concept" (1) *Heythrop Journal* 20 (January 1979): 380–98 and (2) 21 (October 1980): 14–29.

21. *DS* 2879.

22. Boyle, "The Ordinary Magisterium," 17.

23. Ibid., 19.

24. *DS* 2880.

25. Mansi 51, 322.

26. *DS* 3011.

27. *Humani generis* §20.

28. *Lumen gentium* §25.

29. *Humani generis* §20.

30. Ibid., §21.

31. Quoted at a press panel sponsored by the German bishops, October 3, 1963 (*Council Daybook*, Vatican II, Session 1 and 2, 160–61).

32. See T. Howland Sanks, *Authority in the Church: A Study in Changing Paradigms* (Missoula, Mont.: Scholars Press, 1974), 161–73.

33. Walter M. Abbott, S.J., *The Documents of Vatican II* (New York: Guild Press, 1966), 256 n. 172.

34. Christopher Butler, *The Theology of Vatican II*, rev. and enl. ed. (Westminster, Md.: Christian Classics, 1981), 67.

35. Sullivan, *Magisterium*, 99.

36. *Lumen gentium* §25.

37. "Magisterium," in *Encyclopedia of Theology: The Concise Sacramentum Mundi*, ed. Karl Rahner (New York: Seabury, 1975), 3:356.

38. Robert Blair Kaiser, *The Politics of Sex and Religion* (Kansas City: Leaven Press, 1985), 22.

39. Ibid., 17.

40. *Pastor aeternus*, chapter 4.

41. *Lumen gentium* §25.

42. Sullivan, *Magisterium*, 133.

43. George D. Smith, ed., *The Teaching of the Catholic Church* (New York: Macmillan, 1949), 713.

44. *Humanae generis* §37.

45. K. Rahner, "Kritik an Hans Küng," *Stimmen der Zeit* 186 (1970): 367, in John Jay Hughes, "Infallible? An Inquiry Considered," *Theological Studies* 32, no. 2 (June 1971): 196. See also Hans Küng, *Infallible? An Inquiry*, trans. Edward Quinn (Garden City, N.Y.: Doubleday & Company, 1971), 57.

46. *Lumen gentium* §25.

47. *D* 391.

48. Ninth Address of Pope John Paul II to Bishops of the United States, October 15, 1988.

49. Karl Rahner, "On the Concept of Infallibility in Catholic Theology," *Theological Investigations* 14 (New York: Seabury, 1976), 71–72.

50. Francis Sullivan, S.J., "New Claims for the Pope," *The Tablet*, June 18, 1994, 769.

51. This is only the latest and strongest demand from the Pope himself that noninfallible teachings are to be accepted with full religious submission of mind and heart. The demand is already present in the "profession of faith" now required of all those being ordained or installed in any important office in the Church:

> I also firmly accept and hold each and every thing [*omnia et singula*] that is proposed by the same Church definitively [*definite*] with regard to teaching concerning faith and morals.
>
> What is more I adhere [*adhaero*] with religious submission of will and intellect [*religioso voluntatis et intellectus obsequio*] to the teachings which either the Roman Pontiff or the college of bishops enunciate when they exercise the authentic magisterium even if they proclaim those teachings in an act that is not definitive." (*Origins* 18, no. 40 [March 16, 1989]: 663).

Chapter 3 / Probabilism: The Right to Know of Moral Options

1. "*In fide, unitas; in dubiis, libertas; in omnibus, caritas.*"

2. Bernard Häring, C.SS.R, *The Law of Christ: Moral Theology for Priests and Laity* trans. Edwin G. Kaiser, C.PP.S. (Westminster, Md.: Newman Press, 1961), 185.

3. Newman, "Letter to the Duke of Norfolk."

4. Richard A. McCormick, S.J., "Personal Conscience," *Chicago Studies* 13, no. 3 (Fall 1974): 248.

5. Karl Rahner, "Open Questions in Dogma Considered by the Institutional Church as Definitively Answered," *Journal of Ecumenical Studies* 15, no. 2 (Spring 1978): 212.

6. *Gaudium et spes* §51.

7. *Humanae vitae* §14.

8. *Catholic Mind* 66, no. 1225 (September 1968): 54–55.

9. "Vatican Upholds Ban on Sterilization," *Origins: NC Documentary Service* 6, no. 3 (June 10, 1976): 35.

10. *The Code of Canon Law: A Text and Commentary Commissioned by the Canon Law Society of America*, ed. James A. Coriden, Thomas J. Green, and Donald E. Heintschel (New York: Paulist, 1985), 548.

11. Charles E. Curran, et al., *Dissent in and for the Church: Theologians and Humanae vitae* (New York: Sheed & Ward, 1969), 73–76.

12. John Francis Maxwell, "The Development of Catholic Doctrine Concerning Slavery," *World Justice* 11, no. 2 (December 1969): 147–92; 11, no. 3 (March 1970): 291–324; *Slavery in the Catholic Church: The History of Catholic Teaching concerning the Moral Legitimacy of the Institution of Slavery* (Chichester: Rose, 1975).

13. Raymond E. Brown, S.S., "Origins of the Church in the New Testament," lecture on tape at St. Paul's Seminary, University of St. Thomas, October 23, 1992, St. Paul, Minn.

14. Patrick Granfield, *Ecclesial Cybernetics: A Study of Democracy in the Church* (New York: Macmillan Company, 1973), 62–63.

15. *Rerum novarum* §44.

16. *Lumen gentium* §§27, 29.

17. *Veritatis splendor* (1993), §80.

Chapter 4 / Birth Control: The Call for Change

1. Andrew M. Greeley, William McCready, Kathleen McCourt, *Catholic Schools in a Declining Church* (Kansas City: Sheed & Ward, 1976), 133.

2. *Origins: NC Documentary Service* 13, no. 18 (October 13, 1983): 317.

3. *Origins* 13, no. 27 (December 15, 1983): 462.

4. John T. Noonan, Jr., *Contraception: A History of Its Treatment by Catholic Theologians and Canonists*, enlarged ed. (Cambridge: Harvard University Press, 1986), 410.

5. *Origins* 10, no. 17 (October 9, 1983): 263–64.

6. *National Catholic Reporter*, October 8, 1983, 27.

7. *Casti connubii*, December 31, 1930.

8. Robert Blair Kaiser, *The Politics of Sex and Religion: A Case History in the Development of Doctrine, 1962–1984* (Kansas City: Leaven Press, 1985).

9. *The Tablet*, July 23, 1988, 835.

10. Kaiser, *The Politics of Sex and Religion*, 38–39.

11. *Gaudium et spes* §§47–52.

12. Visser was involved in the curia's censure of the Dutch Catechism.

13. From de Riedmatten's summary of the previous history of the commission in a letter of November 27, 1964, to Mr. and Mrs. Patrick Crowley supplied to me by Mrs. Crowley. The Crowley papers of the commission are in the archives of the University of Notre Dame.

14. *Council Daybook* Vatican II, Session 3 (Washington, D.C.: National Catholic Welfare Conference, 1965), 203ff.

15. Ibid., 204.

16. Ibid., 208–9.

17. Ibid., 209–10.

18. Ibid., 214.

19. Häring speaking at Holy Cross Abbey, August 1968.

20. Ibid.

21. Kaiser, *The Politics of Sex and Religion*, 74.

22. Ibid., 88.

23. Ibid., 89.

24. Ibid., 93.

25. John N. Kotre, *Simple Gifts: The Lives of Pat and Patty Crowley* (Kansas City: Andrews and McMeel, 1979), 93.

26. *Gaudium et spes* §49.

27. "*Non posthabitis ceteris matrimonii finibus.*" See Walter M. Abbott, ed., *The Documents of Vatican II* (New York: America Press, 1966), 254, n. 168.

28. *Gaudium et spes* §50.

29. *Gaudium et spes* §51.

30. *Origins* 9, no. 11 (August 30, 1979): 168.

31. Can. 1055.

32. Kaiser, *The Politics of Sex and Religion*, 130.

33. *The Tablet*, 249, no. 8078 (June 3, 1995): 704.

34. Tad Szulc, *Pope John Paul II: The Biography* (New York: Scribner, 1995), 254.

35. Kaiser, *The Politics of Sex and Religion*, 134.

36. Ibid., 134–35.

37. Ibid., 135.

38. Kotre, *Simple Gifts*, 94–97.

39. Kaiser, *The Politics of Sex and Religion*, 135–36.

40. Ibid., 137.

41. Ibid., 138–39.

42. Ibid., 143.

43. See Bruce Vawter, *On Genesis: A New Reading* (New York: Doubleday, 1977), 395–96.

44. Kaiser, *The Politics of Sex and Religion*, 155.

45. Ibid., 174.

46. Mahoney, *The Making of Moral Theology*, 266–67.

47. Norman St. John-Stevens, *The Agonizing Choice: Birth Control, Religion and the Law* (London: Eyre & Spottiswoode, 1971), 112–15.

Chapter 5 / Birth Control: Old Wine in New Wineskins

1. "On the Encyclical 'Humanae vitae,'" *Theological Investigations* 11 (New York: Seabury, 1982), 266.

2. *Humanae vitae* §6.

3. John T. Noonan, Jr., *Contraception: A History of Its Treatment by Catholic Theologians and Canonists*, enlarged ed. (Cambridge: Belknap Press of the Harvard University Press, 1986), is my principal source for the history of the changing tradition on marriage.

4. 1.29, PG 6:373.

5. *Legation on Behalf of Christians* 33, PG 6:965.

6. James A. Brundage, "'Allas! That Evere Love Was Synne': Sex and Medieval Canon Law," *Catholic Historical Review* 82, no. 1 (January 1986): 1–13.

7. *Paedagogus* 2.10.95.3, GCS 12:214.

8. *Stromata* 3.7.57; GCS 15:222.

9. "Third Homily on Genesis 6," GCS 29:47.

10. James A. Brundage, *Law, Sex and Christian Society in Medieval Europe* (Chicago: University of Chicago Press, 1987), 3, 69–70.

11. Samuel Laeuchli, *Power and Sexuality: The Emergence of Canon Law at the Synod of Elvira* (Philadelphia: Temple University Press, 1972), 89.

12. Ibid., 150.

13. See Brundage, *Law, Sex and Christian Society in Medieval Europe*, 89–93.

14. 3.7, PL 77:102.

15. Betram Colgrave and R. A. B. Mynors, eds., *Bede's Ecclesiastical History of the English People* (Oxford: Clarendon Press, 1969), 95–97.

16. *Sentences* 4.26.2.

17. Ibid., 4.31.5.

18. Ibid., 4.31.8.

19. Brundage, *Law, Sex and Christian Society in Medieval Europe*, 241.

20. Ibid., 197–98.

21. *Summa theologiae*, II–II, 154, 12, ad obj. 1.

22. *Summa theologiae*, 3.5.2.1.3.1.

23. John T. Noonan, Jr., "Criticism and Revision of the Usury Theory, 1450–1750" in *The Scholastic Analysis of Usury*, part 2, (Cambridge: Harvard University Press, 1957), 197–362.

24. Jacob Strieder, *Jacob Fugger the Rich: Merchant and Banker of Augsburg, 1459–1525*, trans. Mildred L. Hartsough (New York: Adelphi, 1931), 158–61.

25. *AAS* 22:561; 59.

26. Theodore Mackin, S.J., *Marriage in the Catholic Church: What Is Marriage?* (New York: Paulist Press, 1982), 26ff.

27. *De adulterinis coniugiis*, Liber II, Cap. 12.

28. Canon 1013 1.

29. Heribert Doms, *The Meaning of Marriage* (New York: Sheed & Ward, 1939), xxi–xxii.

30. *AAS* 22:547–48; 23.

31. Ibid., 22:548–49; 24.

32. Ibid., 43:845–46.

33. Ibid., 43:859.

34. *Gaudium et Spes,* §50.

35. Joseph Andrew Selling, *The Reaction to Humanae vitae: A Study in Special and Fundamental Theology* (Ann Arbor: University Microfilms International, 1979), 297.

36. *Humanae vitae* §4.

37. Philippe Delhaye, "A Symposium on '*Humanae vitae*' and the Natural Law" *Louvain Studies* 2, no. 3 (Spring 1969): 212ff.

38. *Humanae vitae* §10.

39. *Digest,* 1.1.1.3, 1.1.1.4, quoted in Brian Tierney, "*Natura id est Deus:* A Case of Juristic Pantheism?" *Journal of the History of Ideas* 24 (1963): 309 (reprint in *Church Law and Constitutional Thought in the Middle Ages* 7 [London: Variorum Reprints, 1979]).

40. *Gaudium et spes,* §51.

41. *Humanae vitae* §11.

42. Ibid., §12.

43. Ferdinando Lambruschini, "Statement Accompanying Encyclical *Humanae vitae,*" *Catholic Mind* 66, no. 1225 (September 1968): 51.

44. *Humanae vitae* §14.

45. Ibid., §12.

46. Karol Wojtyła (John Paul II), *Love and Responsibility,* trans. H. T. Willets (New York: Farrar, Straus, Giroux, 1981), 236. See Peter Hebblethwaite, *In the Vatican* (Bethesda, Md.: Adler & Adler, 1986), 39.

47. Paul Johnson, *Pope John Paul II and the Catholic Restoration* (New York: St. Martin Press, 1981), 32–33.

48. Tad Szulc, *Pope John Paul II: The Biography* (New York: Scribner, 1995), 253.

49. Ibid., 254–55.

50. Letter to author. See Mackin, *Marriage in the Catholic Church,* 276–77.

51. Alison Jolly, *The Evolution of Primate Behavior,* 2d ed. (New York: Macmillan, 1985), chapter 13, "Sex," especially p. 279 on mating during pregnancy.

52. Karl Rahner, "On the Encyclical," 265.

53. John Meyendorff, *Marriage: An Orthodox Perspective,* rev. ed. (Crestwood, N.Y.: St. Vladimir's Seminary Press, 1975), 69–70.

54. Selling, *The Reaction to Humanae vitae,* p. 314.

55. *Humanae vitae* §4.

56. *Origins* 5, no. 31 (January 22, 1976): 491.

Chapter 6 / Birth Control: A Teaching "Not Received"

1. "The Church: Its Strengths and Its Questions," presidential address opening the November 10–14 meeting of the U.S. bishops in Washington, *Origins, NC Documentary Service* 16, no. 23 (November 20, 1986): 395.

2. "On the Encyclical 'Humanae vitae,'" *Theological Investigations* 11 (New York: Seabury, 1982), 267.

3. Joseph Andrew Selling, *The Reaction to Humanae vitae: A Study in Special and Fundamental Theology* (Ann Arbor: University Microfilms International, 1979), 3.

4. Walter M. Abbott, S.J., *The Documents of Vatican II* (New York: Guild Press, 1966), 256 n. 172.

5. For the statements from the bishops' conferences, see John Horgan, ed., *Humanae vitae and the Bishops: The Encyclical and the Statements of the National Hierarchies* (Shannon, Ireland: Irish University Press, 1972).

6. *Human Life in Our Day*, a collective pastoral letter of the American hierarchy, issued on November 15, 1968, at their annual meeting in Washington, D.C. For the conflicting interpretations at the time, see Patrick Granfield, *Ecclesial Cybernetics: A Study of Democracy in the Church* (New York: Macmillan Company, 1973), 80–82.

7. *Ideoque intrinsice inhonestum. AAS,* 60:491.

8. *Humanae vitae* §13.

9. Ibid., §14.

10. *Human Life in Our Day*, 43.

11. Selling, *The Reaction to Humanae vitae*, 13.

12. John Mahoney, *The Making of Moral Theology: A Study of the Roman Catholic Tradition* (Oxford: Clarendon Press, 1987), 291, n. 87.

13. *Annuarium Statisticum Ecclesiae.*

14. Undoubtedly not all of the bishops would have agreed with the statement of their conference. This, however, would be true of all three groups.

15. Jan Grootaers and Joseph A. Selling, *The 1980 Synod of Bishops "On the Role of the Family": Exposition of the Event and an Analysis of Its Texts*, Bibliotheca Ephemeridum Theologicarum Lovaniensium (Leuven: Leuven University Press, 1983), 96.

16. Peter Hebblethwaite, *Paul VI* (New York: Paulist Press, 1993), 594.

17. John Henry Newman, *On Consulting the Faithful in Matters of Doctrine*, ed. with an introduction by John Coulson (New York: Sheed & Ward, 1961).

18. *Humanae vitae* §28.

19. *Lumen gentium* §25.

20. *Origins* 11, nos. 28–29 (December 24, 1981): 447.

21. *Humanae vitae* §25.

22. "An Alternative Proposal: 'The Pope Has Taught Bad Morality,'" *Commonweal* 88, no. 559 (August 23, 1968).

23. Francis X. Murphy, C.SS.R., "Of Sex and the Catholic Church," *Atlantic Monthly* 247, no. 2 (February 1981): 51.

24. *Fons theologiae.*

25. Yves M. Congar, "Reception as an Ecclesiastical Reality," trans. John Griffiths, in Giuseppe Alberigo and Anton Weiler, eds., *Election and Consensus in the Church,* Concilium 77 (New York: Herder and Herder, 1972), 57–66.

26. Karl Rahner, "Magisterium and Theology," *Theological Investigations* 18 (New York: Crossroad, 1983), 61.

27. Thomas Reese, S.J., "The Selection of Bishops," *America* 151, no. 4 (August 25, 1984): 69–71.

28. *Origins* 10, no. 18 (October 16, 1980): 277.

Chapter 7 / Divorce and Remarriage: The Problem and the Teaching of Jesus

1. Andrew M. Greeley, *American Catholics since the Council: An Unauthorized Report* (Chicago: Thomas More, 1985), 152–53.

2. Letter to the author from Andrew Greeley, December 23, 1986.

3. Andrew Hacker, ed., *U.S.: A Statistical Portrait of the American People* (New York: Viking, 1983), 113.

4. *1987 Catholic Almanac* (Huntington, Ind.: Our Sunday Visitor, 1987), 235.

5. Jan Grootaers and Joseph A. Selling, *The 1980 Synod of Bishops "On the Role of the Family": Exposition of the Event and an Analysis of Its Texts,* Bibliotheca Ephemeridum Theologicarum Lovaniensium (Leuven: Leuven University Press, 1983), 100.

6. Theodore Mackin, S.J., *Marriage in the Catholic Church: What Is Marriage?* (New York: Paulist Press, 1982), 158–72.

7. Letter to the author from Andrew Greeley, December 23, 1986.

8. Andrew M. Greeley, *Crisis in the Church* (Chicago: Thomas More, 1979), 130.

9. Canon 1056.

10. Canon 1055, §§1 and 2.

11. Canon 1061, 1.

12. For a study of some of the cases in which this development has taken place see John T. Noonan, Jr., *Power to Dissolve: Lawyers and Marriages in the Courts of the Roman Curia* (Cambridge: Harvard University Press, 1972).

13. James H. Provost, "Intolerable Marriage Situations Revisited," *The Jurist: Studies in Church Law and Ministry* 40, no. 1 (1980): 153–54.

14. In 1975, Italy had no provision for civil divorce. Only the Church courts could grant any kind of relief for broken marriages.

15. *The Tablet*, November 12, 1994, 1455.

16. Ibid., January 14, 1987, 17.

17. Theodore Mackin, S.J., *Divorce and Remarriage* (New York: Paulist Press, 1984), 43–89.

18. George W. MacRae, S.J., *Studies in New Testament and Gnosticism* (Wilmington: Michael Glazier, 1987), 115–29.

19. These approximate dates are taken from *The New Jerome Biblical Commentary (NJBC)*.

20. Most contemporary translations render *apolyōn* as "divorces." However, Mackin suggests that " 'dismisses' reflects more accurately the Rabbinic form of 'divorce' — a unilateral act by the husband, not a decree by an authoritative body" (note from Mackin to the author).

21. Written between 80–85; *NJBC*, 676.

22. Written 64–67; *NJBC*, 596.

23. Written 80–90; *NJBC*, 631.

24. Matt. 19:9 and 5:32.

25. Joseph A. Fitzmyer, S.J., "The Matthean Divorce Texts and Some New Palestinian Evidence," *Theological Studies* 37, no. 2 (June 1976): 197–226.

26. The earliest reference in Fitzmyer's article is to W. K. L. Clarke, "The Excepting Clause in St. Matthew," *Theology* 15 (1927). For rejection of the incest theory see Georg Strecker, *The Sermon on the Mount: An Exegetical Commentary*, trans. O. C. Dean, Jr. (Nashville: Abingdon Press, 1988), 203 n. 29.

27. Walter Bauer, *A Greek-English Lexicon of the New Testament and Other Christian Literature*, trans. and ed. William F. Arndt and F. Wilbur Gingrich, 4th ed. (Chicago: University of Chicago Press, 1952), 699–700.

28. St. Ambrose later tried to solve the problem of Paul's exception by saying that only Christian marriage is from God (Mackin, *Divorce and Remarriage*, 158).

29. "The Greek verb, *mēchōrizétō*, is plainly the hortative subjunctive after the negative participle" (Mackin).

30. Lawrence G. Wrenn, "Marriage — Indissoluble or Fragile?" in Lawrence G. Wrenn, ed., *Divorce and Remarriage in the Catholic Church* (New York: Newman Press, 1973), 135.

31. *NJBC*, 68:120.

32. George Foot Moore, *Judaism in the First Centuries of the Christian Era* (New York: Schocken Books, 1971), 2:126–27.

33. For a popularly written analysis that reaches a similar conclusion using form-criticism see Tübingen New Testament scholar Gerhard Lohfink, *The Bible: Now I Get It! A Form-Criticism Handbook*, trans. Daniel Coogan (Garden City, N.Y.: Doubleday, 1979), 142–51.

Chapter 8 / Divorce and Remarriage: The Tradition and a Call for Change

1. *Ad uxorem*, II:1, *CCSL*, 1 (Turnholt, 1957), 381–82.

2. *Adversus Marcionem*, IV 4, *CCSL*, 1:365.

3. *De exhortatione castitatis*, chapter 5.

4. *In Matthaeum commentarii*, 14, 23; *PG* 10, 781.

5. F. Homes Dudden, *The Life and Times of St. Ambrose* (Oxford: Clarendon Press, 1935), 1:113.

6. In canon 4, Basil described the penitential discipline for the twice-married and the thrice-married before they could be admitted to communion. Father John Meyendorff, Russian Orthodox historian and theologian, writes that "twice-married" refers to those "who enter marriage after either widowhood or divorce." Roy J. Deferrari, Roman Catholic editor of *The Fathers of the Church*, claims that it refers to: "Those who have married after the death of their first spouse." For canon 35 Mackin shows that Deferrari has mistranslated a key word, making Basil and his medieval Orthodox commentators seem to agree with the discipline of the modern Western church. Has one of them been influenced by the contemporary discipline in his own church in his interpretation of the ancient texts?

7. *Against Heresies*, 69, *PG* 41, col. 1024C–1025A.

8. *De Abraham*, I:7, *PL* 14, col. 442.

9. *De Bono Coniugali*, *PL* 40, col. 379.

10. Augustine used Ephesians 5:32 to support the indissolubility of marriage: "This is a great mystery [*mystérion*], and I am applying it to Christ and the Church." No evidence exists in Ephesians that its author had any concern about divorce. Augustine, however, using the Latin Vulgate, where the Greek *mystérion* is rendered *sacramentum*, wrote: " 'This is a great *sacramentum*,' says the Apostle, 'in Christ and in the Church' (Ephesians 5:32). Therefore that which is great in Christ and in the Church is quite small in each and every husband and wife, but is the *sacramentum* of inseparable union." Augustine identified this "sign," that is, *sacramentum*, as the marital bond itself, which can be broken only by death. Later theologians reasoned that since the bond between Christ and the Church can never be broken, so the bond between husband and wife cannot be broken. They transformed a metaphor in Ephesians into law.

11. James A. Brundage, *Law, Sex and Christian Society in Medieval Europe* (Chicago: University of Chicago Press, 1987), 97.

12. John T. Noonan, Jr., "Novel 22," in William W. Bassett, ed., *The Bond of Marriage* (Notre Dame, Ind.: University of Notre Dame Press, 1968), 75. See Brundage, *Law, Sex and Christian Society in Medieval Europe*, 114–17.

13. Thought to be the work of Ambrose of Milan, the commentary was finally recognized in the sixteenth century to be that of an otherwise unknown fifth-century exegete.

14. *Epistola* 94; *PL,* 54:1136–37.

15. Lawrence G. Wrenn, "Marriage — Indissoluble or Fragile?" in Lawrence G. Wrenn, ed., *Divorce and Remarriage in the Catholic Church* (New York: Newman Press, 1973), 138. Was this an "unconsummated" marriage? See Brundage, *Law, Sex and Christian Society in Medieval Europe,* 143–44.

16. Brundage, *Law, Sex and Christian Society in Medieval Europe,* 201.

17. Theodore Mackin, S.J., *Divorce and Remarriage* (New York: Paulist Press, 1984), 279.

18. Brundage, *Law, Sex and Christian Society in Medieval Europe,* 183.

19. Karl Rahner, "Open Questions in Dogma Considered by the Institutional Church as Definitively Answered," *Journal of Ecumenical Studies* 15, no. 2 (Spring 1978): 212.

20. Joseph Gill, S.J., *The Council of Florence* (Cambridge: University Press, 1959), 296–97.

21. Josef Neuner, S.J., and Heinrich Roos, S.J., *The Teaching of the Catholic Church: As Contained in Her Documents,* Karl Rahner, S.J., ed. (Staten Island: Alba House, 1967), 355.

22. *Gaudium et spes* §§47, 49.

23. *Council Daybook,* 138th General Congregation, September 29, 1965 (Washington, D.C.: National Catholic Welfare Conference, 1965), 69.

24. Jan Grootaers and Joseph A. Selling, *The 1980 Synod of Bishops "On the Role of the Family": Exposition of the Event and an Analysis of Its Texts,* Bibliotheca Ephemeridum Theologicarum Lovaniensium (Leuven: Leuven University Press, 1983), 100.

25. *Origins* 10, no. 18 (October 9, 1980): 275.

26. Grootaers and Selling, *The 1980 Synod of Bishops,* 101.

27. Ibid., 330.

28. *Familiaris consortio,* November 22, 1981, §84.

29. *The Tablet,* October 22, 1994, 1360.

30. Ibid., October 1, 1994.

31. Ibid., October 22, 1994.

32. Ibid., November 19, 1994, 1485.

33. Ibid., November 26, 1994, 1525.

34. Andrew M. Greeley, *American Catholics since the Council: An Unauthorized Report* (Chicago: Thomas More, 1985), 15–16.

35. "The baptized person also enjoys rights within the Church: to receive the sacraments" (*Catechism of the Catholic Church* §1269).

36. 1983 Code of Canon Law, canon 1056.

Chapter 9 / Abortion: Catholic Pluralism and the Potential for Dialogue

1. Karl Rahner, "The Problem of Genetic Manipulation," *Theological Investigations* 9 (New York: Herder and Herder, 1972), 236, no. 2.

2. *Science and the Unborn: Choosing Human Futures* (New York: Basic Books, 1988), 77.

3. Clifford Grobstein, *From Chance to Purpose: An Appraisal of External Human Fertilization* (Reading, Mass.: Addison-Wesley, 1981), 27.

4. Abortion — Part I, Hearings of Subcommittee on Constitutional Amendments of Committee of Judiciary of U.S. Senate, 93rd Congress, 1st Session on SJ Res. 119 (Y4J 89/2:A67 pt 1, cited hereafter as Hearing), 1.

5. Hearing, 158.

6. Ibid., 171–72.

7. Boston: St. Paul Editions, 1984, 61–62.

8. *Humanae vitae* §14.

9. Hearing, 164–65.

10. Heribert Jone, *Moral Theology*, trans. Urban Adelman, 3d ed. (Westminster, Md.: Newman Bookshop, 1946), 146.

11. John F. Dedek, *Human Life: Some Moral Issues* (New York: Sheed & Ward, 1972), 50–51.

12. Bernard Häring, *Medical Ethics* (Notre Dame, Ind.: Fides Publishing, 1973), 108–9.

13. *Summa theologiae*, II–II, 64, 7 in Dedek, *Human Life*, 44–45, 55.

14. Letter to the author.

15. See John Connery, S.J., *Abortion: The Development of the Roman Catholic Perspective* (Chicago: Loyola University Press, 1977), 244.

16. "Responding to Persons: Methods of Moral Argument in Debate Over Abortion," *Theology Digest* 21, no. 4 (Winter 1973): 296.

17. John F. Dedek, "The Moral Law," *Chicago Studies* 13, no. 3 (Fall 1974): 237–38.

18. Quoted in John F. Dedek, *Contemporary Medical Ethics* (New York: Sheed & Ward, 1975), 130.

19. Hearing, 318.

20. Ibid., 322–23.

21. Ibid., 288.

22. Ibid., 316.

23. Paul Ramsey, "The Morality of Abortion," in Edward Shils, et al., *Life or Death: Ethics and Options* (Seattle: Reed College, 1968), 85–86.

24. Hearing, 332.

25. Ibid., 342.

26. Andrew M. Greeley, *American Catholics since the Council: An Unauthorized Report* (Chicago: Thomas More Press, 1985), 83.

27. Charles E. Curran, *New Perspectives in Moral Theology* (Notre Dame, Ind.: University of Notre Dame Press, 1976), 190–91.

28. Declaration of April 27, 1974. Cf. *Kirchenzeittung fuer die Doiezese Augsburg,* "Ein schwarzer Tag," May 4–5, 1974. Cited in Franz Scholz, "Problems on Norms Raised by Ethical Borderline Situations: Beginnings of a Solution in Thomas Aquinas and Bonaventure," in Charles E. Curran and Richard A. McCormick, S.J., eds., *Readings in Moral Theology, No. 1: Moral Norms and Catholic Tradition* (New York: Paulist Press, 1979), 180, n. 6.

29. *America* 139, no. 2 (July 15–22, 1978): 29.

30. Richard A. McCormick, *Health and Medicine in the Catholic Tradition: Tradition in Transition* (New York: Crossroad, 1984), 34.

31. Häring, *Medical Ethics,* 117–18.

Chapter 10 / Democracy in the Church:
The Election of Bishops

1. For the question of the identity of James, see *Jerome Biblical Commentary* (Englewood Cliffs, N.J.: Prentice-Hall, 1968), 796.

2. Brian Tierney, "Medieval Canon Law and Western Constitutionalism," *Catholic Historical Review* 52, no. 1 (April 1966): 1–17, reprinted in *Church Law and Constitutional Thought in the Middle Ages* (London: Variorum Reprints, 1979), no. 15.

3. Karol Wojtyła, *The Acting Person,* trans. Andrezej Potocki (Boston: D. Reidel, 1979), 261–300.

4. Ibid., 284–85.

5. Ibid., 286.

6. Ibid., 286–87

7. *Quadragesimo anno* §79.

8. Patrick Granfield, *The Limits of the Papacy: Authority and Autonomy in the Church* (New York: Crossroad, 1987), 125–32.

9. Myles M. Bourke, "Collegial Decision-Making in the New Testament," *The Jurist: Studies in Co-Responsibility* 31, no. 1 (1971): 4–13. Bourke is a former president of the Catholic Biblical Association.

10. Raymond E. Brown, S.S., and John P. Meier, *Antioch and Rome: New Testament Cradles of Catholic Christianity* (New York: Paulist, 1983), 77.

11. See John Fuellenbach, S.V.D., *Ecclesiastical Office and the Primacy of Rome: An Evaluation of Recent Theological Discussion of First Clement* (Washington, D.C.: Catholic University of America Press, 1980), 116.

12. John E. Lynch, "Co-responsibility in the First Five Centuries: Presbyteral Colleges and the Election of Bishops," *The Jurist: Studies in Co-responsibility* 31, no. 1 (1971): 18–21.

13. See William W. Bassett, ed., *The Choosing of Bishops: Historical and Theological Studies* (Hartford: Canon Law Society of America, 1971).

14. *The Apostolic Tradition of Hippolytus*, ed. and trans. Burton Scott Easton (Hamden, Conn.: Archon Books, 1962), 33.

15. *Letter* 67:3–4, *CSEL*,3:737–38, *St. Cyprian: Letters* (1–81), trans. Sister Rose Bernard Donna, in *The Fathers of the Church* 51 (Washington, D.C.: Catholic University Press, 1964), 234.

16. *Letter* 14:4, *CSEL* 3, 2:512; also *Letter* 43.

17. F. Homes Dudden, *The Life and Times of St. Ambrose* I (Oxford: Clarendon Press, 1935), 70–71. For a thorough discussion of the sometimes conflicting evidence see Lynch, "Co-Responsibility in the First Five Centuries," 36–80.

18. *Apologia contra Arianos*, 30, *PG* 25:297.

19. Norman P. Tanner, S.J., ed., *Decrees of the Ecumenical Councils*, vol. 1, *Nicaea to Lateran V* (Washington, D.C.: Georgetown University Press, 1990), 7.

20. Siricius, *Letter* 1:10, *PL* 13:1143.

21. *Letter* 5.2.1, *PL* 13:1157A.

22. *Letter* 4:5, *PL* 50:434, Robert L. Benson, *The Bishop-elect: A Study in Medieval Ecclesiastical Office* (Princeton: Princeton University Press, 1968), 24–25.

23. *Letter* 10:6, *PL* 54:634.

24. *Letter* 167, *PL* 45:1203.

25. *Petentibus, Letter* 14:5, *PL* 54:673.

26. Robert L. Benson, "Reflections on Co-responsibility in the Historical Church," *The Jurist: Studies in Co-responsibility* 31, no. 1 (1971): 58.

27. *The Rule of St. Benedict in Latin and English with Notes* (Collegeville, Minn.: Liturgical Press, 1981), chapter 64. The Rule speaks of "the one selected either by the whole community acting unanimously in the fear of God, or by some part of the community, no matter how small, which possesses sounder judgment" (*Rule*, 65:1. For the various interpretations see 372–75.

28. Benson, "Reflections on Co-responsibility in the Historical Church," 59.

29. Brian Tierney, *The Crisis of Church and State 1050–1300* (Englewood Cliffs, N.J.: Prentice-Hall, 1964), 40.

30. *Tractatus de regia potestate* (1102–1104) quoted in ibid., 83.

31. Benson, "Reflections on Co-responsibility in the Historical Church," 62.

32. Mansi, 21:534.

33. Benson, "Reflections on Co-responsibility in the Historical Church," 63.

34. *Distinctio*, no. 63.

35. Benson, *The Bishop-elect: A Study in Medieval Ecclesiastical Office*, 29.

36. *D.* 63:26.

37. Benson, "Reflections on Co-responsibility in the Historical Church," 71.

38. Benson, *The Bishop-elect: A Study in Medieval Ecclesiastical Office*, 378–79.

39. Kenneth Pennington, *Pope and Bishops: The Papal Monarchy in the Twelfth and Thirteenth Centuries* (Philadelphia: University of Pennsylvania Press, 1984), 58.

40. In *Quanto personam* quoted by Pennington, *Pope and Bishops*, 16.

41. Joseph R. Strayer, *On the Medieval Origins of the Modern State* (Princeton: Princeton University Press, 1970), 28–33.

42. Brian Tierney, "The Continuity of Papal Political Theory in the Thirteenth Century: Some Methodological Considerations," *Medieval Studies* (Toronto) 27 (1965), 245 (reprinted in *Church Law*, 5).

43. William E. Lunt, *Papal Revenues in the Middle Ages* (New York: Columbia University Press, 1934), 1:81–91.

44. Benson, *The Bishop-elect: A Study in Medieval Ecclesiastical Office*, 381, n. 16.

45. Hervé-Marie Legrand, "Theology and the Election of Bishops in the Early Church," in Giuseppe Alberigo and Anton Weiler, eds., *Election and Consensus in the Church*, Concilium 77 (New York: Herder and Herder, 1972), 33–34.

46. Robert Trisco, "The Variety of Procedures in Modern History," in Bassett, *The Choosing of Bishops*, 33–34.

47. Peter Hebblethwaite, *In the Vatican* (Bethesda, Md.: Adler & Adler, 1986), 93–94.

48. Hervé-Marie Legrand, "Theology and the Election of Bishops in the Early Church," 34.

49. Canon 329, §§2 and 3.

50. For the exceptions, see Granfield, *The Limits of the Papacy*, 75–76.

51. Floyd Anderson, ed., *Council Daybook*, Vatican II, Session 1, October 11 to December 8, 1962; Session 2, September 29 to December 4, 1963 (Washington, D.C.: National Catholic Welfare Conference, 1965), 168.

52. Canon 377, §1.

53. Canon 377, §3.

54. *Quadragesimo anno* §79.

55. *Pontificium Consilium ad Christianorum Fovendum*, Vatican City, no. 129, March 25, 1993, 68.

56. *Baptism, Eucharist, and Ministry*, Faith and Order Paper 111 (Geneva: World Council of Churches, 1982), ix.

57. Raymond E. Brown, S.S., *Priest and Bishop: Biblical Reflections* (New York: Paulist Press, 1970), 55.

58. *Unitatis Redintegratio*, §15.

59. Canon 844, §5.

60. *Unitatis Redintegratio* §22.

61. "Reflections of the Roman Catholic Participants," *Lutherans and Catholics in Dialogue IV* (1970), 32.

62. Brown, *Priest and Bishop*, 83.

63. Ibid., 47–86; "Difficulties in Using the New Testament in American Catholic Discussions," *Louvain Studies* 6 (1976), 144–58; "*Episkope and Episkopos:* The New Testament Evidence," *Theological Studies* 41, no. 2 (June 1980): 332.

64. See my article "Intercommunion and Union" *Journal of Ecumenical Studies* 22, no. 3 (Summer 1985): 594–603.

65. Jan Grootaers and Joseph A. Selling, *The 1980 Synod of Bishops "On the Role of the Family": Exposition of the Event and an Analysis of Its Texts,* Bibliotheca Ephemeridum Theologicarum Lovaniensium (Leuven: Leuven University Press, 1983), 102.

66. Vatican City (NC) *Catholic Bulletin,* October 6–12, 1985.

67. George H. Tavard, A.A., "Praying Together: *Communication in Sacris* in the Decree on Ecumenism," in Dom Alberic Stacpoole, O.S.B., *Vatican II Revisited by Those Who Were There* (Minneapolis: Winston, 1986), 214.

Chapter 11 / Democracy in the Church:
The Struggle for Control

1. See Matthew 20:25–27; Mark 10:42–44; Luke 22:25–26; John 13:4–5, 12–17.

2. Raymond E. Brown and John P. Meier, *Antioch and Rome: New Testament Cradles of Catholic Christianity* (New York: Paulist, 1983), 71.

3. Brian Tierney, *The Crisis of Church and State 1050–1300* (Englewood Cliffs, N.J.: Prentice-Hall, 1964), 46–51.

4. Brian Tierney, "The Continuity of Papal Political Theory in the Thirteenth Century: Some Methodological Considerations," *Medieval Studies* (Toronto) 27 (1965): 238–39 (reprinted in *Church Law and Constitutional Thought in the Middle Ages* (London: Variorum Reprints, 1979), no. 5).

5. *Unam sanctam* (1303), DS 875.

6. Brian Tierney, "Boniface VIII, Pope," *New Catholic Encyclopedia,* 2:672.

7. Joseph R. Strayer, *On the Medieval Origins of the Modern State* (Princeton: Princeton University Press, 1970), 56.

8. Quoted in Brian Tierney, "Medieval Canon Law and Western Constitutionalism," *Catholic Historical Review* 52 (1966), reprinted in *Church Law and Constitutional Thought in the Middle Ages,* no. 15.

9. Brian Tierney, *Religion, Law and the Growth of Constitutional Thought 1150–1650* (Cambridge: Cambridge University Press, 1982), 13.

10. Tierney, "Medieval Canon Law and Western Constitutionalism," 9.

11. Pennington, *Pope and Bishops: The Papal Monarchy in the Twelfth and Thirteenth Centuries* (Philadelphia: University of Pennsylvania Press, 1984), 133.

12. Tierney, *Religion, Law and the Growth of Constitutional Thought 1150–1650*, 44–46.

13. Patrick Granfield, *Ecclesial Cybernetics: A Study of Democracy in the Church* (New York: Macmillan, 1973), 179ff.

14. *Summa theologiae*, I–II, 90, 3.

15. Tierney, *Religion, Law and the Growth of Constitutional Thought 1150–1650*, 46.

16. Quoted in "Roots of Western Constitutionalism in the Church's Own Tradition: The Significance of the Council of Constance," in James A. Coriden, ed., *We, the People of God: A Study of Constitutional Government in the Church* (Huntington, Ind.: Canon Law Society of America, 1968), 117–18.

17. Pennington, *Pope and Bishops: The Papal Monarchy in the Twelfth and Thirteenth Centuries*, 133.

18. See Patrick Granfield, *The Limits of the Papacy: Authority and Autonomy in the Church* (New York: Crossroad, 1987), 60–61.

19. *De sententia excommunicationis* quoted in Brian Tierney, "Grosseteste and the Theory of Papal Sovereignty," *Church Law*, no. 6.

20. Tierney, "Medieval Canon Law and Western Constitutionalism," 16.

21. *Lumen gentium* §12.

22. Yves M. Congar, "Towards a Catholic Synthesis," in Jürgen Moltmann and Hans Küng, eds., *Who Speaks for the Church?* Concilium 148 (New York: Seabury, 1981), 74.

23. John Kenneth Galbraith, "Economic Development: Engine of Democracy," *New York Times*, August 25, 1987.

24. Brian Tierney and Sidney Painter, *Western Europe in the Middle Ages: 300–1475*, 3d ed. (New York: Alfred A. Knopf, 1978), 253–67.

25. Ozment, *The Age of Reform, 1250–1559: An Intellectual and Religious History of Late Medieval and Reformation Europe* (New Haven: Yale University Press, 1980), 91–92.

26. VI 3.16.1 *Periculoso*; in letter to the author.

27. Joseph A. Komonchak, "Issues behind the Curran Case: The Church and Modernity — From Defensiveness to Engagement," *Commonweal* 114, no. 2 (January 30, 1987): 44.

28. *Lumen gentium* §12.

29. B. C. Butler, "Authority in the Church," *The Tablet* 231, no. 7141 (May 21, 1977): 479.

30. See Juan Luis Segundo, S.J., *Theology and the Church: A Response to Cardinal Ratzinger and a Warning to the Whole Church*, trans. John W. Diercksmeier (Minneapolis: Winston Press, 1985), 27–29.

31. *Lumen gentium* §12.

32. *Origins* 17, no. 16 (October 1, 1987): 256.

33. Karol Wojtyła, *The Acting Person*, trans. Andrezej Potocki (Boston: D. Reidel, 1979), 287.

Index

New Testament Church
   democratic decision–making,
      154–55
   teachers in, 154–55
New York Times, 22, 23
Noonan, John T., Jr.
   birth control commission, 58,
      59, 67–68
   direct–indirect abortion, 140
   on *Humanae vitae*, 85
NORC. *See* National Opinion
      Research Center (NORC)

Olivi, Pietro, 26
On Chaste Marriage, 71, 126
   intercourse during the sterile
      period, 79–80
   primary and secondary ends
      of marriage, 80–81
   prohibition of contraception,
      45, 52, 88
*On Consulting the Faithful in Mat-
      ters of Doctrine* (Newman),
      98
On the Family (John Paul II), 99
On Human Life. See Humanae vitae
"On Reserving Priestly Ordina-
      tion to Men Alone" (John
      Paul II), 40
"On Responsible Parenthood"
      (Vatican II), 8
Ordinary, universal magis-
      terium, 25, 31–32
   John Paul II, 39–40
Orthodox Church
   divorce and remarriage, 108,
      119–20
   Synod on the Family and, 38,
      108
Ottaviani, Alfredo, 57, 69
   birth control commission, 63
Outler, Albert C., 142

Papal infallibility
   defined at Vatican I, 26
   taught by Pietro Olivi, 26
   uses of, 27
Papal office
   centralizing power, 163, 164

medieval canonists, 182
sources of revenue, 165
*Pastoral Constitution on the Church
      in the Modern World*, 53, 54,
      69–70
   conscience, 7
   vocabulary used by Paul VI,
      83, 88
Pastoral Rule (Gregory the Great),
      75
Paul, Saint
   divorce and remarriage, 110
   marriage, 75
   slavery, 46, 47
Paul VI, 20, 137. *See also Humanae
      vitae*
   birth control commission, 71,
      72, 149
   natural law, 83–84
   *Vatican Declaration on Sexual
      Ethics*, 88
   and Vatican II, 34
Paul VI (Hebblethwaite), 97
Pius IX, 46
   Immaculate Conception, 27, 30
   ordinary, universal
      magisterium, 31–32
   and papal infallibility, 26
Pius V, 77
Pius VI, 166
Pius VII, 165
Pius X, 4, 16
Pius XI. *See also On Chaste
      Marriage*
   direct abortion, 145–46
   subsidiarity principle, 153, 167
Pius XII, 71
   assent to teachings in
      encyclical letters, 33
   Assumption defined, 27, 30
   direct abortion, 145–46
   Divino Afflante Spiritu, 3
   Humani generis, 3, 32
   marital intercourse, 77
   ordination, 28, 39
   prohibition of contraception,
      45
   use of sterile period to avoid
      conception, 81–82